Rule in International Politics

There is hardly any aspect of social, political, and economic life today that is not also governed internationally. Drawing on debates around hierarchy, hegemony, and authority in international politics, this volume takes the study of the international "beyond anarchy" a step further by establishing the concept of rule as the defining feature of order in the international realm. The contributors argue that the manifold conceptual approaches to sub- and superordination in the international should be understood as rich conceptualizations of one concept: rule. Rule allows constellations of sub- and superordination in the international to be seen as multiplex, systemic, and normatively ambiguous phenomena that need to be studied in the context of their interplay and consequences. This volume draws on a variety of conceptualizations of rule, exploring, in particular, the practices of rule as well as the relational and dynamic characteristics of rule in international politics.

Christopher Daase is Professor of International Organizations at Goethe University Frankfurt am Main, and Co-Director of the Peace Research Institute Frankfurt (PRIF).

Nicole Deitelhoff is Professor of International Relations and Theories of Global Orders at Goethe University Frankfurt am Main, and Director of the Peace Research Institute Frankfurt (PRIF).

Antonia Witt is Head of the Research Group "African Intervention Politics" at the Peace Research Institute Frankfurt (PRIF).

Rule in International Politics

Edited by

Christopher Daase

Peace Research Institute Frankfurt and Goethe University Frankfurt

Nicole Deitelhoff

Peace Research Institute Frankfurt and Goethe University Frankfurt

Antonia Witt

Peace Research Institute Frankfurt

CAMBRIDGE
UNIVERSITY PRESS

CAMBRIDGE
UNIVERSITY PRESS

Shaftesbury Road, Cambridge CB2 8EA, United Kingdom

One Liberty Plaza, 20th Floor, New York, NY 10006, USA

477 Williamstown Road, Port Melbourne, VIC 3207, Australia

314–321, 3rd Floor, Plot 3, Splendor Forum, Jasola District Centre, New Delhi – 110025, India

103 Penang Road, #05–06/07, Visioncrest Commercial, Singapore 238467

Cambridge University Press is part of Cambridge University Press & Assessment, a department of the University of Cambridge.

We share the University's mission to contribute to society through the pursuit of education, learning and research at the highest international levels of excellence.

www.cambridge.org
Information on this title: www.cambridge.org/9781009307697

DOI: 10.1017/9781009307703

First published 2023
First paperback edition 2024

A catalogue record for this publication is available from the British Library

ISBN 978-1-009-30771-0 Hardback
ISBN 978-1-009-30769-7 Paperback

Contents

Contributors

KAREN J. ALTER is Norman Dwight Harris Professor of International Relations and Professor of Political Science and Law at Northwestern University, a permanent visiting professor at the iCourts Center for Excellence, University of Copenhagen Faculty of Law, and Co-Director of the Research Group on Global Capitalism and Law at Northwestern University. Alter's research focuses on the construction of global economic rules, the politics of international regime complexity, and the global and regional judicialization of international relations. Alter is author of the award-winning book *The New Terrain of International Law: Courts, Politics, Rights* (Princeton University Press, 2014); *Transplanting International Courts: The Law and Politics of the Andean Tribunal of Justice* (Oxford University Press, 2017, with Laurence Helfer); *The European Court's Political Power* (Oxford University Press, 2009); and *Establishing the Supremacy of European Law* (Oxford University Press, 2001). She has also authored more than sixty articles and book chapters on the politics of international law, comparative international courts, and international regime complexity.

CHRISTOPHER DAASE is Professor of International Organizations at Goethe University Frankfurt am Main, and Co-Director of the Peace Research Institute Frankfurt (PRIF). He is the speaker of the Regional Research Cluster "Transformation of Political Violence" (TraCe). His research focuses on international security policy; asymmetric conflicts and terrorism; deterrence and arms control; recognition in international politics; as well as forms of international resistance, opposition, and dissidence. He has published widely on these themes, including as a co-author in "Rule and Resistance in Global Governance" (*International Theory*, 2021) and "Opposition and Dissidence: Two Modes of Resistance against International Rule" (*Journal of International Political Theory*, 2018), both with Nicole Deitelhoff, and as an editor of *Rule and Resistance beyond the Nation State* (co-edited, Rowman & Littlefield International, 2019) and *Recognition in International Politics* (co-edited, Palgrave, 2015).

NICOLE DEITELHOFF is Professor of International Relations and Theories of Global Orders at Goethe University Frankfurt am Main, and Director of the Peace Research Institute Frankfurt (PRIF). She is a co-speaker of the Excellence Research Initiative "ConTrust: Trust in Conflict" and speaker of the "Research Institute Social Cohesion" (RISC). Her research covers contestation and crises of institutions and international norms; the foundations of political rule and its legitimation; forms of international resistance, opposition, and dissidence; as well as democracy and social cohesion. Among her recent publications are "Keeping Your Enemies Close? The Variety of Social Movements' Reactions to International Organizations' Opening Up" (*International Studies Review*, 2021, with Felix Anderl and Priska Daphi), "Rule and Resistance in Global Governance" (*International Theory*, 2021, with Christopher Daase), "Things We Lost in the Fire: How Different Types of Contestation Affect the Validity of International Norms" (*International Studies Review*, 2020, with Lisbeth Zimmermann), and "What's in a Name? Contestation and Backlash against International Norms and Institutions" (*British Journal of Politics and International Relations*, 2020).

IAN HURD is Professor of Political Science and Director of the Weinberg College Center for International and Area Studies at Northwestern University. His most recent work is *How to Do Things with International Law* (Princeton University Press, 2017), an examination of the political uses of international law. His research and teaching are on international law and politics, in theory and in practice, and political science research methods. His book *After Anarchy: Legitimacy and Power in the UN Security Council* (Princeton University Press, 2008) won the Chadwick Alger Prize at ISA and the Myres McDougal award from Policy Sciences Association. He is also the author of a leading textbook for students of international organizations and global governance, *International Organizations: Politics, Law, Practice* (4th edition, Cambridge University Press, 2020).

DAVID A. LAKE is the Gerri-Ann and Gary E. Jacobs Professor of Social Sciences and Distinguished Professor of Political Science at the University of California, San Diego. A past president of both the International Studies Association (2010–2011) and the American Political Science Association (2016–2017), he has published widely in international relations theory and international political economy. His recent books include *Hierarchy in International Relations* (Cornell University Press, 2009) and *The Statebuilder's Dilemma: On the Limits of Foreign Intervention* (Cornell University Press, 2016). He is currently completing a book on *Indirect Rule: The Making of U.S. International Hierarchy.*

JULIA C. MORSE is Assistant Professor of Political Science at the University of California, Santa Barbara. Her research focuses on international organizations and global governance with particular attention to issues of rule complexity and compliance. Her research has been published in *International Organization*, *International Studies Quarterly*, *The Review of International Organizations*, and *Journal of Politics*. Her article "Contested Multilateralism" (2014, co-authored with Robert Keohane) theorizes about the creation of regime complexes, arguing that when state coalitions are dissatisfied with existing international institutions, they may create or seek out alternative multilateral venues to challenge the existing institutional status quo.

NICHOLAS ONUF is Professor Emeritus in the Department of Politics and International Relations at Florida International University, Miami. His interests range broadly in international, legal, political, and social theory. His books include *World of Our Making* (Routledge, 1989), *The Republican Legacy in International Thought* (Cambridge University Press, 1998), *Making Sense, Making Worlds* (Routledge, 2013), *The Mightie Frame: Epochal Change and the Modern World* (Oxford University Press, 2018), and *International Theory at the Margins* (Bristol University Press, 2023).

OLE JACOB SENDING is Director of Research and Research Professor at the Norwegian Institute of International Affairs. His research interests include the character of global governance arrangements, the changing form of state sovereignty, and the evolving features of power politics. His research on global governance focuses on the role of expertise, the dynamics of authority constitution, and the nexus between public and private actors. His most recent publications on these issues include "Consultancies in Public Administration" in *Public Administration* (2022) and "Contracting Development" in *Review of International Political Economy* (2020), both with Leonard Seabrooke.

ANTONIA WITT is Head of the Research Group "African Intervention Politics" and a senior researcher at the Peace Research Institute Frankfurt (PRIF), Germany. Her research focuses on the legitimacy and authority of international organizations, African regional organizations, Global International Relations, and the local politics of African interventions. She is the author of *Undoing Coups: The African Union and Post-coup Intervention in Madagascar* (Zed Books, 2020) and the co-author of *International Organizations under Pressure: Legitimating Global Governance in Challenging Times* (Oxford University Press, 2019). Her work has been published, inter alia, in the *Review of International Studies*, *Millennium*, *Journal of Intervention and Statebuilding*, and the *South African Journal of International Affairs*.

MICHAEL ZÜRN is Director of the Global Governance unit at WZB Berlin Social Science Center and Professor of International Relations at the Freie Universität Berlin. Since 2019, he is a speaker of the DFG-funded Cluster of Excellence "Contestations of the Liberal Script" (SCRIPTS). Previously, he served as Founding Dean of the Hertie School of Governance. His work focuses on the emergence and functioning of inter- and supranational institutions and organizations, and their impact on political orders. His publications focus, among others, on the legitimacy and effectiveness of international institutions. His most recent book publications are *The Democratic Regression* (co-authored, Suhrkamp, 2021), *Struggle over Borders* (co-authored, Cambridge University Press, 2019), and *A Theory of Global Governance* (Oxford University Press, 2018).

Acknowledgements

The idea for this book was born during the lecture series "Beyond Anarchy: Rule and Authority in the International System" at the Cluster of Excellence "The Formation of Normative Orders" at Goethe University Frankfurt. This lecture series, organized in the fall of 2013 by the Chairs of Christopher Daase and Nicole Deitelhoff, and the debates we had since then laid the foundation for many of the chapters in this volume. Although almost a decade has passed since then, the problem of rule in international politics has not become less of a puzzling albeit omnipresent issue for International Relations scholarship. We are therefore enormously thankful for the great support we had for pursuing this initial idea and for eventually turning it into a book. We want to thank in particular Ben Kamis, Jannik Pfister, and Philip Wallmeier for their invaluable support in the organization of the lecture series back then. We also owe great thanks to Felix Anderl, Nele Kortendiek, Sebastian Schindler, Philip Wallmeier, Tobias Wille, and Lisbeth Zimmermann for their inspiring inputs as discussants at our 2017 author workshop at the Cluster of Excellence in Frankfurt. For their great editorial and research support during the preparation of the final manuscript, we want to thank our student assistants Selina Fatim Diaby, Laura Fischer, Janne Linder, Franziska Schreiber, and Maike Wäscher, as well as Viola Niemack for her untiring organizational and emotional support in this process. Carla Welch has immensely supported us with language editing, and we thank Ruth Martin for a professional index. We are very grateful to the two anonymous reviewers for thoroughly commenting on our manuscript and for giving us the opportunity to sharpening our arguments. Finally, we want to thank John Haslam, Tobias Ginsberg, and Chris Hudson from Cambridge University Press as well as Mugesh Karthikeyan for professionally guiding us through the publication process.

Introduction

1 The Elephant in the Room of International Relations

Rule in the Study of International Politics

Christopher Daase, Nicole Deitelhoff, and Antonia Witt

From health to migration and cross-border trade and from policing to democratic elections, there is hardly any aspect of social, political, and economic life today that is not also governed internationally. The proliferation of international rules and standards, the mushrooming of international courts and tribunals, the ever-growing authority of international and regional organizations, the power of business firms and transnational non-state actors to shape international policies, and the persistent global inequality, both material and nonmaterial, all these emphasize that the international system is infused with structures of sub- and superordination that affect the conduct of actors across the globe, whether states or individuals. This observation is not new to the discipline of International Relations (IR). In fact, it has sparked lively debates on how to conceptualize these developments, centered on distinct theoretical lenses such as hegemony,[1] hierarchies,[2] status,[3] empire,[4] and international authority.[5] No matter which of these approaches is preferred, one thing they have in common is that they all set out to describe the international "beyond anarchy," questioning and replacing the anarchy *problematique* that has defined the field of IR for so long.[6]

This volume is part of and draws on these debates, but at the same time it aims to take the study of the international "beyond anarchy" a step further by establishing the concept of rule as the defining feature of order in the international realm. More specifically, we argue that the manifold conceptual approaches to sub- and superordination in the international should be understood as rich conceptualizations of one concept: rule. With this, we aim at advancing a research agenda that defines rule as a systematic approach to studying international politics.[7] Unlike in the anarchy *problematique*, our approach sees rule – and not its absence – as the problematic aspect of the international, allowing an exploration of competing conceptualizations of rule and how they materialize in diverse empirical realms. Drawing on the works of W. B. Gallie and John Rawls, we distinguish between concept and conceptions based on the idea that a concept is an abstract notion, while conceptions are the particular instantiations and specifications of such an abstract notion.[8] As we will argue in this introduction, the burgeoning yet fragmented IR literature on the character of the international "beyond anarchy" has largely been based on different conceptions of the nature of this international that are rooted in one overarching concept of rule. We define rule broadly as constellations of formally or informally institutionalized sub- and superordination with the aim of affecting the distribution of basic goods and influence and of stabilizing expectations, regardless of whether these constellations are primarily of sociocultural, economic, or military nature. Thus, like the elephant in the room, *rule as an empirical phenomenon* has always been there in the study of international politics, addressed in different and disconnected strands of IR research. However, since the latter focused on different conceptions of rule, the relevance and potential of *rule as a theoretical concept* for understanding the international has not been systematically developed.

By promoting the concept of rule, we aim to show that rule can serve both as an integrating and a diagnostic tool for the study of the international "beyond anarchy." First, the concept of rule allows us to identify the specific characteristics of the different conceptualizations used in IR scholarship and, in turn, builds bridges between and encourages critical engagement across what have so far been largely distinct and often disconnected literatures. Second, bringing together what have so far been separate conceptual debates, the concept of rule renders visible the multiplicity and heteronomy of different forms of sub- and superordination in the international. While, as we will explain in more detail in this introduction chapter, discussions around hierarchy, hegemony, and international authority shed light on different forms and constellations of sub- and superordination, it is important to note that reducing the international "beyond anarchy" to either of these artificially restricts our empirical gaze to what are, in fact, only specific instances of rule. In short, rule allows constellations of sub- and superordination in the international to be seen as more multiplex, systemic, and normatively ambiguous phenomena that need to be studied in the context of their interplay and consequences. Third, the concept of rule also helps identify blind spots in the existing scholarship on the international "beyond anarchy," thus making a substantial contribution to moving the debate forward. Specifically, in this volume, we identify two such blind spots in particular: the practices of rule and the relational and dynamic characteristics of rule, which the contributions in Part II and Part III of this volume, respectively, will spell out in more detail.[9] In sum, as we demonstrate in this volume, understanding the international through the concept of rule, as opposed to its various conceptualizations, thus underlines the nonuniform and dynamic characteristics of the international "beyond anarchy," which should be taken into account in a concept that is both integrative and diagnostic. We argue that rule is a concept that meets precisely these criteria.

In the remainder of this introduction chapter, we define the concept of rule vis-à-vis more substantial conceptualizations of it. We first summarize IR scholars' more recent works on three key conceptual lenses – hierarchy, hegemony, and authority – which are the most established and productive debates on studying the international "beyond anarchy" to date. While hierarchy has broadened IR scholars' study of constellations of sub- and superordination in the international, the concept is not specific enough to enable a systematic study and comparison of what we call rule; unless understood as "governance hierarchy," it is not a replacement for anarchy as a fundamental ordering principle of the international.[10] Hegemony and authority, in turn, we argue, are specific conceptualizations of rule. We contend that these two (and possibly other) conceptualizations of rule can be distinguished from one another based on their different understandings of the means and sources through which rule is established and exercised, and with regard to their normative assessments of rule, that is, whether rule is seen as a problem of or as a solution for international politics. They have also been predominantly applied to understanding and explaining different phenomena of international politics, such as interstate relations in the case of hegemony and global governance in the case of international authority. In Part III of this introduction chapter, we outline our understanding of the concept and conceptualizations of rule that underpin this volume. We define rule as constellations of formally or informally institutionalized sub- and superordination with the aim of affecting the distribution of basic goods and influence and of stabilizing expectations, regardless of whether these constellations are primarily of sociocultural, economic, or military nature. The individual chapters in this volume all consider a more substantial conceptualization of rule and in so doing expressly refer to the concept laid out in this introduction chapter. Based on the individual contributions, Part IV highlights the multiplicity and complexity of rule in the international system and Part V summarizes why this book matters for advancing our understanding of global politics.

What Is There "Beyond Anarchy"?

Notwithstanding the continuing attraction of the anarchy assumption in IR, today there is a growing, if fragmented, research agenda that seeks to describe and explain the international system "beyond anarchy." These debates are specifically centered on three conceptual lenses – hierarchy, hegemony, and authority – all of which emphasize different forms of sub- and superordination in international politics. In the following subsections, we briefly delve into the three strands of theoretical discussion, describing how they relate to the overarching concept of rule.

Of the three conceptual lenses, hierarchy is the broadest. Studies on international hierarchy constitute a burgeoning field of IR research that has produced important insights into how hierarchies emerge and fade, thus demonstrating the extent to which the international is organized hierarchically. As a concept, however, hierarchy is at once too broad and too limited to grasp the prevalence of different forms of rule in the international realm.[11] Although the study of international hierarchies allows us to identify the manifold forms of sub- and superordination that exist in international politics, the concept as such does not entail an explicit expectation as to the effects of such hierarchies, or more specifically, how they affect the conduct of actors in the international realm. Hegemony and authority, in contrast, are more narrowly defined approaches to the international "beyond anarchy" and have so far been predominantly applied to different empirical contexts. The debate on hegemony has a long pedigree in debates on world order, concentrating on how specific cultural, economic, and political structures and resources position some actors to affect the conduct of others. The debate on international authority, in turn, is deeply embedded in the study of global governance in IR. Focusing on the reasons for deference, authority research highlights the specific attributes of actors or institutions to explain why actors obey the commands or requests of others. Thus, both hegemony and authority make a clear conceptual reference to the effects of constellations of sub- and superordination on the conduct of actors and are therefore, as we will lay out in the following, specific but different conceptions of rule.

Hierarchy

Despite the prominent assumption that the international system is made up of equal units, various strands of IR theories have, if only implicitly, questioned this premise for a long time. This is especially true for power transition theories that understand the international order as a vertical one with the most powerful state at the top, always wary of rising challengers attempting to surpass it.[12] Even apart from these approaches, however, functional differentiation and stratification among states have been persistent features of both international politics and its theorization. For realists, for instance, the unequal distribution of capabilities among states has ranked them vertically and allowed some to command others and function as guardians of the international order (see also the subsection "Hegemony" further below). Furthermore, changes in this unequal distribution of capabilities have been interpreted as major threats to international stability and entailing a risk of violent conflict in the international system, as in theories of hegemonic stability.[13] Similarly, world systems theory and other Marxist theories have demonstrated the emergence and prevailing effects of the core–periphery relations resulting from imperialism and the global reach of capitalism.[14] Notwithstanding this factual inequality among the units of the international system, however, it is only recently that hierarchies – that is "any system through which actors are organised into vertical relations of super- and subordination"[15] – have come to form a burgeoning research agenda as such, leading some to even speak of a new field of "hierarchy studies."[16] Today, this field is marked by great diversity, uniting scholars from various strands of IR theory. As argued by Ayşe Zarakol, scholarship in this field "converges on two insights: first, that hierarchies are a ubiquitous feature of international (i.e. interstate) politics and, second, that they generate social, moral and behavioural dynamics that are different from those created by other arrangements."[17]

Broadly speaking, the study of hierarchy in the international system has so far taken two quite different forms, resulting in two contrasting approaches. These approaches diverge in their meta-theoretical assumptions, in what they identify as the main sources of international hierarchies, and in the normative assessments of the latter, that is, to what extent hierarchies are considered a problem of or a solution to international politics. The first approach, often referred to as "narrow," considers international hierarchy the result of contractual, usually dyadic relationships between states. This account has been most prominently advanced by David Lake but can also be found in works such as John Ikenberry's *Liberal Leviathan.*[18] For Lake, hierarchy is the exercise of authority – that is, rightful rule – by a dominant state over subordinate states on a particular set of issues. Subordinate states are willing to give up a portion of their freedom and subordinate themselves to the authority of dominant states in exchange for security and order. Hierarchy is then defined by "the extent of the authority exercised by the ruler over the ruled."[19] In this approach, hierarchy is the result of a bargain between states, based on mutual consent, which ranks states according to their different roles and responsibilities and thereby structures the international system based on the functions different states perform for the system. Rather than a problem, hierarchy is therefore a solution to the disorder that is likely to emerge in an international system marked by anarchy.

Contrary to this agency-focused account of international hierarchy, other scholars advance an understanding of hierarchy as resulting from deep-seated, historically grown, and changing structures of inequality that define actors' uneven power and status in the international system. In such a reading, hierarchies have always been a characteristic feature of the international system.[20] For scholars advocating this perspective, hierarchy is not the result of a voluntary bargain between dominant and subordinate states, but rather these states are said to already be enmeshed in structures of inequality that delineate their realm of action and define their position within a system of vertical differentiation. In other words, actors – whether states or otherwise – of the international system are already "born into" a structured world that not only defines roles and positions but also establishes who is a legitimate actor in the first place.[21] In this regard, scholars have identified international hierarchies as resulting from historically grown and prevailing racism and imperial relationships,[22] from the international expansion of law,[23] from international norms such as sovereignty,[24] self-determination,[25] or gender equality,[26] and from the unequal distribution of wealth.[27] Though materialism has played an important role in this strand of hierarchy research, many scholars have demonstrated the importance of intersubjective factors, such as discourse, habitus, embodiment, and stigma, for hierarchies to have an impact on everyday international life.[28]

This diverse field of studies on international hierarchies has revealed the theoretical and empirical limits of the anarchy assumption and has helped to make visible the manifold ways in which the international realm is shaped by structured relationships of sub- and superordination. Indeed, one of the great advantages of this research agenda has been its emphasis on the existence of hierarch*ies* rather than a single hierarchy in the international realm.[29] As a concept for the study of different forms of rule in the international realm, however, hierarchy is at once too broad and too limited.

First, the theoretical and empirical breadth of approaches to international hierarchy results in conceptual vagueness. While some see this as an advantage that will enable them to identify lines of critical engagement across different approaches,[30] such critical engagement has so far not come to fruition and is unlikely to bridge the gaping meta-theoretical divide that sets scholars of hierarchy apart. The narrow conception of hierarchy as contracted authority cannot serve as an integrating conceptual framework due to its emphasis on voluntarism and legitimacy, which may not hold for a general concept in international politics.[31] Given the conceptual merging of hierarchy and authority, it also raises the question as to what value hierarchy has as a concept in itself.

The broad understanding of hierarchy, in turn, is prone to gloss over conceptual differences between hierarchy, inequality, and systems of rule and may thus lose sight of the particular forms of differentiation and stratification prevalent in international politics.[32]

Second, as several authors have pointed out, the existence of hierarchical relations is not incompatible with the assumption of the international system being marked by anarchy. In fact, as argued by Jack Donnelly, the juxtaposition of hierarchy and anarchy is a false one, as at least etymologically speaking, hierarchy and anarchy are not mutually exclusive. Anarchy translates as "without a leader (*archos*) or rule (*arche*)." Thus "neither super-ordination nor differentiation … has any logical relationship to (an)archy; that is, to government or its absence."[33] Hence, discussion of hierarchies – broadly understood as differentiation and stratification – does not conceptually question but in fact qualifies international anarchy.[34] One possible way out would be to focus on what Meghan McConaughey et al. call "governance hierarchy" as a particular form of hierarchical relations based on the intention to command,[35] which is – as we will explain further – precisely what the concept of rule does.

Hegemony

A second prominent perspective for the study of the international "beyond anarchy" is hegemony. However, as in the case of hierarchy, it must be noted that some approaches, especially more traditional ones, emphasize that hegemony does not override the anarchy of the international system.[36] Hegemony is neither a uniformly used concept nor a coherent theory. Rather, it is a basic term from a larger family of theories dealing with a specific aspect of sub- and superordination in international politics.[37] Originating in debates about world order structures, what theories of hegemony have in common is a focus on capabilities, that is, the means by which rule is established and maintained. Realist and liberal approaches emphasize material capabilities, such as military and economic power. However, for hegemony to emerge, there must also be the will to apply these capabilities and to exercise leadership.[38] Depending on which of these aspects (power or will) is given priority, a distinction can be made between more realist or more liberal approaches to hegemony. Constructivist and critical theories, by contrast, stress ideational and cultural resources of power.[39] In addition, they emphasize the problematic effects of hegemony, namely domination, while realist and liberal approaches tend to see hegemony as a solution to cooperation problems and a formula for legitimate order and stability.

At the heart of realist theories is the material ability of strong states to force weaker ones into obedience.[40] John Mearsheimer defines a hegemon as a "state that is so powerful that it dominates all the other states in the system."[41] While classical realists and structural realists argue that unilateral concentrations of power can only be short-lived and are balanced by the countervailing power of other states, theorists of international hegemony argue that strong states can establish a stable unipolar order if they use their power to generate some sort of international public goods.[42] Public goods might include not only ensuring an open and free world economy but also providing international security. The prevention of Great Power wars and the protection of relatively weak states is, according to Robert Gilpin, a crucial source of the "prestige" that hegemons enjoy: "To some extent the lesser states in an international system follow the leadership of more powerful states, in part because they accept the legitimacy and utility of the existing order."[43] According to Stephen Brooks and William Wohlforth, the strength of this effect increases with the power of the hegemon: "The stronger the leading state is and the more entrenched its dominance, the more improbable and thus less constraining counterbalancing dynamics are."[44] Under these conditions, unipolar systems may well be more stable than multi- or bipolar systems, as maintained by hegemonic stability theory.

While realist approaches to hegemony see the availability of superior power resources as crucial to create a stable order, liberal approaches understand them as necessary but not sufficient. Instead, liberal approaches focus more on the will to lead. According to Robert Keohane, hegemony is defined "as a situation in which one state is powerful enough to maintain the essential rules governing interstate relations, and *willing to do so*."[45] Along these lines, John Ikenberry has described the emergence of the liberal world order after World War II as a "rule and regime-based order created by a leading state."[46] In the liberal world order, Ikenberry points out, "order is also established and maintained through the exercise of power by the leading state, but power is used to create a system of rule that weaker and secondary states agree to join."[47] In a more recent essay, John Ikenberry and Daniel Nexon developed these ideas further and proposed that hegemony no longer be considered an independent variable and its consequences examined, but to focus on the practices of hegemonic politics and what effects they have on the hegemonic order.[48] This move, the authors argue, allows some of the criticism put forward by critical theories to be integrated, for example, that the concept of hegemony has a Western normative bias and overlooks the fact that the liberal order is anything but favorable or benign for large parts of the world, especially for actors in the Global South.[49]

This line of argument is systematically spelled out in the critical tradition of IR, which relies on the Gramscian notion of "cultural hegemony."[50] While traditional Marxist approaches were primarily concerned with the economic power of social classes institutionalized in the capitalist system of domination, Antonio Gramsci and critical theory approaches recognized the deeper connection between economic and cultural power and domination. The concept of cultural hegemony addresses the structural power of norms, rules, and procedures that generates various actors, with their identities, interests, and positions in the system in the first place.[51] The resulting unequal distribution of opportunities to participate in shaping international politics leads to the stabilization of unequal exchange relations and the institutionalization of structures of sub- and superordination between center and periphery,[52] a structure that is, *inter alia*, powerfully reinforced by Western concepts of international law, as theorists of Third World Approaches to International Law have stressed.[53]

Although the prospect of combining material power and ideas[54] that draw more heavily on critical theory approaches that problematize the cultural foundations of hegemonic orders[55] and emphasize contestation rather than compliance to better understand contemporary developments[56] is promising, some reservations about the concept of hegemony remain. First, the concept of hegemony oscillates between the realist focus on powerful coercion and the liberal focus on legitimate leadership and thus obscures the crucial aspect of the precarious legitimacy of hegemonic orders instead of clarifying it.[57] Second, hegemony has always been and remains a concept largely related to states and interstate relations and thus underestimates the growing influence of international organizations (IOs) or non-state actors. Doing so, it reinforces a static and state-centric view of world politics instead of exploring its dynamic nature. Third, the normative overtones of the concept are also persistent, either identifying hegemony as a benevolent order per se or denouncing it as inherently illegitimate (e.g., as domination). Thus, while hegemony captures a specific aspect of sub- and superordination in international politics, namely the variety of means by which rule is established and maintained, it seems that hegemony studies do not fully exploit this potential.

Authority

Lastly, what is probably the most prominent IR debate concerning instances of rule is that which centers on the concept of authority. Authority is generally understood as the right of one actor to command

and induce deference from some other actor(s) on a particular issue. Similar to hegemony, the authority debate emerged within debates about world order, in particular, in the context of a proclaimed turn to global governance.[58] The governance turn was accompanied by an increased scholarly concern for the growing competencies of IOs and non-state actors, such as corporations and civil society organizations in the making, and the enforcement of international rules.[59] The starting point of this research agenda is the observation by Ian Hurd and others that states adhere to international norms, rules, and agreements not only because they fear external coercion or act out of self-interest but also, and not least, because they believe that these norms, rules, and agreements are legitimate.[60] This insight removed the traditional link between state, authority, and territory making it "possible to imagine other actors that might be authoritative."[61] Authority is thus something that, on the one hand, actors accrue, but on the other hand, it is also a systemic feature when patterns of authority change the structure of the international system.[62] Central questions in this strand of research are therefore how international authority shapes relations between states, how other actors in the international realm, such as IOs, non-governmental organizations (NGOs), international courts, and other transnational actors gain – or lose – authority, and how legitimacy is made, contested, and defended.[63]

The study of international authority in IR has so far predominantly focused on the different sources of deference, that is, the reasons for actors to obey commands or fulfill requests. No matter what the different approaches argue are the particular reasons for this deference – rational calculation,[64] a sense of moral obligation,[65] or a reflexive insight into one's own cognitive limitations[66] – all approaches share the idea that deference occurs because actors perceive the claim to authority as legitimate, that is, as rightful.

The various approaches to international authority in IR differ with regard to two dimensions: (1) the question of where this authority, or rather the deference to authority, comes from, that is, the sources of deference and (2) how the various approaches conceptualize the link between authority and legitimacy. Regarding the sources of deference, David Lake defines authority, in the spirit of Max Weber, as rightful and legitimate rule: "That is, an authoritative ruler has the right to command subordinates to perform certain actions and, because the commands are rightful, the ruled have the duty to comply."[67] For Lake, this rightfulness can be attributed to a contract between ruler and ruled that is advantageous for both (see subsection "Hierarchy"). Other approaches, in contrast, hold that socialization into a specific set of norms and principles brings about rightfulness.[68] William Wohlforth et al., for instance, have studied the "moral authority" of states and found that even small and middle powers can raise their international status by contributing as "good powers" to "system maintenance," for example, by participating in peace missions. Moral authority does not change a state's material capabilities, but it helps it negotiate its place in the imagined stratification order of sub- and superordination.[69] Lastly, another strand of literature refers to reflexive insights into cognitive limits as a source of deference. For instance, Michael Zürn highlights the rise of epistemic authority based on superior expertise that makes others defer to the requests of the actor in the superior position.[70] Similarly, Deborah Avant and her colleagues stress expertise as one important source but also highlight other actor attributes to explain deference.[71] Finally, approaches that take a rather critical perspective of global governance reject the claim of actor or institutional attributes, instead focusing on the practices and techniques that make claims to authority effective.[72] Nico Krisch and others have shown that international authority flows not only from formal structures and procedures but also, as "liquid authority," from informal practices, inter-institutional cooperation, and functional effectiveness.[73] Similarly, Ole Jacob Sending has analyzed the competing practices that make certain actors become authoritative in the first place.[74] Alongside these different understandings of the sources of deference, the approaches also consider varying understandings of the link between authority and legitimacy. In one approach, for example, authority basically equals legitimate authority.[75] In IO and global governance research, authority is often perceived as delegated authority: states delegate certain tasks and responsibilities to IOs, thereby conferring authority, and this authority is legitimate because it is voluntarily delegated.[76] But through authority, IOs can also gain independence and agency, which they can, in turn, extend and increase through their own actions.[77] Particularly in crisis situations, IOs have the opportunity to expand and solidify their authority through "emergency powers."[78]

In another approach, Karen Alter and her colleagues studying international courts argue that authority does not guarantee legitimacy, whether delegated or not.[79] Only when international courts/IOs satisfy and justify this authority through the appropriate procedures and successful performance does legitimacy emerge, and with it the willingness of the actors concerned to abide by the organization's decisions and rules. Thus, authority can be more or less legitimate.[80] This concerns what Michael Zürn calls the authority–legitimacy link. In *A Theory of Global Governance*, Zürn describes the increase of authority nested in trans- and international institutions and the need for new forms of legitimacy that is often not available to them because suitable political structures and processes are absent.[81] As a consequence, the rise of authority in international institutions is likely to produce politicization by civil society and contestation by states.[82]

In both of these approaches, authority is inextricably linked to legitimacy, that is, the belief of the ruled that a rule, institution, or leader has the right to govern their conduct.[83] Even though the sources of this belief vary between the approaches, compliance with a command or request made by an authority holder is a matter of choice. This understanding, however, narrows the applicability of authority as a concept quite substantially. As Vincent Pouliot has highlighted, it particularly neglects all those relations of sub- and superordination in which the subordinate actors have only limited alternatives to obedience. For many actors in the international sphere, lacking material power or, even more importantly, social and cultural capital, there is no choice but to submit.[84] In sum, the study of international authority has advanced IR scholars' understanding of the international "beyond anarchy" in important ways. As a conceptual lens, however, authority only helps us grasp particular constellations of sub- and superordination in the international realm that affect the conduct of others and the distribution of resources: namely, those consciously – albeit for varying reasons – obeyed and considered more or less legitimate by subordinate actors.

The Concept of Rule in the International System

The study of international hierarchies, hegemony, and authority has profoundly influenced the way IR scholars have come to think about and research order in the international realm, demonstrating the manifold ways in which the international has been and continues to be shaped by constellations of sub- and superordination. But as the previous section and the discussion of the various theoretical approaches have highlighted, there is no consensus on what constitutes these constellations of sub- and superordination and on what basis to identify and normatively assess them. Are constellations of sub- and superordination in the international the effect of the unequal distribution of (cultural, economic, and political) means of affecting the conduct of subordinate actors? Or are such constellations to be identified based on the various reasons for which subordinate actors willingly obey commands from superior actors? And are such forms of sub- and superordination a solution to international politics or rather the most problematic aspect of the latter?

Given these differences, it cannot be our aim to come up with one thick, uniform concept. Also from an empirical point of view, a single concept seems impossible, given the observable multiplicity of empirical forms of sub- and superordination in the international, which, to a certain extent, would necessarily make such a concept ignorant. As a consequence, we therefore do not consider such a thick, uniform concept to be of particular value, for it might actually hamper rather than advance the generation of knowledge on international politics. And yet, valuing empirical complexity and multiplicity should neither contradict the search for conceptual advancement nor impede critical engagement between the different conceptions. This is, in fact, a common feature of many of the core concepts of political life, such as the widely discussed concept of power in international relations.[85] Hence, in order to facilitate a conceptual discussion within IR, there is a need for an overarching concept that allows the integration of various conceptions, as well as diagnosis of the essence of (different forms of) sub- and superordination in the international realm and their effects on the conduct of actors. We argue that rule, understood as a constellation of formally or informally institutionalized sub- and superordination with the aim of affecting the distribution of basic goods and influence and of stabilizing expectations, can serve as precisely such an overarching, integrating, and diagnostic concept.

In seeking to advance rule as such an overarching concept, we draw on the distinction between "concept" and "conceptions." The notion of differentiating between "concept" and "conceptions" can already be found in W. B. Gallie's work on essentially contested concepts.[86] Introducing the distinction between the two, Gallie's aim was to understand how essentially contested concepts, such as trust, power, or justice, could nevertheless be understood as referring to one kind of phenomenon. According to Gallie, it is the conditions for the application of a given concept that are contested, deriving from divergent theoretical or ethical positions held by different actors. Gallie therefore reserved these divergent positions for distinguishing between conceptions of the respective phenomena. Similarly, John Rawls used the distinction between concept and conceptions of justice to highlight the difference between a normative concept of justice and various conceptions that would apply a specific set of principles, such as his conception of "justice as fairness."[87] Thus, while a concept denotes an abstract notion, conceptions are the particular instantiations and specifications of such an abstract notion. While concept and conceptions often use the same denominator – such as "power" for structural vs. institutional power[88] or "justice" as in "justice as fairness" vs. "justice as freedom"[89] – this is not necessarily the case. What is crucial is not the denomination but the existence of specific instantiations of a given concept, stemming from the varying theoretical and ethical positions people hold.

Using this distinction between concept and conceptions, we propose that rule be considered as a concept that leaves ample room for different, more substantial conceptions, varying with regard to (1) the means through which rule is established and enacted, (2) the sources of and reasons for deference on the side of the subordinate actors, and (3) the normative resources for assessing different forms of rule.

This means that our concept of rule does not specify how rule is constituted and on what means its exercise relies. It is also neutral in its normative assessment, whether rule is a solution to problems of international politics or in fact one of the problems of international politics. Moreover, in terms of empirical focus, the concept of rule is open to being applied to very different situations of international life, from interstate relations to transnational social movements. All these specifications can be located in various conceptions of rule.

While we argued that hierarchy is underdetermined with regard to rule unless an intention or ability to command on the part of the superordinate actor is added, hegemony and authority are in fact specific instantiations, hence conceptions of rule. Concretely, *hegemony* is a conception of a constellation of sub- and superordination based on the unequal distribution of key means to affect the conduct of subordinate actors. Depending on which strand of hegemony research is studied, such means can be economic and political, established in active leadership (liberal/realist hegemony), or they can be cultural, becoming effective in ideological prescription (critical hegemony). In terms of normative assessment, the two strands of hegemony research take opposing perspectives: while for the first, hegemony is legitimate as it rests on a willingness to obey on the part of subordinate actors, the latter strand stresses the problematic and potentially illegitimate aspects of hegemony, focusing in particular on situations in which hegemony is resisted (domination). *Authority*, in turn, is a particular conception of a constellation of sub- and superordination exercised through the voluntary obedience of those ruled and thus imbued with legitimacy. Unlike hierarchy and despite their substantial differences, these conceptions, by definition, refer to the formally or informally endorsed claim of superordinate actors that they have the right to affect the conduct of subordinates as a central characteristic of structures of sub- and superordination. Hence, they all refer to the same core concept: rule.

The Multiplicity of Rule in the International System

None of the contributions to this volume question the existence of constellations of sub- and superordination in the international system. Their purpose is therefore not to detect but to problematize these structures of sub- and superordination, be it in theoretical, empirical, or normative terms. Each contribution starts from the observation that there are particular types and structures of rule and aims to investigate the causes of their emergence, their forms of existence, and their social effects. In so doing, each contribution spells out a specific conception of rule by drawing to the core concept as defined in this introduction. The need to do this emerges from the insight that, unlike the nation-state, which still serves as the unrivaled conceptual role model for political rule, there is neither a unified system of rule in the international realm, nor a clear and identifiable set of institutions and agents that constitute and manage structures of rule. While there are clear examples of institutionalized forms of rule based on material coercion, the overall image of rule in the international system is much more amorphous. Forms of rule emerge in different spaces and in more or less institutionalized constellations and therefore have to be traced in their multiple dimensions, that is, in the practices of actors constituting and enacting rule, the changing institutional conditions for rule, and the resulting consequences for the distribution of power and wealth. Apart from demonstrating this multiplicity of rule in the international system, the contributions in this volume also substantially advance the study of international structures of sub- and superordination by shedding light on two hitherto understudied dimensions: the practices of rule as well as its relational and dynamic character, which the chapters in Parts II and III address in more detail.

Outline of the Book

The volume is divided into three parts: Part I focuses on theorizing rule, bringing together different theoretical approaches to both the concept and to concrete yet different conceptions of rule. Michael Zürn opens this Part I by introducing a particular conception of rule, namely "reflexive authority." According to Zürn, authority involves "a form of power that is based neither exclusively on coercion, nor on the manipulation of incentives, and also not on persuasion, but it includes the recognition of inequality among actors" (Zürn, this volume), which he calls "voluntary subordination." Hence, it is the puzzle of obedience or deference that lies at the core of Zürn's approach to constellations of sub- and superordination in the international system. Distinguishing between three different forms of authority – contracted, inscribed, and reflexive – he aims to demonstrate that authority rests on actors' insights into the limitations of their own rationality and information base, because they conclude that without authoritative institutions or agents, certain goods and values could not be sufficiently provided for. Zürn argues that while contracted authority conflates authority with cooperation, inscribed authority cannot deal with the prevalence of contestation against authority. Only the reflexive form of authority that centers around actors' insights into the need for certain forms of authority can explain the puzzle of deference.

David Lake in his chapter theorizes about the conditions for rule to come into being, concretely, why one particular form of rule emerges and not others. Starting from the premise that rules are not only the result of rulers' own interest, but are structured by the existing rules and rule makers, Lake uses an organizational ecology approach to explain the rise of a particular kind of ruling body in the international system: private governance organizations (PGOs) whose rule(s) favor free market neoliberalism. Lake demonstrates how the reluctance of states to invest authority in intergovernmental organizations induces the disproportionate growth because these are most likely to have the resources to engage in rulemaking.

Nicholas Onuf approaches the problem of rule by taking up and elaborating on ideas he first developed with Frank F. Klink in the late 1980s, starting from the socially constitutive effects of rules. Onuf argues that rules are what make rule possible and consequently identifies three different kinds of rules (instruction, directive, and commitment rules) and their corresponding forms of rule (hegemony, hierarchy, and heteronomy). Although hegemony and hierarchy are possible forms of rule, the international system is best described as heteronomous, as it consists of rules that simultaneously regulate the mutual recognition of state equality *and* the unequal distribution of their privileges. Onuf's heuristic also provides a departure point for understanding the proliferation of rule(s) globally as a defining feature of modernity.

The chapters in Part II, while building on different conceptualizations of rule, all focus on the practice of rule as enacted by a multitude of agencies in the international realm, such as state representatives, transnational organizations, and regional mediators. Ole Jacob Sending's chapter presents a conception of rule that is based on the rulemaking practices of actors, which Sending calls "auto-authority." He starts from the observation that many forms of transnational governance are valued particularly because they are effective without being coercive, that is, they rely on nonbinding measures. As Sending highlights, this effectiveness is the effect of a form of authority that is neither delegated nor contracted, but that emerges solely from the practice of engaging in rulemaking. Hence, in order for IR scholars to explain forms of rule, Sending concludes, the important thing is not to look at different sources of legitimacy but rather to investigate the practices of actors engaging in rulemaking and their authority-constituting consequences.

Sending illustrates his argumentation with examples from the formation of a global population policy and the global governance of health.

Antonia Witt's chapter moves to another kind of actor involved in practicing rule: regional organizations. She introduces the idea of the region as a site of rule, formalized in the growing authority of regional organizations to define governance principles for their member states. Concretely, the chapter analyzes the connection between international authority and authority in/of states, thus offering a relational reading of authority that focuses on the constitutive connections between different sites of authority. With a case study on the African Union's (AU) anti-coup policy, Witt analyzes how the authority to define what counts as legitimate authority in states both reproduces the state as a locus of legitimate authority and denies it that very authority. Unlike most of the existing literature, which studied the authority of IOs based on the sources of IO authority, Witt offers a reading of IO authority through the practices of enacting authority and the effects this has in specific locations.

International law has become a key field both for practices and for the study of international rule. Ian Hurd investigates in his chapter whether there is such a thing as an international rule of law by analyzing the practices of state parties in relation to international law. Based on a comparison between the logic of the domestic rule of law and that of the international rule of law, Hurd demonstrates that, while the international rule of law might not work as a neutral institutional framework to help states solve their conflicts, it nevertheless functions as a kind of constitutional meta norm that structures states' arguments and practices regarding international law. Thus, even though the international rule of law is "fiction," it is an effective fiction in the sense that state practices working on this fiction end up making the international rule of law into a form of international rule.

Lastly, Part III advances our understanding of the relational and dynamic aspects of rule, in particular its relation to resistance. Christopher Daase and Nicole Deitelhoff introduce a conception of rule that rejects the hitherto dominant focus on recognition. Instead, the two authors propose a conception of rule that is tied to resistance. Based on an eclectic reading of different traditions of theories of rule, they stipulate that there is no rule without resistance. Even though rule might aim at suppressing resistance or might take such a subtle shape that it hardly encounters resistance, conceptually, rule is bound to resistance. Without a minimum of opposition and objection to orders, a recourse to rule would not be necessary. Even legitimate rule, which Weber calls authority, is legitimate only to a certain degree. Although one can assume a general willingness to obey, it only makes sense to speak of rule *or* authority if there is also the chance of dissent and the possibility of resistance, because even legitimate rule (authority) is the assertion of interests *against the will* of others. As a consequence, the authors argue, not only obedience and the will to comply but also dissent and the will to resist have to be part of every conception of rule. Furthermore, from such a perspective, the shape of rule can be linked to the resistance it gives rise to. To demonstrate this relationship, Daase and Deitelhoff introduce four illustrative case studies on state and non-state forms of resistance and how they indicate and influence forms of rule.

Karen Alter, in extension to the chapter by Ian Hurd, explores state resistance against international law rather than the regularity of state practice that brings about the authority of the international rule of law. Specifically, Alter's focus is on recent waves of state contestation against international law. She distinguishes between ordinary and extraordinary contestation, the latter being aimed at pushing back international law, while the former "takes place within a legal field, when lawyers, stakeholders, judges, and government officials debate and contest over the meaning of international law" (Alter, this volume). As Alter highlights, it is the extraordinary contestations that are of concern, as they have the potential to tear down the very fabric of international law.

The question of the conditions under which resistance can become a threat to existing orders of rule is also at the center of Julia Morse's contribution. Morse focuses on the politics of anti-globalist leaders in the US, Europe, and beyond who portray their positions as being against an international that is increasingly shaped by authority. The goal of such leaders of restoring national sovereignty and reducing the power of international institutions is therefore framed as resistance to global rule. Morse identifies three possible alternative strategies to undermine the international liberal order: (1) challenging international regimes by breaking their rules or withdrawing completely, (2) demanding changes in institutional designs or rules, and (3) forming new institutions that run counter to the objectives of the old ones. So far, Morse holds, the robustness of international institutions in the face of anti-globalist challenges indicates the continuous authority of global governance arrangements. In the long run, however, unilateral strategies might have grave repercussions for global governance. Morse's chapter therefore demonstrates that the analysis of strategies of resistance not only reveals the preferences of the challengers but also "signals something about the nature of rule and authority in the international system," and "has long-term consequences for the authoritativeness of the regime complex" (Morse, this volume).

Why Rule Matters

Over the last two decades, in particular, a lot has been written about different forms of inequality and stratification, about hierarchies and authority in world politics, making abundantly clear that constellations of sub- and superordination are not new to the scene of international relations but have existed all along. Some of these constellations come with the explicit or implicit aim of affecting the conduct of actors, stabilizing expectations, and shaping the distribution of power and resources. We call these constellations rule. What differentiates international politics from national politics is that these constellations do not align themselves in one coherent scheme of rule but give rise to a wide array of different forms and structures of rule that compete and overlap.[90] To refer to the international system as either anarchical or hierarchical is an inadequate description, rather characterizing it as a heterarchy would be more fitting.[91]

But if rule has existed in international politics all along, why did it take so long for IR scholarship to tackle it systematically? There is no simple answer to this question. One of the reasons for the long neglect lies in conceptual developments in the field, the most important of which was the currency anarchy gained as an imaginary and ordering principle of the international system in the 1980s through Kenneth Waltz's seminal book *Theory of International Politics*.[92] His move to equate rule with (formal) hierarchy worked as an effective showstopper to any serious engagement with rule in international politics for quite some time; this might even hold true today given the fact that most IR scholars working on related issues prefer to refer to hierarchies, hegemony, and international authority instead of rule. Nevertheless, the fact that today there is more research on hierarchies, hegemony, and authority is probably also related to the impressive institutionalization, and, as part of it, formalization of world politics during the last two decades, which made rule more visible, on the one hand, and harder to escape, on the other.[93]

Looking at the contributions in this volume, we believe it was the right decision to cast our net more widely and address the multiplicity of rule in the international realm through the integrating and diagnostic concept introduced here.[94] In fact, as an initial conclusion, this volume demonstrates that a focus on rule, as defined in this introduction and explicated in the ensuing chapters, has at least three advantages: first, it makes the relational and processual dimension of forms of sub- and superordination visible, which in turn means grasping rule neither as static nor as given, but as dynamically constituted, contested, and changed through agency. This raises questions such as what kind of practices make rule possible and under what conditions can particular actors successfully rule or make a claim to authority, to which the contributions by Lake, Sending, Hurd, Witt, and Onuf, in particular, provide answers. Second, understanding the forms and functions of rule helps to make sense of the myriad forms of resistance and contestation that we observe in world politics today. Not all forms of inequality point to rule, but nor do all forms of contestation. Understanding the interaction between rule and resistance, as demonstrated in the contributions by Daase and Deitelhoff, Alter, and Morse, allows us to assess the longevity as well as the conditions for erosion of particular systems of rule, an aspect also discussed in Zürn's contribution to this volume. A critical conclusion drawn by all contributions is that even though resistance is rising, the current international order demonstrates an impressive "stickiness." And lastly, deepening our understanding of international rule facilitates a normative interrogation of the structures of inequality and hierarchy that we can observe in world politics by laying bare the ruling function of those structures. The chapters by Lake, Sending, and Witt explicitly pursue such a critical objective. Rendering rule visible is a crucial precondition for it to be subjected to informed critique. Especially in times of anti-globalist movements, rising populism, and nationalism, such informed critique may become the inevitable basis for the formulation of real alternatives.

References

Acharya, Amitav. 2014. "Global International Relations (IR) and Regional Worlds: A New Agenda for International Studies." *International Studies Quarterly* 58(4): 647–659.

Acharya, Amitav. 2017. "After Liberal Hegemony: The Advent of a Multiplex World Order." *Ethics & International Affairs* 31(3): 271–285.

Alter, Karen J. 2014. *The New Terrain of International Law*. Princeton and Oxford: Princeton University Press.

Alter, Karen J., Laurence R. Helfer, and Mikael Rask Madsen. 2018. "International Courts in a Complex World," in Karen Alter, Laurence R. Helfer, and Mikael Rask Madsen (eds.), *International Court Authority*. Oxford: Oxford University Press, pp. 3–23.

Anderl, Felix. 2022. *Broken Solidarities: How Open Global Governance Divides and Rules*. Bristol: Bristol University Press.

Anderl, Felix, Christopher Daase, Nicole Deitelhoff, Victor Kempf, Jannik Pfister, and Philip Wallmeier (eds.). 2019. *Rule and Resistance beyond the Nation State: Contestation, Escalation, Exist*. London: Rowman & Littlefield International.

Anghie, Anthony. 2006. "The Evolution of International Law: Colonial and Post-Colonial Realities." *Third World Quarterly* 27(5): 739–753.

Anghie, Anthony, and Bhupinder S. Chimni. 2003. "Third World Approaches to International Law and Individual Responsibility in Internal Conflicts." *Chinese Journal of International Law* 2(1): 77–103.
Anievas, Alexander, Nivi Manchanda, and Robbie Shilliam (eds.). 2015. *Race and Racism in International Relations: Confronting the Global Colour Line.* London: Routledge.
Ashley, Richard K. 1988. "Untying the Sovereign State: A Double Reading of the Anarchy Problematique." *Millennium: Journal of International Studies* 17(2): 227–262.
Avant, Debora D., Martha Finnemore, and Susan K. Sell (eds.). 2010. *Who Governs the Globe?* Cambridge: Cambridge University Press.
Barder, Alexander D. 2017. "International Hierarchy." *Oxford Research Encyclopedia of International Studies*, https://oxfordre.com/internationalstudies/view/10.1093/acrefore/9780190846626.001.0001/acrefore-9780190846626-e-95 (last accessed July 25, 2022).
Barder, Alexander D. 2015. *Empire Within: International Hierarchy and Its Imperial Laboratories of Governance.* London: Routledge.
Barkawi, Tarak, and Mark Laffey. 2002. "Retrieving the Imperial: Empire and International Relations." *Millenium: Journal of International Studies* 31(1): 109–127.
Barnett, Michael. 2001. "Authority, Intervention, and the Outer Limits of International Relations Theory," in Thomas M. Callaghy et al. (eds.), *Intervention and Transnationalism in Africa: Global-Local Networks of Power.* Cambridge: Cambridge University Press, pp. 47–65.
Barnett, Michael N., and Martha Finnemore. 1999. "The Politics, Power, and Pathologies of International Organizations." *International Organization* 53(4): 699–732.
Barnett, Michael N., and Martha Finnemore. 2004. *Rules for the World: International Organizations in Global Politics.* Ithaca: Cornell University Press.
Barnett, Michael N., and Raymond Duvall. 2004. *Power in Global Governance.* Cambridge: Cambridge University Press.
Bially Mattern, Janice, and Ayşe Zarakol. 2016. "Hierarchies in World Politics." *International Organization* 70(3): 623–654.
Bieler, Andreas, and Adam David Morton. 2004. "A Critical Theory Route to Hegemony, World Order, and Historical Change: Neo-Gramscian Perspectives in International Relations." *Capital & Class* 28(1): 85–113.
Black, Julia. 2017. "'Says Who?' Liquid Authority and Interpretive Control in Transnational Regulatory Regimes." *International Theory* 9(2): 286–310.
Brooks, Stephen G., and William C. Wohlforth. 2008. *World Out of Balance: International Relations and the Challenge of American Primacy.* Princeton and Oxford: Princeton University Press.
Buchanan, Allen. 2003. *Justice, Legitimacy, and Self-Determination: Moral Foundations of International Law.* Oxford: Oxford University Press.
Buckel, Sonja, and Andreas Fischer-Lescano. 2009. "Gramsci Reconsidered: Hegemony in Global Law." *Leiden Journal of International Law* 3: 437–454.
Cerny, Philip G., and Alex Prichard. 2017. "The New Anarchy: Globalization and Fragmentation in World Politics." *Journal of International Political Theory* 13(3): 378–394.

Chimni, B. S. 2003. "Third World Approaches to International Law: A Manifesto," in Anthony Anghie et al. (eds.), *The Third World and International Order*. Leiden: Martinus Nijhoff Publishers, pp. 47–74.

Clapham, Christopher. 1998. "Degrees of Statehood." *Review of International Studies* 24(2): 143–157.

Clark, Ian. 2011. *Hegemony in International Society*. Oxford: Oxford University Press.

Cox, Robert W. 1981. "Social Forces, States and World Orders: Beyond International Relations Theory." *Millennium: Journal of International Studies* 10(2): 126–155.

Cox, Robert W. 1983. "Gramsci, Hegemony and International Relations: An Essay in Method." *Millennium: Journal of International Studies* 12(2): 162–175.

Daase, Christopher, and Nicole Deitelhoff. 2019. "Opposition and Dissidence." *Journal of International Political Theory* 15(1): 11–30.

Deitelhoff, Nicole, and Christopher Daase. 2021. "Rule and Resistance in Global Governance." *International Theory* 13(1): 122–130.

Donnelly, Jack. 2006. "Sovereign Inequalities and Hierarchy in Anarchy: American Power and International Society." *European Journal of International Relations* 12(2): 139–170.

Donnelly, Jack. 2015. "The Discourse of Anarchy in IR." *International Theory* 7(3): 393–425.

Donnelly, Jack. 2017. "Beyond Hierarchy," in Ayşe Zarakol (ed.), *Hierarchies in World Politics*. Cambridge: Cambridge University Press, pp. 243–265.

Drezner, Daniel W. 2019. "Counter-Hegemonic Strategies in the Global Economy." *Security Studies* 28(3): 505–531.

Frank, André G. 1979. "Unequal Accumulation: Intermediate, Semi-Peripheral, and Sub-Imperialist Economies." *Review* 2(3): 281–350.

Gallie, Walter B. 1956. "Essentially Contested Concepts." *Proceedings of the Aristotelian Society* 56(1): 167–198.

Gill, Stephen (ed.). 1993. *Gramsci, Historical Materialism, and International Relations*. Cambridge: Cambridge University Press.

Gill, Stephen. 2003. *Power and Resistance in the New World Order*. Basingstoke: Palgrave Macmillan.

Gilpin, Robert. 1980. *War and Change in World Politics*. Cambridge: Cambridge University Press.

Goh, Evelyn. 2013. *The Struggle for Order: Hegemony, Hierarchy, and Transition in Post-Cold War East Asia*. Oxford: Oxford University Press.

Grovogui, Siba N'Zatioula. 1996. *Sovereigns, Quasi Sovereigns, and Africans: Race and Self-Determination in International Law*. Minneapolis and London: University of Minnesota Press.

Gruffydd Jones, Branwen. 2008. "Race in the Ontology of International Order." *Political Studies* 56: 907–927.

Havercroft, Jonathan and Alex Prichard. 2017. "Anarchy and International Relations Theory: A Reconsideration." *Journal of International Political Theory* 13(3): 252–265.

Heupel, Monika, and Michael Zürn (eds.). 2017. *Protecting the Individual from International Authority: Human Rights in International Organizations*. Cambridge: Cambridge University Press.

Hobson, John M., and Jason C. Sharman. 2005. “The Enduring Place of Hierarchy in World Politics: Tracing the Social Logics of Hierarchy and Political Change.” *European Journal of International Relations* 11(1): 63–98.

Hooghe, Liesbet, and Gary Marks. 2015. “Delegation and Pooling in International Organizations.” *Review of International Organizations* 10(3): 305–328.

Hooghe, Liesbet, Tobias Lenz, and Gary Marks. 2019. “Contested World Order: The Delegitimation of International Governance.” *The Review of International Organizations* 14: 731–743.

Hooghe, Lisbet, Gary Marks, Tobias Lenz, Jeanine Bezuijen, Besir Ceka, and Sved Derderyan. 2017. *Measuring International Authority: A Postfunctionalist Theory of Global Governance*. Vol III. Oxford: Oxford University Press.

Hopf, Ted. 2013. “Common-Sense Constructivism and Hegemony in World Politics.” *International Organization* 67(2): 317–354.

Hurd, Ian. 1999. “Legitimacy and Authority in International Politics.” *International Organization* 53(2): 379–408.

Hurrell, Andrew. 2007. *On Global Order: Power, Values, and the Constitution of International Society*. Oxford: Oxford University Press.

Ikenberry, G. John. 2011. *Liberal Leviathan: The Origins, Crisis, and Transformation of the American World Order*. Princeton and Oxford: Princeton University Press.

Ikenberry, G. John, and Daniel Nexon. 2019. “Hegemony Studies 3.0: The Dynamics of Hegemonic Orders.” *Security Studies* 28(3): 395–421.

Katzenstein, Peter J., and Lucia A. Seybert (eds.). 2018. *Protean Power: Exploring the Uncertain and Unexpected in World Politics*. Cambridge: Cambridge University Press.

Keene, Edward. 2013. “International Hierarchy and the Origins of the Modern Practice of Intervention.” *Review of International Studies* 39(5): 1077–1090.

Keohane, Robert O. 1984. *After Hegemony: Cooperation and Discord in World Political Economy*. Princeton and Oxford: Princeton University Press.

Kindleberger, Charles P. 1981. “Dominance and Leadership in the International Economy.” *International Studies Quarterly* 25(3): 242–254.

Koskenniemi, Martti. 1997. “Hierarchy in International Law: A Sketch.” *European Journal of International Law* 8: 566–582.

Kreuder-Sonnen, Christian. 2019. *Emergency Powers of International Organizations: Between Normalization and Containment*. Oxford: Oxford University Press.

Krisch, Nico. 2017. “Liquid Authority in Global Governance.” *International Theory* 9(2): 237–260.

Kustermans, Jorg, and Rikkert Horemans. 2022. “Four Conceptions of Authority in International Relations.” *International Organization* 76(1): 204–228.

Lake, David A. 2009. *Hierarchy in International Relations*. Cornell: Cornell University Press.

Lentner, Howard H. 2005. “Hegemony and Autonomy.” *Political Studies Review* 53(4): 735–752.

Lukes, Steven. 1974. *Power: A Radical View*. London: Macmillan.

MacDonald, Paul K. 2018. “Embedded Authority: A Relational Network Approach to Hierarchy in World Politics.” *Review of International Studies* 44(1): 128–150.

Macdonald, Kate, and Terry Macdonald. 2017. “Liquid Authority and Political Legitimacy in Transnational Governance.” *International Theory* 9(2): 329–351.

Mallavarapu, Siddharth. 2021. "Imperialism, International Law, and War: Enduring Legacies and Curious Entanglements," in Lothar Brock, and Hendrik Simon (eds.), *The Justification of War and International Order*. Oxford: Oxford University Press, pp. 45–64.

McConaughey, Meghan, Paul Musgrave, and Daniel H. Nexon. 2018. "Beyond Anarchy: Logics of Political Organization, Hierarchy, and International Structure." *International Theory* 10(2): 181–218.

Mearsheimer, John J. 2001. *The Tragedy of Great Power Politics*. New York: W. W. Norton & Company.

Meiches, Benjamin. 2019. "The Charge of Genocide: Racial Hierarchy, Political Discourse, and the Evolution of International Institutions." *International Political Sociology* 13(1): 20–36.

Morse, Julia C., and Robert O. Keohane. 2014. "Contested Multilateralism." *Review of International Organizations* 9: 385–412.

Murphy, Craig. 1994. *International Organization and Industrial Change*. Oxford: Oxford University Press.

Nedal, Dani K., and Daniel H. Nexon. 2019. "Anarchy and Authority: International Structure, the Balance of Power, and Hierarchy." *Journal of Global Security Studies* 4(2): 169–189.

Nexon, Daniel H., and Iver B. Neumann. 2017. "Hegemonic-Order Theory: A Field-Theoretical Account." *European Journal of International Relations* 24(3): 662–686.

Nye, Joseph S. 1990. *Bound to Lead: The Changing Nature of American Power*. New York: Basic Books.

Onuf, Nicholas, and Frank F. Klink. 1989. "Anarchy, Authority, Rule." *International Studies Quarterly* 33(2): 149–173.

Organski, Abramo F. K. 1958. *World Politics*. New York: Alfred A. Knopf.

Parmar, Inderjeet. 2019. "Transnational Elite Knowledge Networks: Managing American Hegemony in Turbulent Times." *Security Studies* 28(3): 532–564.

Paul, T. V., Deborah W. Larson, and William C. Wohlforth (eds.). 2014. *Status in World Politics*. Cambridge: Cambridge University Press.

Pouliot, Vincent. 2016. *International Packing Orders: The Politics and Practice of Multilateral Diplomacy*. Cambridge: Cambridge University Press.

Pouliot, Vincent. 2017. "Against Authority: The Heavy Weight of International Hierarchy," in Ayşe Zarakol (ed.), *Hierarchies in World Politics*. Cambridge: Cambridge University Press, pp. 113–133.

Pouliot, Vincent. 2021. "Global Governance in the Age of Epistemic Authority." *International Theory* 13(1): 144–156.

Rawls, John. 1971. *A Theory of Justice*. Cambridge: The Belknap Press of Harvard University Press.

Risse, Thomas (ed.). 2013. *Governance without the State? Policies and Politics in Areas of Limited Statehood*. New York: Columbia University Press.

Rosenau, James N., and Ernst-Otto Czempiel (eds.). 1992. *Governance without Government: Order and Change in World Politics*. Cambridge: Cambridge University Press.

Schmidt, Brian C. 2018. *Hegemony: A Conceptual and Theoretical Analysis*. Berlin: DOC Research Institute.

Scholte, Jan Aart. 2020. "Rethinking Hegemony as Complexity," in Piotr Dutkiewicz, Tom Casier, and Jan Aart Scholte (eds.), *Hegemony and World Order*. London: Routledge, pp. 78–97.

Sending, Ole J. 2015. *The Politics of Expertise: Competing for Authority in Global Governance*. Ann Arbor: Michigan University Press.

Sending, Ole J. 2017. "Recognition and Liquid Authority." *International Theory* 9(2): 311–328.

Sending, Ole J., and Iver B. Neumann. 2006. "Governance to Governmentality: Analyzing NGOs, States, and Power." *International Studies Quarterly* 50(3): 651–672.

Slaughter, Anne-Marie. 2017. "The Return of Anarchy?" *Columbia Journal of International Affairs*, Special 70th Anniversary Issue: The Next World Order, Vol. 70, https://jia.sipa.columbia.edu/return-anarchy (last accessed July 14, 2022).

Spanu, Maja. 2020. "The Hierarchical Society: The Politics of Self-determination and the Constitution of New States after 1919." *European Journal of International Relations* 26(2): 372–396.

Tallberg, Jonas, Karin Bäckstrand, and Jan Aart Scholte (eds.). 2018. *Legitimacy in Global Governance: Sources Processes, and Consequences*. Oxford: Oxford University Press.

Tallberg, Jonas, and Michael Zürn. 2019. "The Legitimacy and Legitimation of International Organizations: Introduction and Framework." *Review of International Organizations* 14(4): 581–606.

Tammen, Ronald L., Jacek Kugler, and Douglas Lemke. 2017. "Foundations of Power Transition Theory," Oxford Research Encyclopedia of Politics, https://oxfordre.com/politics/view/10.1093/acrefore/9780190228637.001.0001/acrefore-9780190228637-e-296 (last access July 26, 2022).

Towns, Ann E. 2012. "Norms and Social Hierarchies: Understanding International Policy Diffusion 'From Below'." *International Organization* 66(2): 179–209.

Towns, Ann E., and Bahar Rumelili. 2017. "Taking the Pressure: Unpacking the Relation between Norms, Social Hierarchies, and Social Pressures on States." *European Journal of International Relations* 23(4): 756–779.

Viola, Lora, Duncan Snidal, and Michael Zürn. 2015. "Sovereign (In)Equality in the Evolution of the International System," in Stephan Leibfried et al. (eds.), *The Oxford Handbook on Transformations of the State*. Oxford: Oxford University Press, pp. 221–236.

Wallerstein, Immanuel. 1974. *The Modern World-System: Capitalist Agriculture and the Origins of the European World-Economy in the Sixteenth Century*. New York: Academic Press.

Wallerstein, Immanuel. 1979. *The Capitalist World Economy: Essays*. Cambridge: Cambridge University Press.

Waltz, Kenneth N. 1979. *Theory of International Politics*. Reading: Addison-Wesley.

Webb, Michael C., and Stephen D. Krasner. 2009. "Hegemonic Stability Theory: An Empirical Assessment." *Review of International Studies* 15(2): 183–198.

Witt, Antonia. 2022. "Beyond Formal Powers: Understanding the African Union's Authority on the Ground." *Review of International Studies* 48(4): 626–645.

Wohlforth, William C., Benjamin de Carvalho, Halvard Leira, and Iver B. Neumann. 2018. Moral Authority and Status in International Relations: Good States and the Social Dimension of Status Seeking. *Review of International Studies* 44(3): 526–546.

Wolf, Reinhard. 2019. "Taking Interaction Seriously: Asymmetrical Roles and the Behavioral Foundations of Status." *European Journal of International Relations* 25(4): 1186–1211.

Zarakol, Ayşe. 2010. *After Defeat: How the East Learned to Live with the West.* Cambridge: Cambridge University Press.

Zarakol, Ayşe (ed.). 2017a. *Hierarchies in World Politics.* Cambridge: Cambridge University Press.

Zarakol, Ayşe. 2017b. "Theorising Hierarchies: An Introduction," in Ayşe Zarakol (ed.), *Hierarchies in World Politics.* Cambridge: Cambridge University Press, pp. 1–14.

Zürn, Michael. 2018. *A Theory of Global Governance: Authority, Legitimacy, and Contestation.* Cambridge: Cambridge University Press.

Notes

1 Goh 2013; Ikenberry 2011; Ikenberry and Nexon 2019.

2 Bially Mattern and Zarakol 2016; Lake 2009; MacDonald 2018; Viola et al. 2015; Zarakol 2017a.

3 Paul et al. 2014; Wolf 2019.

4 Barder 2015; Barkawi and Laffey 2002.

5 For instance, Krisch 2017; Sending 2015; Zürn 2018; see also Donnelly 2015.

6 On the "anarchy *problematique*," see Ashley 1988, but also see Slaughter 2017 on the "return of anarchy" in light of growing anti-globalization and anti-internationalization trends, as well as Havercroft and Prichard 2017 and Cerny and Prichard 2017 for theoretical discussions on the lasting currency of the concept of anarchy.

7 See Donnelly's (2017: 265) early call for such an agenda and, of course, the seminal article by Onuf and Klink 1989; see also Anderl 2022; Anderl et al. 2019; Daase and Deitelhoff 2019: 16.

8 Gallie 1956; Lukes 1974; Rawls 1971.

9 For an account of both aspects, see, for example, earlier works by Pouliot 2016; Sending 2015.

10 Donnelly 2006; McConaughey et al. 2018: 186.

11 See also Donnelly 2017.

12 The classic work by Organski 1958; overview in Tammen et al. 2017.

13 Kindleberger 1981.

14 Cox 1981; Gill 2003; Wallerstein 1979.

15 Zarakol 2017b: 1.

16 McConaughey et al. 2018: 184; for an overview, see Barder 2017; Mattern and Zarakol 2016; Zarakol 2017a.

17 Zarakol 2017b: 2.
18 Ikenberry 2011; Lake 2009.
19 Lake 2009: 9.
20 Hobson and Sharman 2005.
21 Pouliot 2016; Pouliot 2017: 122.
22 Anievas et al. 2015; Barkawi and Laffey 2002; Gruffydd Jones 2008; Meiches 2019.
23 Anghie 2006; Koskenniemi 1997; Mallavarapu 2021.
24 Grovogui 1996; Keene 2013.
25 Spanu 2020.
26 Towns 2012; Towns and Rumelili 2017.
27 Wallerstein 1979.
28 Pouliot 2016; Zarakol 2010.
29 Donnelly 2017: 247.
30 Bially Mattern and Zarakol 2016; Zarakol 2017b: 9.
31 For a critical discussion, see Pouliot 2017: 122–124.
32 Donnelly 2017: 265.
33 Donnelly 2006: 141.
34 See also MacDonald 2018.
35 McConaughey et al. 2018: 186.
36 See for instance Gilpin 1980: 7, 28.
37 Ikenberry and Nexon 2019: 396.
38 Clark 2011: 18; Lentner 2005; Schmidt 2018.
39 Anghie 2006; Buckel and Fischer-Lescano 2009.
40 Waltz 1979: 131.
41 Mearsheimer 2001: 41.
42 Webb and Krasner 2009.
43 Gilpin 1980: 30.
44 Brooks and Wohlforth 2008: 48.
45 Keohane 1984: 34, our emphasis.
46 Ikenberry 2011: 70.
47 Ikenberry 2011: 74.
48 Ikenberry and Nexon 2019.
49 Acharya 2014: 37.
50 Cox 1983; Bieler and Morton 2004.
51 Cox 1983; Gill 1993; Murphy 1994.
52 Frank 1979; Wallerstein 1974.
53 Anghie 2006; Anghie and Chimni 2003; Chimni 2003.
54 Hopf 2013.
55 Nexon and Neumann 2017; Parmar 2019.
56 Acharya 2017; Drezner 2019.
57 See Lentner 2005.
58 Hurrell 2007; Rosenau and Czempiel 1992.
59 Avant et al. 2010; Barnett and Finnemore 1999, 2004; Sending and Neumann 2006: 653.
60 Hurd 1999: 400.
61 Barnett 2001: 64.
62 Nedal and Nexon 2019: 6.

63 Alter 2014; Alter et al. 2018; Hooghe et al. 2019; Hurd 1999; Tallberg and Zürn 2019; Tallberg et al. 2018; for an overview, see Kustermans and Horemans 2022.
64 Lake 2009.
65 Hurd 1999.
66 Zürn 2018.
67 Lake 2009: 8.
68 Hurd 1999; Zürn calls this form of authority "inscribed authority" (2018: 43).
69 Wohlforth et al. 2018.
70 Zürn 2018; see also Zürn, this volume.
71 Avant et al. 2010: 11–14.
72 Sending and Neumann 2006.
73 Black 2017; Krisch 2017; Macdonald and Macdonald 2017.
74 Sending 2015.
75 Hurd 1999; Lake 2009.
76 Hooghe and Marks 2015; Hooghe et al. 2017.
77 Alter et al. 2018; Barnett and Finnemore 2004; Heupel and Zürn 2017.
78 Kreuder-Sonnen 2019.
79 Alter et al. 2018; see also Morse and Keohane 2014.
80 See also Tallberg and Zürn 2019.
81 Zürn 2018: 95–104.
82 Deitelhoff and Daase 2021.
83 Buchanan 2003; Tallberg et al. 2018: 8–10.
84 Pouliot 2017: 119, 2021; Sending 2017; Witt 2022.
85 Barnett and Duvall 2004; Katzenstein and Seybert 2018.
86 Gallie 1956.
87 Rawls 1971: 5.
88 Barnett and Duvall 2004: 12.
89 Rawls 1971.
90 Even this is rather a matter of degree not of category if empirical statehood across the globe is taken into account, where areas of limited statehood and the structures of rule and authority prevalent therein demonstrate the limitations of the ideal of a uniform power constituting state order that is still upheld (Clapham 1998; Risse 2013).
91 See also Daase and Deitelhoff 2019; Donnelly 2017: 256; McConaughey et al. 2018; Scholte 2020.
92 Waltz 1979.
93 Deitelhoff and Daase 2021.
94 See also Donnelly 2017, 265.

Part I

Theorizing Rule

2 Authority in International Relations

Contracted, Inscribed, or Reflexive?

Michael Zürn[1]

In the last two decades, students of International Relations (IR) have increasingly added terms like "governance," "authority," "domination," "stratification," and "rule" to their repertoire. They reject the notion of anarchy and point to elements of rule in the global system. This chapter aims at contributing to this shift by focusing on the use of the concept of authority for the analysis of global governance institutions. In line with the introduction to this volume, authority is considered as a specific mode of "formally or informally institutionalized sub und superordination."[2]

Different from the introduction,[3] both authority and rule are considered in this chapter as analytical concepts to grasp (different) forms of domination that are based on recognition. Authority is a functionally differentiated form of a right to do something; it is specialized in the sense that it is limited to certain tasks and functions. The authority of the driving instructor is an example. In contrast, "rule" or "systems of rule" refers to a social relationship as a whole – as in the master–slave relationship. We, therefore, can speak of political rule if it is systematic in the sense that it can potentially take action regarding all conceivable issues. Whereas rule, in this use of the term, is encompassing or systemic, and it often involves the recognition that force can be used to enforce rules, authority is more limited to specific issues and functions, and it does not necessarily involve the acceptance of rule enforcement.

Both authority and systems of rule refer to institutionalized forms of domination (sub- and superordination) that are not merely based on coercion and incentives. In focusing on such mutually recognized forms of domination, the concepts of authority and rule point to a social paradox. They involve a form of power that is based neither exclusively on coercion, nor only on the manipulation of incentives, and also not only on persuasion, but it includes the recognition of inequality among actors. The exercise of authority and rule is based on an asymmetric relationship that is acknowledged by both sides: by the superordinate and the subordinate. Authority and rule thus involve "voluntary subordination" but still point to a power relationship. It is a "social paradox" that is at the core of these concepts.

I argue in this chapter that this social paradox is especially accentuated when it comes to the context of global governance and International Organizations (IOs). In this context, authority is more prevalent than systems of rule. I present three theoretical solutions to the social paradox and, thus, three conceptions of authority. In the section "International Authority as Social Paradox," I elaborate on the social paradox of international authority in the context of global governance. This part is followed by a brief discussion of the two dominant conceptions of the concept of authority in IR. Both the notion of contracted authority and the idea of inscribed authority are presented as possible responses to the paradox, but they are also criticized for their shortcomings in the global governance context. Against this background, I develop in the following section the conception of reflexive authority that aims at avoiding the weaknesses of the other two approaches. In the concluding part, I take up the critique of the conception of reflexive authority.

International Authority as Social Paradox

The exercise of power includes all instances in which an actor *A* brings an actor *B* to think or do something that they would not have thought or done otherwise.[4] In this definition, if we replace actor *A* by something that comprises not only actors but also structures, the definition becomes even more encompassing.[5] In any case, power can come in different forms. First, those who do something that they actually do not want to do may be forced to do so. In this version, an actor does something because they fear the consequences of not doing so – either a punishment or a withdrawal of incentives. Power is involved secondarily when someone gets persuaded or manipulated to change beliefs in a way that affects their behavior. In this case, the subordinate does something because they get convinced by the power of the better argument or by some form of cognitive manipulation that certain behavior is appropriate. These two logics have dominated the thinking about cooperation and institutions in IR for the last decades. They came in different conceptions and juxtapositions, such as the logic of consequentiality and the logic of appropriateness,[6] or, in another take, the logic of bargaining and the logic of arguing,[7] or strategic and deliberative action.[8]

In contrast, the concept of authority points to the logic of deference as a third form of power. It is based on the acceptance of a decision or an interpretation because it comes from a certain source. It is a belief in certain qualities of authority that make subordinates adapt their beliefs and behavior. The foundational treatment of the concept in modern social sciences probably is the one by Max Weber in his sociology of domination. He defines rule as "the chance that certain specific (or all) commands will be obeyed by a given group of persons."[9] It thus does not include every mode of exercising "power" or "influence" over other persons. Rule ("authority") in this sense may be based in individual cases on the most diverse motives of docility: from dull habituation to purely instrumental considerations. Yet a certain minimum of willingness to obey, that is, an interest (based on ulterior motives or genuine acceptance) in obedience, belongs to every genuine relationship of rule."[10]

The "interest in obedience" requires explanation. The paradoxical core of the concept of authority has been pointed out by many of the best-known social theorists. Max Horkheimer, for instance, talks about "affirmed dependency,"[11] while Pierre Bourdieu labels the same phenomenon the "complicity of the dominated."[12] The deference to commands of others sounds paradoxical and invokes theories about the sources of abnormality. Indeed, the authoritarian personality[13] and the Milgram experiment[14] are still among the most often cited works on authority. Yet these seminal theories about the social origins of mindless obedience do not help much to understand the pervasive and partially productive role of authority relationships in many modern societies and the global political system.

The notion of interest in obedience becomes even more puzzling when it comes to IR and global governance. In global governance, authority is often exercised by international and transnational institutions. Such institutions are mostly associated with IOs. The actors who run authority-holding IOs are international administrators (secretariats) as well as the executives of important states and corporations. Subordinates of these authorities are members of the world society consisting of both states and civil societies; that is, state executives, non-governmental organizations (NGOs), multinational enterprises, interest groups, and sometimes individuals. International and transnational authority holders depend on the recognition of audiences, namely their constituencies and external observers. But why should the Australian government, for instance, have an interest in being obedient to the World Trade Organization (WTO)? And why should the Austrian people accept a directive by the European Union (EU) to open borders for migrants?

It is for four reasons that interest for deference sounds especially peculiar when it comes to global governance. First of all, nations and their governments mostly strive for sovereignty and are willing to renounce it only under specific circumstances. Why should social actors that usually strive for autonomy or even dominance accept their subordination without being forced, incentivized, or persuaded to do so? Secondly, the global governance authorities are young. The absolute majority of IOs are the product of state interactions after World War II, and transnational authorities developed mainly from the 1980s onward. Unlike the authority relationship between some individuals and, say, clerics, global governance institutions were not prior to the birth of most nation-states; it was rather the other way around. Many nations and states were not born into a pre-existing practice of authority of global governance. Thirdly, states and the societies governed by them have established numerous mechanisms of questioning any kind of obligation in the international realm – both within the government and outside in the form of expertise in the parliament, universities, and think tanks. Finally, global governance authorities target, among others, states that have considerably more resources at their disposal than any conceivable IO. All IOs, including the EU, have less staff than any of the big cities in Europe. This makes authority in global governance again different from traditional authority relationships in which the authority usually possesses more resources and capacities than the individuals obedient to authority. It seems that the notion of "affirmed dependency" or the "complicity of the dominated" poses even more of a social paradox for global governance institutions than it does in authority relationships between institutions and individuals.

In the remainder of the chapter, I will briefly distinguish two dominant responses to this paradox in global governance research.[15] On the basis of a critique of these two versions dominant in IR – the former broadly associated with a rationalist and the latter with a constructivist understanding of international institutions – I lay out a third response. The notion of "reflexive authority" builds on a service conception of authority.[16] In contrast to contracted and inscribed authority, it sees authority in global governance as deriving from epistemic foundations that include the permanent monitoring of authorities.[17]

Conceptions of International Public Authority

Authority relationships have for a long time been only implicitly part of IR. Some influential authors – loosely associated with realist thinking – for instance, see the international system as a progression of hegemonic constellations based on both hard and soft power.[18] Besides, theories of imperialism emphasize the mutual recognition of hierarchical structures as important within imperial settings.[19] In institutionalist theory, the analysis of authority relationships is more recent. To the extent that international institutions are seen as deviating from the consent principle by pooling and delegating authority, the concept is used to study relationships between international institutions on the one hand and states, societies, or individuals on the other.[20] A similar and parallel development took place in the discipline of international law.[21]

The recent contributions usually follow one of two conceptions of authority. The first conception may be labeled "contracted authority." It conceives authority relationships in the international realm as an outcome of a social contract between the later authority holders and their constituency. Such a relationship depends on generating benefits for both sides. A second approach to resolving the paradox can be labeled "inscribed authority." It conceives authority relationships as a result of socialization processes. Based on a critique of these two versions dominant in IR – the former broadly associated with a rationalist and the latter with a constructivist understanding of international institutions – I lay out a third response that I label "reflexive authority." It sees authority in global governance as deriving from epistemic foundations that include the permanent monitoring of authorities.

Contracted Authority

In this understanding, the foundation of authority is a contract. In contracts, autonomous actors agree on a treaty that is of advantage for all who subscribe to it. This liberal conception of authority is reason-based, locates authority mainly in institutions and law, and can be traced back to Hobbes and Locke.[22] In IR, this view is mostly associated with the influential work of David Lake,[23] as well as with the works authored by Alex Cooley and Liesbet Hooghe and colleagues,[24] among others. The essential elements of this conception of authority are commands, legitimacy, and interests.

"One speaks of authority if *B* regards *A*'s command as legitimate and correspondingly has an obligation to obey. ... Whereas power is evidenced in its effects irrespective of their cause, authority exists only to the extent that *B* recognizes an obligation resting on the legitimacy of *A*'s command."[25] It is mostly "legal-rational authority" based on a codified order that needs to be studied in this perspective.[26] Social contracts are then the major source of legitimacy.

This conception of authority hinges on rational interests. Lake puts it very explicitly: "Both dominant and subordinate states have to be better off in hierarchic than in strictly anarchic relations for the contract to be fulfilled."[27] In this view, the conferral of authority is negotiated, and it allows one actor to exercise authority to the extent that it serves the interests of both sides. Authority, therefore, needs to be bought by the dominant actors and holds only for as long as the contract is beneficial for both sides.

According to Lake's analysis,[28] smaller partners recognize US leadership in certain issue areas in return for protection and the provision of collective goods on a bilateral basis. This dyadic understanding of authority leaves little room for the authority of international or transnational organizations. In the dyadic version, *A* and *B* are both states. The dominant state *A* uses contracts as instruments to exercise authority over *B*. The contracts and, thus, international institutions are epiphenomena of the state interactions.

More recent versions of this conception have moved to a triadic conception. In the triadic version, contracts may lead to the pooling or delegation of authority to international institutions. The contractualist version of international authority, however, does not lose sight of the interests that stand behind the establishment of third parties exercising authority. It is open to the possibility that any given IO or third party reflects underlying power constellations.

Such a contractualist conception of authority has a number of advantages. First of all, it is a relational concept of authority emphasizing mutual recognition and thus avoiding any conception that considers authority as a property of an actor based on certain capacities. The second strength derives from building on a clearly identified micro-mechanism. Authority, especially if understood as based on mutual recognition, is not just there as a structure that empowers and constrains actors, but it is also affected by actors and their actions.

At the same time, the contractualist conception of international authority has two critical weaknesses. First, contracted authority is based on – as Vincent Pouliot puts it – excessive voluntarism.[29] The contract view seems to assume that authority depends completely and at all times on legitimacy. As soon as legitimacy – or mutual recognition – is gone, so is authority. Jason Sharman moves the point forward by stating that "[i]f parties are free to bargain, transact or break off negotiations as best suits their individual interests, this suggests a 'horizontal' market interaction on the basis of formally equal parties, rather than one premised on super- and subordination."[30] The contractualist notion of international and transnational authority thus runs in danger of becoming identical with cooperation under anarchy, losing sight of the forms of authority and dominance via global governance institutions. There is little room for illegitimate authority, and the concept has a built-in tendency to become affirmative.

This leads to my second objection. The social paradox of authority is solved by explaining away deference. If the recognition of authority can be explained completely as a contract with reference to pre-defined interests, then it is the outcome of bargaining and not the authority relationship as such that is accepted. To put it differently, in this conception, actors comply "only" content dependently with the contract and do not defer content independently to an authority, which is, according to Joseph Raz, the central feature of an authority relationship.[31] Deference to the authority evaporates in this concept.

Inscribed Authority

Socialization-based accounts of authority give priority to the social order in which individuals are situated. Authority, in this view, is a relationship in which habits are activated and reproduced by actors. Contemporary proponents of this view emphasize that even modern relationships are not based on freedom and autonomy but on socializations that reflect relations of production, the distribution of social capital, or sedimented discourses.[32] In IR, this view is associated with the influential work of Michael Barnett and Martha Finnemore, Ian Hurd, Deborah Avant, and colleagues, as well as Emanuel Adler and Vincent Pouliot.[33]

Michael Barnett and Martha Finnemore define authority as the "ability of one actor to use institutional and discursive resources to induce deference from others."[34] The foundation of deference is legitimacy. Ian Hurd is most explicit in spelling out the role of legitimacy in authority relationships. He claims that "[a] rule will become legitimate to an individual (and therefore become behaviorally significant) when the individual internalizes its content and reconfigures his or her interests according to the rule. When this happens, compliance becomes habitual (in the sense of being the default position) ...."[35] In this understanding, authority is based on shared understandings and is legitimate in the sense that actors have been successfully socialized into them.

It is essentially habits and practices that preexist to which actors get used to performing competently.[36] These are also the mechanisms through which authority relationships and stratification reproduce themselves.

The conception of inscribed authority also has significant strengths. Most importantly, it does not need to reduce authority relationships to mutual interests. It thus allows criticizing social relationships from a normative perspective, even if the relationship is accepted by all participants. The shared understanding of inequality underlying such a relationship needs to be carved out. The conception of inscribed authority aims exactly at that. It takes deference seriously.

For the analysis of authority relationships in global governance, such a perspective also displays weaknesses, however. First of all, given the context, it depends too much on habits. Most states and non-state global governance actors were there before global governance institutions were established. States have invented some of those global governance institutions without first being socialized by them. When France and the United Kingdom (UK) joined the International Monetary Fund (IMF), they either believed in the need to establish a global governance authority in this area or were forced by the US to join in – it was hardly because the structure of the international system socialized them to do so. Moreover, in the inscribed view of authority, fundamental resistance seems to be the primary form of contestation. Since actors have internalized deference, they must free themselves from their socialization and the dominant discourses. Resistance is usually the way to do this.[37] The degree of simple opposition and voice that can be observed in the international realm[38] seems too pervasive for a conception based on internalized habits.[39]

The strong emphasis on internalization in the conception of inscribed authority points to a second weakness. A conception that bases deference completely on internalization seems to miss some of the features of authority relationships in global governance. Deference to reflexive international and transnational authorities is often not internalized but is permanently under observation. Moreover, even in those cases in which deference to the authority gets internalized over time, the norms postulated by the authority may or may not be internalized. The payment of taxes to states, for instance, is rather grudgingly accepted without being transformed into an internalized desire to pay, even if the state, as an authority, is recognized or even internalized. If internalization is emphasized as a micro-mechanism sustaining authority relationships, it neglects the specific features of global governance institutions and also underestimates their degree of instability and contestation.

Reflexive Authority

Building on the conceptions of contracted and inscribed authority and the stated criticisms, I aim at developing a third conception of public authority consisting of reflexivity and requests based on epistemic foundations. This conception claims that authority builds on another logic of action than the logic of appropriateness or the logic of consequentiality. It is neither learning or the quality of a specific argument nor the manipulation of the subordinate's preferences through incentives that leads to deference but the recognition of the authority as worth observing. Authority is a form of power – as Hannah Arendt has put it – that is marked by "recognition by those who are asked to obey; neither coercion nor persuasion is needed."[40]

Reflexivity and Its Epistemic Foundations

In general, current authority relationships in global governance do not reproduce long-standing practices. Against this contextual background, authority is conceptualized as reflexive. Reflexive authority relationships include enlightened and critical subordinates that recognize authorities because they acknowledge their limitations. Reflexive authority thus has advantages for both the authority holders *and* the constituencies. In this sense, I follow the "service conception" of authority as developed by Joseph Raz.[41]

The reflexivity in reflexive authority relationships is twofold. On the one hand, it speaks to an element of enduring reflection about the worthiness of the authority that runs counter to the notion of internalization. While reflexive authority involves dispensing with an exact examination of the specific judgment or decision on the side of subordinates, it at the same is scrutinized by permanent monitoring and consideration of the standards that make an authority appealing and trustworthy. For instance, most people would believe in the climate models of a Nobel laureate without checking all the parameters and equations, which would take a considerably long time. At the same time, the credentials and the reputation of the authority are checked permanently. Authority relationships, therefore, become their own theme in the sense that there is always the possibility of questioning and redesigning the relationship.

On the other hand, the recognition of authority does not exclusively derive from a rationalist conception based on predefined interests; it rather stems from reflections about the limits of rationality. It is, therefore, especially in situations without predefined interests that reflexive authority plays out. By providing information and new perspectives, the authority may shape the preferences. In the case of reflexive authority, the recognition of external authorities is based on the knowledge about the limitations of one's own rationality and information base.[42] In turn, authorities offer either superior knowledge or an impartial perspective, or both.[43]

Reflexive authorities depend on the epistemic constructions that identify the limits of subordinates and the realm of the superiority of an authority. In contrast to the contractual notion of international authority, reflexive authority emphasizes the role of knowledge orders as the constitutive background of authority relationships and deference.[44] Yet, the notion of reflexive authority does not depend on the assumption that those who are considered as authorities are indeed closer to the truth. Rather it points to the relevance of the social process in which superior knowledge or an impartial perspective is established. The focus on the social processes of knowledge production highlights the role of science therein. The whole notion of "scientification" of social processes[45] indicates the importance of science in this process.

Science has shown its effectiveness in the course of history. At the same time, it has developed reputational mechanisms – such as the ranking of universities, prizes for outstanding scientists, and citation indexes – that tell us which scientific opinion is more scientific. As a consequence, those who question authorities often need to question science as well. Critics of genetically modified foods, for instance, tend not to challenge the scientific quality of studies that point to the nonhazardousness of these products. Instead, they cast doubts on whether science can assign ethical considerations an appropriate place and whether science can take into account the "unknown unknowns." Most strategies that aim at questioning authority, therefore, involve epistemic challenges to the dominant knowledge order.

Requests

Most accounts of inscribed and contracted authority see commands at the core of the exercise of authority. Reflexive authority does not work exclusively with "commands to do x" but includes "requests to consider y." Requests can come either indirectly in the form of behavioral implications of interpretations or directly in the form of demands. In both cases, it is not possible to speak of commands. Most analysts of international authority, therefore, avoid statements like "The WTO commands the government of the US to reduce tariffs," or "The World Health Organization (WHO) commands France to invest more in health."

Reflexive public authorities rather request to take into account reasons as a means to pursue international or global goals. Even when the WHO directly requests a new vaccination, states do not take this as a command. This applies especially to all the cases of indirect demands that are put forward by international authorities, such as the Programme for International Student Assessment (PISA) benchmarking for the quality of high schools. In this case, the authority of international and transnational institutions is based on something that is labeled "secondary reasons" in pragmatist philosophy. Especially when one is uncertain about the primary reasons for making a decision (e.g., "Is the food good in this restaurant?"), secondary reasons ("If they have a certificate, it must be good") become decisive. This deference to the certification scheme, however, excludes neither an own judgment afterward ("The food was, despite the recommendation, mediocre") nor the possibility of shifting to another certification scheme after negative experiences have multiplied.

Different reflexive authorities may thus compete with each other allowing for forum shopping on the side of the subordinates. It follows that the exercise of authority is not always based on a prior delegation of authority. Self-nominated authorities can formulate rules, requests, and recommendations in the first place, which then subsequently become authoritative.[46]

Moreover, in the reflexive conception of authority, it is not the perceived "duty to follow" that is decisive. One usually does not follow a restaurant guide because one feels a duty to do so. Secondary reasons do not create a "duty" to follow. Indeed, states usually follow IO prescriptions because they feel that the authority is doing a good service.

Epistemic and Political Authority

Two basic types of authority can be identified: the authority to make decisions and the authority to provide interpretations. The authority to make decisions can be called "political authority," and the authority to make interpretations "epistemic authority." In both cases, international and transnational authorities make decisions that affect the freedom of the constituent units and justify this with reference to a common good. In this sense, they both represent a form of public authority.[47] The epistemic foundation of authority applies to both political and epistemic authorities. The recognition of political authority as having an impartial or third perspective that allows them to make requests justified with reference to a common good depends as much on knowledge construction as it does on the recognition of valid information production in the case of epistemic authority. Both types of reflexive authority are founded in epistemic constructions.

In the case of "political authority," stipulations, rules, and norms are viewed as "binding" for a certain collective. Political authority rests on the acknowledgment that there needs to be an institution that is authorized to make collectively binding decisions to promote the common good and prevent chaos. Political authorities, thus, have the right to make decisions that violate the particular interests of members in the short term. Political authority rests on a cognitive framework that permits a common interpretation of the common good.

On the international and transnational level, newly institutionalized political authorities have emerged in the last decade. The principle that a given territory is governed exclusively by the national government no longer holds. International institutions circumvent the consent principle by making decisions through forms of majority voting or the informal dominance of hegemonic powers. Majority decisions and the exercise of dominance by strong countries enhance the capacity of international institutions to act by avoiding vetoes by single states and overcoming blockades. Today, roughly two-thirds of all IOs – in which at least one major power participates – have the possibility of taking decisions by a majority vote.[48] Moreover, states are increasingly delegating power directly to IOs. The authority index developed by Liesbet Hooghe and Gary Marks shows a marked increase in the last decades.[49] The development that is captured in the International Authority Database (IAD) points to a very similar level of rise.[50]

To the extent that the new international institutions exercise political authority, they set rules that reduce the room to maneuver for national states and govern formerly purely domestic affairs either directly or indirectly. Especially powerful states aim to use such authorities to exercise influence outside of their territory; at the same time, they often try to limit the authorities' influence on their own affairs. Especially powerful states, therefore, keep the possibility of evaluation and of shifting loyalty, and they even create circumstances to extend these options. The notions of "counter-multilateralism"[51] and "deliberate fragmentation"[52] point to this strategy: States recognize "multiple" authorities with overlapping competencies in order to put pressure on authorities to act not against their interests, as well as to keep the option of shifting loyalty.

The other basic type of authority can be labeled "epistemic authority." Epistemic authorities provide interpretations that structure the behavior of others. Epistemic authority is based on expert knowledge and moral integrity. The views and positions of an authority are adopted because they appear to be both knowledgeable and nonpartisan at the same time. Epistemic authority is based on the assumption that knowledge and expertise are unequally distributed, but a common epistemological framework makes it possible to ascertain knowledge inequality. An epistemic authority need not, in all cases, convince people factually and in detail. It is, therefore, not the quality of the specific argumentation, but rather the general reputation of an institution or a person that is decisive. What is involved is governance by reputation,[53] most often in the form of governance by numbers[54] or indicators.[55]

The significance of institutions with purely epistemic authority has unquestionably increased on the transnational level. It particularly includes influential and "credible" NGOs such as Greenpeace – in the environmental area – or Amnesty International – in the area of human rights – which are active in setting as well as monitoring norms. The growth of transnationally active NGOs has been enormous; the access to IOs has increased dramatically as well, by a factor of three since 1975.[56]

A special version of this type of public authority arises when an epistemic authority is assigned to that status by political institutions. Then we may speak of "politically assigned epistemic authorities" (PAEAs). It is especially this type of authority that has gained enormously in importance and changed the constellation in the exercise of public power. At the international as well as the transnational level, such PAEAs have moved into the focus of attention, particularly during the past two decades. The rating agencies, the Intergovernmental Board for International Public Sector Accounting, the International Panel for Climate Change, the international evaluation institutions in the area of environmental policy in general, the Organization for Economic Co-operation and Development in the area of educational policy and international courts are all political institutions that have become more influential over the past two decades by formulating recommendations based on expertise. In general, the authority of IOs has risen steeply regarding the policy functions of agenda setting, knowledge generation, and norm interpretation,[57] pointing to the growing relevance of PAEAs. In these cases, the epistemic authority comes with some institutional resources and means to achieve compliance with the requests. PAEAs thus blur the distinction between epistemic and political authority.

Perpetuation and Legitimation

While it is true that an authority relationship may, in some cases, emerge spontaneously – for instance, in crisis situations – and does not require prior delegation, the future of this relationship will not forget the spontaneous moment. If there is a fire in a theater, a few may turn out to coordinate the exit movement without any such preassignment. If the same group of people that spend the evening in the theater would sit in an airplane and an emergency were to arise, it is likely that the passengers would look at the same people asking for instructions. Any authority relationship has, therefore, a tendency to be not a one-shot instance but to be durable for at least some time. Such a transformation of the spontaneous moment can come in the form of either "objectification" or in the form of "institutionalization."

An authority relationship is "objectivized"[58] if the knowledge order that underlies the relationship becomes a dominant worldview or ideology that reaches beyond the immediately involved actors to external audiences.[59] It is then broadly accepted that the authority holder represents the "objective," "non-particularistic" perspective. Scientists with public appeal are a case in point. To the extent that they get broadly accepted by external audiences, objectification points also to social pressure and coercion. If an actor rejects insights from such an "authority" that are seen as "objective" and unquestionable, the danger of social exclusion and being seen as weird arises. The voluntariness of subordination is then reduced.

Objectivized authority can transform into indirect coercion when third parties are dependent on those who acknowledge an authority. An institution carrying out quality tests about consumer products, for instance, may, in the first place, only influence those consumers who are reading the journal reporting the test. Consumers often follow the "request" of the test, although it is in no way binding. At the same time, epistemic authorities may induce deference from the producer of consumption goods indirectly by affecting the behavior of consumers. If the tester enjoys high credibility and affects consumer choice strongly, then their ideas about a good product become "indirectly binding" for the producer via the pressure of a third party, that is, a large share of consumers.

The other form of perpetuation of authority is *institutionalization*. An authority relationship is institutionalized when the decisions and interpretations are *a priori* delegated or pooled.[60] Governments represent an ideal type for this form of authority perpetuation. Also, IOs can be seen as an institutionalized authority. Since the establishment of international institutions involve sunk costs that are lost if one exits, and breaking a commitment in addition often leads to reputational losses, the cost-free voluntariness of subordinations is reduced the very moment authority is institutionalized.

When authority is objectivized or institutionalized, it perpetuates, and in this way, it involves elements of coercion. Every institutionalized authority, therefore, tends to legitimate its practice in order to arouse the belief in its legitimacy.[61] This distinction between "legitimacy beliefs" and "legitimation processes" is important because it helps to disentangle authority and legitimacy while still maintaining their close link via the notion of legitimation processes.[62]

Such a conceptual separation between authority and legitimacy contradicts the use in some areas of social sciences, where an understanding of authority is often defined as "legitimate power." Also, in IR, many conceptions link legitimacy so closely to authority as to make "legitimate authority" a pleonasm, and the two notions become virtually indistinguishable.[63] The key implication of this view is spelled out by Hurd openly: "The phrase 'legitimate authority' is redundant."[64] This fusionist view ("authority is legitimate power") leads to counterintuitive implications. First, if legitimacy and authority are two sides of a coin, then the more authority an institution has, the more legitimate it must be.

From a normative point of view (external perspective), this is absurd, because only the unconstrained master would enjoy full legitimacy. It is also problematic from an empirical perspective, which looks at internal perspectives on authority since institutions sometimes acquire new institutional competencies without necessarily being seen as more legitimate by all affected actors. Second, the fusionist view does not allow for the distinction between authority holders and institutionalized authority. One may consider, for instance, a specific practice of an authority holder (a specific government) as illegitimate while still recognizing the authority (the government) in principle.[65]

Forms of Contestation

In contrast to the fusionist view, legitimacy can most generally be described as the "generalized perception or assumption that the *actions* of an entity are desirable, proper, or appropriate within some socially constructed system of norms, values, beliefs, and definitions."[66] The legitimacy of a public authority thus refers to the acceptance of an institution's "activities" or "practices": the exercise of authority as appropriate among its constituencies (internal legitimacy) and outside observers (external legitimacy). It is, therefore, primarily these practices and much less the constitutive act that drives legitimation efforts by those claiming authority.[67] The views and beliefs of the audiences (i.e., constituencies and observers) are seen as the outcome of a process in which, on the one hand, authority holders and other supporters (most often deliberately) seek to make a political institution more legitimate by boosting beliefs that authority is exercised appropriately. This process is called legitimation – the permanent attempt to arouse and nurse the beliefs in legitimacy. On the other hand, where actors seek to undermine the legitimacy of a political institution, one can speak of delegitimation. Legitimation and delegitimation processes provide the link between authority and legitimacy. Both authority and legitimacy are based on the willingness to follow, but the process of recognition refers to different levels. The first level refers to the recognition of authority as desirable in principle to achieve certain goals and common good. The second level of recognition is about the appropriate exercise of authority.

Without first-level recognition, there would be no institutionalization of authority, nor any pooling of authority or delegation to IOs in the first place. Whereas a commonly recognized authority can advance the common good, it certainly does not always do so. The authority may be a necessary condition for achieving a common good, but it is certainly not sufficient. Only if the authority is being appropriately exercised in line with commonly shared normative principles, it serves its social purpose it is supposedly made for. Whereas the first-level recognition of authority refers to the recognition of the social purpose and the *ex-ante* acceptance of capacities, the second-level recognition of legitimacy refers to the practice of exercising authority and the *ex-post* acceptance of activities. To exemplify, anarchists in the late nineteenth century questioned all the authorities in many states in Europe (they did not think that the state should have authority at all), while most communists were in favor of a strong state but questioned the actual regime's legitimacy (they questioned the specific exercise of authority). In a nutshell, legitimacy beliefs involve a judgment about the exercise of an authority. In this sense, the concept of legitimacy is parasitic on the concept of authority. Legitimacy beliefs form in an ongoing process of legitimation and delegitimation.

By distinguishing authority and legitimacy as two different levels of recognition and by emphasizing the reflexivity of subordinates, it becomes easier to grasp different forms of contestation or politicization.[68] To begin with, by pointing to requests as means of exercising authority, the conception of reflexive authority considers "noncompliance" as a contestation of a given decision or interpretation without challenging the legitimacy or authority of an institution. The EU, for instance, does not comply with the substantial judgment of the WTO Dispute Settlement Body but still pays the fine for noncompliance. In this way, the EU acknowledges the authority and the legitimacy of the institution but rejects a given request or policy. Secondly, acts of "delegitimation" point to efforts that target a given exercise of authority for not meeting the criteria of legitimacy, such as impartiality, democratic participation, fair distribution, or the rule of law. It is common for such delegitimation efforts that they are targeted at politics, but they do not necessarily challenge the polity. Much criticism of the EU refers to its lack of legitimacy without questioning European authorities as such. Similarly, most of those who saw the Trump administration exercising authority illegitimately do not question the authority of the presidency as such. Both noncompliance and delegitimation represent forms of opposition to given policies or the politics underlying them. Finally, one may point to the comparatively rare instances where the authority as such is contested. The Brexit campaign, for instance, challenged the need for European authorities as a whole and did not stop at criticism of the exercise of European authority. One may label this form of contestation as "dissidence."[69] These three types of contestation aim at different targets (see Table 2.1). The targets essentially replicate the distinction between policy, politics, and polity.

Table 2.1 *Contracted, inscribed, and reflexive authority*

	Contracted Authority	Inscribed Authority	Reflexive Authority
Commands (including enforcement) or requests	Commands derived from contracts	Internalized commands	Requests
Logic of action	Interest-based compliance	Socialization-based appropriateness (learned competence)	Reflected deference
Agent or structure	Actor interests	Inscribed in structures	Actors based on epistemic foundations
Fusionist or separate	Fusionist	Fusionist	Separate
Primary form of contestations	Noncompliance	Resistance	Noncompliance, delegitimation, and dissidence

To sum up the conceptual discussion of authority, reflexive authority is different from both the contractualist and the inscribed conception of authority. In reflexive authority relationships, the authority holder sends requests instead of commands to constituencies who know about their limitations but tend to monitor the authorities closely. Reflexive authority is based on the acceptance of a knowledge order that reproduces the authority relationship. Whereas reflexive authority can – under special circumstances – transform into habituation, especially on the side of those members of the constituency that lack informational and monitoring capacities, this is not a part of the definition. The concept of reflexive authority is compatible with the idea of "liquid authority."[70] Whereas liquid authority mainly sheds light on the form (or the aggregate state) of international and transnational institutions, reflexive authority looks at its social foundation. The ongoing contestation of the underlying episteme of international and transnational authorities, the deliberate and permanent monitoring of these authorities, and strategies developed to maintain room for maneuver despite recognizing authorities, in principle, are the features of reflexive authority that induce liquidity.

Conclusion: On the Critique of Reflexive Authority

Authority involves the social paradox of voluntary subordination that is especially accentuated when it comes to the context of global governance and IOs. After a critical discussion of the two dominant conceptions of the concept of authority in IR – the notion of contracted authority and the idea of inscribed authority – I developed the conception of reflexive authority that aims at avoiding the weaknesses of the other two approaches. It builds on another logic of action than the logic of appropriateness or the logic of consequentiality. It is neither learning nor the quality of a specific argument, nor a manipulation of the subordinate's preferences through incentives that lead to deference, but the recognition of the authority as worth observing. In this sense, it is cognition or the power of an episteme that creates authority. In this conclusion, I take up a specific set of criticisms of this reflexive conception of authority.

Some scholars reject the concept of authority as such and suggest others in order to highlight inequality in global politics. I use the work of Christopher Daase and Nicole Deitelhoff,[71] as well as Vincent Pouliot,[72] as representatives of this strand of research. For them, the concept of authority is incomplete since it builds on agreement and consensus and thus cannot grasp processes of domination and the (re-)production of inequality in the global system. Vincent Pouliot, for instance, writes: "To say the subordinates abide by a given domination structures out of choice or decision … implies that they somewhat approve it."[73] Yet, from his practice theory point of view, "subordinates are forced into reproducing the structures. Hierarchy is reproduced through faking it."[74] Similarly, Christopher Daase and Nicole Deitelhoff argue that authority is a liberal concept and, therefore, it is based on consent and legitimacy, thus overlooking the role of contestation and coercion.[75] Instead, they suggest the concept of rule and seek sites of resistance in order to identify rule.

To start with, the use of the concept of authority should not necessarily include the assumption of its legitimacy. If one accepts the statement that institutionalized authority always requires legitimation but not every institutionalized authority is legitimate, then there is the possibility of unsuccessful legitimation and illegitimate authority. An authority is illegitimate if it is regularly exercised in a way that is not considered as legitimate either by external observers (including normative theorists) or by subordinates. If the exercise of authority is seen as not serving the social purpose that it has been created for and as not acting impartial, then legitimacy beliefs drop, yet the authority may still be recognized. Most revolutions against authoritarian states have been targeted against the exercise of the authority, not against the need for the state to exercise authority. In these cases, the recognition of the state remained, while its exercise of authority was not considered legitimate. In any case, the reflexive conception is open to kinds of contestation. Contestation is built into the notion of reflexivity, since international authorities are permanently confronted with critical audiences. Against this background, we demonstrated that the rise of authority leads to a rise of politicization and contestation and to legitimation struggles.[76]

Moreover, even in those cases in which the authority as such is questioned, this does not necessarily cause the authority to disappear. Authority can be effective if legitimacy beliefs are absent. The reason for this is objectification and institutionalization. If states have agreed to confer authority to an IO, it does not suffice to withdraw recognition. As long as the institution exists and maintains a certain level of recognition by the other members, the request formulated comes with a sense that it has to be obliged with. In some cases, the conferral of authority even includes the right to enforcement. Authority then mingles with force, but the power is in this case still based on the recognition of the authority. Enforcement and the threat of enforcement are used when recognition does not work.

In addition, authorities may indirectly exercise force. Many lenders adopt the judgment of rating agencies – a transnational authority – as guidance without inspecting the judgments in each individual case. Rating agencies thus exercise authority over lenders. Yet in this way, rating agencies also exert pressure on states to follow the policies that give them a good rating; otherwise, borrowing becomes impossible or at least more costly. In this indirect way, the objectification of epistemic authority may create a coercive effect. Again, authority may lead to constellations that forces subordinates to comply.

Pouliot is, therefore, correct in emphasizing that "one cannot infer either a positive cost-benefit calculus or 'third degree internalization' simply from compliant behavior."[77] Indeed, authority needs not to be reduced to consent. Rather, authority regularly translates into super- and subordination to the extent that they are perpetuated. In this case, authorities usually contain elements of force in addition to deference.

Moreover, international authority does not only lead to super- and subordination between IOs and states, it also reinforces inequalities between states. As long as international institutions are intergovernmental bodies based on consent, their effect on sovereign equality is ambivalent but often positive overall. Although both procedural and substantive rules are likely to reflect power inequalities in these institutions, the legal equality expressed in the consent principle acts as an equalizing force. Insofar as international institutions exercise authority, however, the consent principle is undermined, and a centralization of power takes place. The rise of authority leads to the institutionalization of inequality among states.[78]

As a consequence, the more the consent principle in world politics is replaced with international and transnational authority, the more institutionalization of inequality between states can be observed. While inequality between states has certainly been prior to the institutionalization of authority, it is especially in the context of the rise of international authority that inequality gets institutionalized and "lowly states" get aware of their "place." The rise of international authority thus fosters "a practical understanding of the roles and ranks that different countries play through their ambassadors."[79] It is no coincidence that "international pecking orders" can be best illustrated by the "informal hierarchies of standing among permanent representatives and their teams posted to major IO headquarters."[80] At the same time, the rise of international authority empowers IOs in their relationship with most states. This is a liquid relationship which can be much more easily contested than the inequality between states.

Finally, Daase and Deitelhoff introduce the term "rule" as a non-consensual and non-liberal alternative to authority.[81] While I maintain that legitimacy is not part of the concept of authority (at least not in the conception of reflexive authority) and that the concept of rule also involves an element of recognition, I concur with Daase and Deitelhoff that there are indeed good reasons to distinguish – in contrast to Weber – between authority and rule/domination. In my view, however, the two terms should be distinguished according to their scope, and not according to the mode of action they involve.

International authorities play out in specifically defined and circumscribed contexts: They may be part of a system of loosely coupled spheres of authority, as in global governance, or they may be part of a system of rule as in the constitutionalized nation-state. While both international and national courts hold authority, the modern state – with its monopoly of the legitimate use of force and a general responsibility for the development of a given society – exercises rule.

Such a distinction based on scope maintains the commonality between authority and rule. None of the two concepts should be equated with either solely coercion or solely consent. Both rule and authority depend – at least to some extent – on social recognition. Both concepts contain – to some extent – the social paradox of voluntary subordination. Coercion usually plays a larger role in a system of rule than in the case of specific authorities. Accordingly, an illegitimate system of rule backed up by force can, therefore, stay longer than an illegitimate authority. Yet it seems mistaken to state that rule is based on coercive power and authority on consent. A system of rule based on coercion alone cannot exist for long either.[82]

References

Adler, Emanuel, and Vincent Pouliot. 2011. "International Practices." *International Theory* 3(1): 1–36.

Adorno, Theodor W., Else Frenkel-Brunswik, Daniel. J. Levinson, and R. Nevitt. Sanford. 1950. *The Authoritarian Personality*. New York: Harper.

Alter, Karen, Laurence Helfer, and Mikael Madsen. 2016. "How Context Shapes the Authority of International Courts." *Law and Contemporary Problems* 79(1): 1–36.

Arendt, Hannah. 1970. *On Violence*. New York: Harcourt, Brace and World.

Avant, Deborah D., Martha Finnemore, and Susan K. Sell. 2010. "Who Governs the Globe?," in Deborah D. Avant, Martha Finnemore, and Susan K. Sell (eds.), *Who Governs the Globe?* New York: Cambridge University Press, pp. 1–34.

Barker, Rodney. 2001. *Legitimating Identities: The Self-Presentations of Rulers and Subjects*. Cambridge: Cambridge University Press.

Barnett, Michael, and Raymond Duvall (eds.). 2005. *Power in Global Governance*. Cambridge: Cambridge University Press.

Barnett, Michael, and Martha Finnemore. 2004. *Rules for the World: International Organizations in Global Politics*. Ithaca: Cornell University Press.

Benvenisti, Eyal, and George W. Downs. 2009. "National Courts, Domestic Democracy, and the Evolution of International Law." *European Journal of International Law* 20(1): 59–72.

Biersteker, Thomas J., and Rodney B. Hall (eds.). 2002. *The Emergence of Private Authority in Global Governance*. Cambridge: Cambridge University Press.

Black, Julia. 2017. "'Says Who?' Liquid Authority and Interpretive Control in Transnational Regulatory Regimes." *International Theory* 9(2): 286–310.

Blake, Daniel, and Autumn Payton. 2008. "Voting Rules in International Organizations: Reflections of Power or Facilitators of Cooperation?" Paper presented at the ISA's 49th Annual Convention, 2008, San Francisco, CA.

Borchardt, Knut, Edith Hanke, and Wolfgang Schluchter (eds.). 2013. *Max Weber Gesamtausgabe I/23. Wirtschaft und Gesellschaft: Soziologie*. Tübingen: Mohr Siebeck.

Börzel, Tanja, and Michael Zürn. 2021. "Contestations of the Liberal International Order: From Liberal Multilateralism to Postnational Liberalism." *International Organization* 75(2): 282–305.

Bourdieu, Pierre. 1990. *The Logic of Practice*. Stanford: Stanford University Press.

Bourdieu, Pierre. 1991. *Language and Symbolic Power*. Cambridge: Polity Press.

Breitmeier, Helmut, Oran R. Young, and Michael Zürn. 2006. *Analyzing International Environmental Regimes. From Case Study to Database*. Cambridge: MIT Press.

Bull, Hedley. 1977. *The Anarchical Society. A Study of Order in World Politics*. Basingstoke/London: MacMillan.

Butler, Judith P. 1996. *Excitable Speech: A Politics of the Performative*. New York: Routledge.

Cooley, Alexander. 2005. *Logics of Hierarchy: The Organization of Empires, States, and Military Occupations*. Ithaca: Cornell University Press.

Daase, Christopher, and Nicole Deitelhoff. 2015. "Jenseits der Anarchie: Widerstand und Herrschaft im internationalen System." *Politische Vierteljahresschrift* 56(2): 299–318.

Daase, Christopher, Nicole Deitelhoff, Ben Kamis, Jannik Pfister, and Philip Wallmeier (eds.). 2017. *Herrschaft in den Internationalen Beziehungen*. Wiesbaden: Springer VS.

Davis, Kevin E., Benedict Kingsbury, and Sally Engle Merry. 2012. "Indicators as a Technology of Global Governance." *Law & Society Review* 46(1): 71–104.

de Wilde, Pieter, Anna Leupold, and Henning Schmidtke. 2016. "Introduction: The Differentiated Politicisation of European Governance." *West European Politics* 39(1): 3–22.

de Wilde, Pieter, and Michael Zürn. 2012. "Can the Politicization of European Integration Be Reversed?" *Journal of Common Market Studies* 50(S1): 137–153.

Doyle, Michael W. 1986. *Empires*. Ithaca: Cornell University Press.

Elster, Jon. 1986. *Ulysses and the Sirens: Studies in Rationality and Irrationality*. Cambridge: Cambridge University Press.

Elster, Jon. 1995. "Strategic Uses of Arguments," in Kenneth J. Arrow, Robert H. Mnookin, Lee Ross, and Amos Tversky (eds.), *Barriers to Conflict Resolution*. New York: W.W. Norton, pp. 236–257.

Elster, Jon. 1999. "Arguing and Bargaining in Two Constituent Assemblies." *University of Pennsylvania Journal of Constitutional Law* 2: 345.

Enoch, David. 2014. "Authority and Reason-Giving." *Philosophy and Phenomenological Research* 89(2): 296–332.

Galtung, Johan. 1972. "Eine strukturelle Theorie des Imperialismus," in Dieter Senghaas (ed.), *Imperialismus und strukturelle Gewalt. Analysen über abhängige Produktion*. Frankfurt a. M.: Suhrkamp, pp. 29–104.

Geis, Anna, Frank Nullmeier, and Christopher Daase (eds.). 2012. *Der Aufstieg der Legitimitätspolitik. Rechtfertigung und Kritik politisch-ökonomischer Ordnungen* (Leviathan Sonderband 40/27). Baden-Baden: Nomos.

Habermas, Jürgen. 1985. *The Theory of Communicative Action. Reason and the Rationalization of Society*. Boston: Beacon Press.

Habermas, Jürgen. 1996. *Between Facts and Norms: Contributions to a Discourse Theory of Law and Democracy*. Cambridge: MIT Press.

Hooghe, Liesbet, Gary Marks, Tobias Lenz, Jeanine Bezuijen, Besir Ceka, and Svet Derderyan. 2017. *Measuring International Authority. A Postfunctionalist Theory of Governance, Volume III*. Corby: Oxford University Press.

Horkheimer, Max. 1987a [1936]. "Allgemeiner Teil," in Max Horkheimer (ed.), *Studien über Autorität und Familie*. Lüneburg: Dietrich zu Klampen Verlag, pp. 3–76.

Horkheimer, Max, ed. 1987b [1936]. *Studien über Autorität und Familie*. Lüneburg: Dietrich zu Klampen Verlag.

Hurd, Ian. 1999. "Legitimacy and Authority in International Politics." *International Organization* 53(2): 379–408.

Hurd, Ian. 2007. *After Anarchy: Legitimacy and Power in the United Nations Security Council*. Princeton: Princeton University Press.
Hutter, Swen, and Edgar Grande. 2014. "Politicizing Europe in the National Electoral Arena: A Comparative Analysis of Five West European Countries, 1970–2010." *Journal of Common Market Studies* 52(5): 1002–1018.
Kelley, Judith, and Beth Simmons. 2015. "Politics by Number: Indicators as Social Pressure in International Relations." *American Journal of Political Science* 59: 1146–1161.
Kennedy, Paul. 1989. *The Rise and Fall of the Great Powers: Economic Change and Military Conflict from 1500 to 2000*, New York: Knopf.
Kojéve, Alexandre. 1975. *Hegel: Eine Vergegenwärtigung seines Denkens*. Frankfurt a.M.: Suhrkamp.
Krisch, Nico. 2017. "Liquid Authority in Global Governance." *International Theory* 9(2): 237–260.
Lake, David A. 2009. *Hierarchy in International Relations*. Ithaca: Cornell University Press.
Lake, David A. 2010. "Rightful Rules: Authority, Order, and the Foundations of Global Governance." *International Studies Quarterly* 54(3): 587–613.
Lindblom, Charles Edward. 1977. *Politics and Markets: The World's Political-Economic Systems*. New York: Basic Books.
March, James G., and Johan P. Olsen. 1998. "The Institutional Dynamics of International Political Orders." *International Organization* 52(4): 943–969.
Milgram, Stanley. 1974. *Obedience to Authority: An Experimental View*. London: Tavistock.
Modelski, George. 1987. *Long Cycles in World Politics*. Seattle: University of Washington Press.
Morse, Julia C., and Robert O. Keohane. 2014. "Contested Multilateralism." *The Review of International Organizations* 9(4): 385–412.
Münkler, Herfried. 2005. *Imperien. Die Logik der Weltherrschaft – vom Alten Rom bis zu den Vereinigten Staaten*. Berlin: Rowohlt.
Nullmeier, Frank, Anna Geis, and Christopher Daase. 2012. "Der Aufstieg der Legitimitätspolitik: Rechtfertigung und Kritik politisch-ökonomischer Ordnungen," in Anna Geis, Frank Nullmeier, and Christopher Daase (eds.), *Der Aufstieg der Legitimitätspolitik. Rechtfertigung und Kritik politisch-ökonomischer Ordnungen* (Leviathan Sonderband) 40/27. Baden-Baden: Nomos, pp. 11–40.
Peters, Birgit, and Johan Karlsson Schaffer. 2013. "The Turn to Authority Beyond States." *Transnational Legal Theory* 4(3): 315–335.
Pouliot, Vincent. 2016a. "Hierarchy in Practice: Multilateral Diplomacy and the Governance of International Security." *European Journal of International Security* 1(1): 5–26.
Pouliot, Vincent. 2016b. *International Pecking Orders: The Politics and Practice of Multilateral Diplomacy*. New York: Cambridge University Press.
Pouliot, Vincent. 2017. "Against Authority: The Heavy Weight of International Hierarchy," in Ayşe Zarakol (ed.), *Hierarchies in World Politics*. Cambridge: Cambridge University Press, pp. 113–134.
Pouliot, Vincent, and Jean-Philippe Thérien. 2018. "Global Governance in Practice." *Global Policy* 9(2): 163–172.

Raz, Joseph. 2006. "The Problem of Authority: Revisiting the Service Conception." *Minnesota Law Review* 90(4): 1003–1044.

Raz, Joseph. 2009. *The Authority of Law: Essays on Law and Morality*. Oxford and New York: Oxford University Press.

Ruggie, John G. 1975. "International Responses to Technology: Concepts and Trends." *International Organization* 29(3): 557–583.

Ruggie, John G. 2004. "Reconstituting the Global Public Domain – Issues, Actors, and Practices." *European Journal of International Relations* 10(4): 499–531.

Schmelzle, Cord. 2015. *Politische Legitimität und zerfallene Staatlichkeit*. Frankfurt am Main: Campus-Verlag.

Schuppert, Gunnar Folke. 2010. *Staat als Prozess: Eine staatstheoretische Skizze in sieben Aufzügen*. Frankfurt, a. M.: Campus.

Sending, Ole Jacob. 2015. *The Politics of Expertise: Competing for Authority in Global Governance*. Ann Arbor: University of Michigan Press.

Sending, Ole Jacob. 2017. "Recognition and Liquid Authority." *International Theory* 9(2): 311–328.

Sharman, Jason C. 2013. "International Hierarchies and Contemporary Imperial Governance: A Tale of Three Kingdoms." *European Journal of International Relations* 19(2): 189–207.

Simmerl, Georg and Michael Zürn. 2016. "Internationale Autorität: Zwei Perspektiven." *Zeitschrift für Internationale Beziehungen* 23(1): 38–70.

Suchman, Marc C. 1995. "Managing Legitimacy: Strategic and Institutional Approaches." *The Academy of Management Review* 20(3): 571–610.

Tallberg, Jonas, Thomas Sommerer, Theresa Squatrito, and Christer Jönsson. 2013. *The Opening Up of International Organizations: Transnational Access in Global Governance*. Cambridge: Cambridge University Press.

Tallberg, Jonas and Michael Zürn. 2019. "The Legitimacy and Legitimation of International Organizations: Introduction and Framework." *The Review of International Organization* 14(4): 581–606.

Triepel, Heinrich. 1938. *Die Hegemonie. Ein Buch von führenden Staaten*. Stuttgart: Kohkhammer.

Venzke, Ingo. 2013. "Understanding the Authority of International Courts and Tribunals: On Delegation and Discursive Construction." *Theoretical Inquiries in Law* 14(2): 381–409.

Viola, Lora A., Duncan Snidal, and Michael Zürn. 2015. "Sovereign (In)equality in the Evolution of the International System," in Evelyne Huber, Matthew Lange, Stephan Leibfried, Jonah Levy, Frank Nullmeier, and John Stephens (eds.), *The Oxford Handbook of Transformations of the State*. Oxford: Oxford University Press, pp. 221–236.

von Bogdandy, Armin, Philipp Dann, and Matthias Goldmann. 2010. "Developing the Publicness of Public International Law: Towards a Legal Framework for Global Governance Activities," in Armin von Bogdandy, Rüdiger Wolfrum, Jochen von Bernstorff, Philipp Dann, and Matthias Goldmann (eds.), *The Exercise of Public Authority by International Institutions. Advancing International Institutional Law*. Heidelberg: Springer, pp. 3–32.

von Bogdandy, Armin and Ingo Venzke. 2014. *In wessen Namen? Internationale Gerichte in Zeiten globalen Regierens*. Berlin: Suhrkamp.

Wallerstein, Immanuel. 1974. *The Modern World-System I. Capitalist Agriculture and the Origins of the European World-Economy in the Sixteenth Century*. New York: Academic Press.

Weber, Max. 1978 [1925]. "Chapter III. The Types of Legitimate Domination [Die Typen der Herrschaft]," in Guenther Roth, and Claus Wittich (eds.), *Max Weber. Economy and Society. An Outline of Interpretative Sociology*. Berkeley: University of California Press, pp. 212–301.

Weber, Max. 2013. "Kapitel I. Soziologische Grundbegriffe," in Knut Borchardt, Edith Hanke, and Wolfgang Schluchter (eds.), *Max Weber Gesamtausgabe I/23. Wirtschaft und Gesellschaft: Soziologie*. Tübingen: Mohr Siebeck, pp. 147–215.

Weingart, Peter. 2008. *Die Stunde der Wahrheit? Zum Verhältnis der Wissenschaft zu Politik, Wirtschaft und Medien in der Wissensgesellschaft*. Weilerswist: Velbrück Wissenschaft.

Wiener, Antje. 2014. *A Theory of Contestation*. Berlin, Heidelberg: Springer.

Zürn, Michael. 2018. *A Theory of Global Governance. Authority, Legitimacy, and Contestation*. Oxford: Oxford University Press.

Zürn, Michael, Martin Binder, and Matthias Ecker-Ehrhardt. 2012. "International Authority and Its Politicization." *International Theory* 4(1): 69–106.

Zürn, Michael, Alexandros Tokhi, and Martin Binder. 2021. "The International Authority Database." *Global Policy* 12(4): 430–442.

Notes

1 This chapter builds on and expands the arguments of chapter two in *A Theory of Global Governance: Authority, Legitimation and Contestation* (Zürn 2018). Earlier versions of this chapter were presented at the workshop "Beyond Anarchy: Rule and Authority in the International System," Cluster of Excellence "Normative Orders" at Goethe University Frankfurt, May 25–26, 2017, as well as the workshop on "International Public Authority" at Max Planck Institute for Comparative Public Law and International Law, Heidelberg, September 20–21, 2017. I want to thank the participants of these workshops for their comments as well as Nicole Deitelhoff, Jürgen Habermas, Sebastian Schindler, and Ole Jacob Sending for especially extensive and intriguing ones.

2 Daase et al., this volume: 2.

3 Daase et al., this volume.

4 Weber 2013: 211.

5 See Barnett and Duvall 2005.

6 March and Olsen 1998.

7 Elster 1995, 1999.

8 Habermas 1985, 1996.

9 The proposition that Weber used authority (Autorität) and rule (Herrschaft) synonymously is based on an edition in which the sociology of domination was authorized by Weber himself (Borchardt et al. 2013). Contrary to earlier versions edited by Marianne Weber and Johannes Winckelmann, he uses the two terms consistently interchangeably. See Simmerl and Zürn (2016) for a more detailed discussion. The following quote is *my translation* of this most recent edition.

10 Weber 2013: 449; translation M. Z.
11 Horkheimer 1987a [1936].
12 Bourdieu 1990.
13 Adorno et al. 1950.
14 Milgram 1974.
15 For a more extensive discussion, see Zürn 2018.
16 See Barnett and Finnemore 2004; Raz 2006; Sending 2015.
17 See also Sending, this volume.
18 See Kennedy 1989; Modelski 1987; Triepel 1938.
19 Doyle 1986; Münkler 2005. Especially dependency theorists focused on the cooptation of local elites as a necessary condition for the functioning of a system of inequality (see Galtung 1972; Wallerstein 1974).
20 See also chapters by Alter and Hurd, this volume. Early contributions are Biersteker and Hall 2002.
21 The work of Armin von Bogdandy and colleagues has been pathbreaking (von Bogdandy and Venzke 2014; von Bogdandy et al. 2010) in international law. See also, more recently, the work of Black 2017 and Krisch 2017.
22 See, e.g., Enoch 2014; Schmelzle 2015.
23 Lake 2009, 2010.
24 See Cooley 2005 and Hooghe et al. 2017, respectively.
25 Hooghe et al. 2017: 14.
26 See also Barnett and Finnemore 2004.
27 Lake 2009: 93.
28 Lake 2009, 2010.
29 Pouliot 2017.
30 Sharman 2013: 190.
31 Raz 2006.
32 Cf. Adorno et al. 1950; Bourdieu 1991; Butler 1996; Horkheimer 1987b [1936]. Hegel's analysis of the relationship between the master and the slave has been foundational for this thinking (Kojéve 1975: 48–89). In an existential struggle, the master prevails and enforces subordination of the slave. Yet the relationship remains interdependent: The master depends on the recognition and work of the slave, which in turn is a source of emancipation for the slave.
33 See Adler and Pouliot 2011; Avant et al. 2010; Barnett and Finnemore 2004; Hurd 1999, 2007; Pouliot 2016b, respectively.
34 Barnett and Finnemore 2004: 5. See also Avant et al. 2010: 9.
35 Hurd 2007: 31. See also Hurd, this volume.
36 Adler and Pouliot 2011; Pouliot and Thérien 2018. See also Sending, this volume.
37 See, however, Wiener 2014, who emphasizes permanent contestation in the enactment of norms.
38 See Zürn et al. 2012.
39 See Daase and Deitelhoff, Alter, and Morse, this volume.
40 Arendt 1970: 45.
41 See Raz 2006. This also is in line with the starting point of the influential discussion in Michael Barnett and Martha Finnemore (2004: 21): "The authority of IOs … lies in their ability to present themselves as impersonal and neutral – as not exercising power but instead serving others." See also Sending 2015.

42 Reflexive authority resembles the self-binding logic of Ulysses when confronted with the sirens that is in addition reflective in the sense that it permanently monitors its own reflexivity (see Elster 1986).
43 Joseph Raz (2009) offers five – more fine-grained – reasons for accepting an authority: The authority is wiser than the subject; it has a steadier, less biased will; it prevents self-defeating action; it reduces transaction costs; it is better placed to make the decision.
44 See also Sending 2017; Venzke 2013.
45 Weingart 2008.
46 See Sending, this volume.
47 See also von Bogdandy et al. 2010.
48 Blake and Payton 2008; Breitmeier et al. 2006.
49 Hooghe et al. 2017.
50 Zürn et al. 2021.
51 Morse and Keohane 2014.
52 Benvenisti and Downs 2009.
53 Schuppert 2010: 94.
54 Kelley and Simmons 2015.
55 Davis et al. 2012.
56 See Tallberg et al. 2013: 68.
57 Zürn et al. 2012.
58 "Objectivization" in this context does not mean that something becomes an objective truth, but that an authority relationship becomes generalized in the sense that many actors consider it as intersubjectively true and existent.
59 See also Sending, this volume.
60 See Hooghe et al. 2017.
61 Barker 2001; Geis et al. 2012; Weber 1978 [1925]: 213.
62 See Nullmeier et al. 2012; Tallberg and Zürn 2019.
63 See, e.g., Ruggie 2004.
64 Hurd 2007: 61.
65 See the contributions by Alter et al. (2016) and Peters and Karlsson Schaffer (2013), who argue similarly in defending the separation of authority and legitimacy.
66 Suchman 1995: 574 (emphasis added).
67 See also Sending, this volume.
68 Politicization mainly refers to moving issues into the realm of public choice, thus presupposing the possibility of making collectively binding decisions on that matter. Full-scale politicization consists of three components: (a) the growing "salience" of an issue, involving (b) a "polarization of opinion" about this issue, and (c) an "expansion of actors and audiences" engaged (see, e.g., de Wilde and Zürn 2012; de Wilde et al. 2016; Hutter and Grande 2014). In this use of the term, politicization is a more specific form of the more generic concept of contestation.
69 See, Daase and Deitelhoff, this volume for the distinction between opposition and dissidence.
70 Krisch 2017.
71 Daase and Deitelhoff 2015; Daase et al. 2017.
72 Pouliot 2016a, 2016b, 2017.

73 Pouliot 2017: 5.
74 Pouliot 2017: 5.
75 Daase and Deitelhoff 2015.
76 Börzel and Zürn 2021; Zürn et al. 2012.
77 Pouliot 2017: 6.
78 See Viola et al. 2015.
79 Pouliot 2017: 11.
80 Pouliot 2016b: 6, 2017: 10.
81 Daase and Deitelhoff 2015; see also Daase and Deitelhoff, this volume.
82 Lindblom 1977.

3 Ruling the World

Organizational Ecology and Bias in Global Governance

David A. Lake[1]

Rules are always made by someone for some purpose, but – to paraphrase Karl Marx – rulers do not make rules as they please. Which rules get made and their purpose are structured by the existing constellations of rules and rule-makers. Thus, the ecology of governance organizations (GOs) matters for what is or is not ruled, what legitimate powers any governor may hold, and whose political preferences are instantiated in rules. The array of actors who comprise the system of global governance has grown dramatically. Especially notable has been the growth of private governance organizations (PGOs), such as the International Accounting Standards Board (IASB) and the Forest Stewardship Council (FSC), discussed briefly later.[2] As described by Sending (this volume), PGOs exert a form of "auto-authority" that is neither contracted nor delegated from some other rule-making authority. The rise of PGOs has been greeted enthusiastically by many who see them as progressive manifestations of global civil society, and I should note that I intuitively share this enthusiasm. But our understanding of how and why PGOs have arisen is incomplete. Most analysts explain the growth of PGOs as a response to essential functions otherwise unfulfilled in global politics. This is not incorrect. Yet, our understanding of the emergence of PGOs is enriched by organizational ecology.

Drawing on ecological theory, I posit that the rise of PGOs is a response to disagreements between states that block the creation of what might otherwise be effective intergovernmental organizations (IGOs). Observers have, of course, recognized that disagreements between states have blocked action by IGOs and opened the door for PGOs. An organizational ecology approach, however, grounds this observation in a larger theory with three specific implications. First, an organizational ecology approach stresses the importance of looking at governance as a field and not just a single population of agents.[3] In other words, the approach turns our attention to the interactions of populations of organizations. It also prompts us to ask what is missing? What is absent is often as important as what is present, and organizational "holes" are revealed only by theory and plausible counterfactuals. Second, the approach highlights that ecologies are interactive and complex with often unintended consequences. Like all evolutionary theories, organizational ecology presumes there is no designer who manipulates situations to bring about an intended result. Rather, what we observe is the product of local decisions by many different agents who then set the conditions within which others act and, in our case, make rules. Third, an ecological approach helps us understand how populations are both competitive and synergistic. In global governance, organizations compete to set rules and, by attracting adherents, gain resources from a pool that is in the short run fixed. Too many sets of rules are equivalent to no rules at all – each actor can then simply follow the rules they prefer[4] – and all organizations require resources to survive. In this way, competition is a form of resistance as theorized by Daase and Deitelhoff (this volume), though not by the ruled but, in this case, by other potential rulers. At the same time, the ways in which private transnational governance has evolved promotes specialization and differentiation between agents and, thus, creates new populations. Where public regulation often fuses rule-making, monitoring, and enforcement in a single organization (e.g., the United States Food and Drug Administration), private governance is dependent on the cooperation of the regulated entities and, thus, cannot commit to objectivity. As a result, new populations of independent auditors and monitors have arisen to implement private regulations, a synergistic response to how a particular ecological niche has been filled.

Finally, and more generally, an organizational ecology approach prompts the question of whether the particular, path-dependent ecology that has emerged is socially optimal. This is more a question than a conclusion, but one worth asking. All rules are biased, reflecting the interests of some actors and not others. Who governs matters. Although PGOs represent global civil society, their structure, organizational needs, and the requirement of self-financing risk creating a neoliberal bias in global governance. This is not so much a matter of counting PGOs at the international level compared to, say, the domestic array of GOs within democratic states. Rather, it flows from the diffuse nature of support for civic PGOs versus the concentrated interests of business PGOs that are already filling governance niches. How biased in favor of business this emergent ecology is depends, in part, on the counterfactual of what regulation by IGOs might entail. Would IGOs represent better the interests of labor, consumers, and other diffuse social actors than the stakeholder models of the current system of private governance? This is a challenging question without a clear answer, but one with important normative implications.

The literature on global governance has moved, appropriately, from a focus on states to IGOs and now to PGOs.[5] This chapter shifts the level of analysis to the field of GOs and draws on principles of ecology to understand systems of governance. These principles are summarized in the first section "An Ecological Approach to Organizations." "Global Governance: Concepts, Definitions, and Populations" identifies the types of GOs that exist alongside states. "Governance Organizations and State Structure" looks at the ecologies of limited states and how their rich arrays of organizations "check and balance" one another. This section introduces the ideas that follow from an organizational ecology perspective in a context that is already relatively well understood. "The Ecology of Global Governance" reasons by analogy to the system of global governance, focusing on how disagreements between states have blocked the formation of IGOs and left open governance niches that are then filled by PGOs. This process is illustrated briefly in the cases of financial accounting and forest sustainability. The final section "Biased Rule in the Global Ecology" turns to possible alternative organizational ecologies and their welfare implications. The key question here is the porousness of public governance structures in states and through states in IGOs to the influence of special interests versus the structural influence of business in stakeholder models of private governance.

An Ecological Approach to Organizations

Although the literature on organizational ecology is now large, few scholars have applied its insights to questions of global governance.[6] The hallmark of an ecological approach is "population thinking."[7] Although the unit of analysis is the organization, the level of analysis is the organizational field. A population is defined as a collection or set of organizations that are "alike in some respect,"[8] relatively homogenous,[9] or have a "common dependence on the material and social environment."[10] An organizational field, in turn, is the set of "organizations that, in the aggregate, constitute a recognized area of institutional life."[11] The field, in short, is the population of organizational populations, including the absence of some types of organizations that might be expected theoretically or that have been found in other similar environments. In neither case is the focus on any specific organization, except insofar as it is representative of a population. The relevant population or field is an analytic question defined by the theorist on the basis of pragmatic judgments derived from the research question.[12]

A second hallmark is resource scarcity. Populations are assumed to be constrained by the need for resources. In the natural world, resources are food and water, sunshine, mates, and other essentials. For organizations, resources include revenue, members, and possibly legitimacy.[13] As with populations, what constitutes a resource is a pragmatic judgment postulated by the analyst. In the section "Biased Rule in the Global Ecology," I emphasize the importance of resources for PGOs in configuring their interests and, in turn, the rules they adopt. Those organizations that are most efficient in acquiring resources are most likely to survive; those that are less well suited to this task will not. The tighter is the resource environment, the greater the selection pressure on organizations. Resource scarcity, however, does not imply that organizations are "optimal" in any sense.[14] Due to various regulatory mechanisms, it may be impossible for a new, more "efficient" organization to gain a foothold within the population or field. Path dependence is a characteristic of many systems that may lead them far from efficient outcomes.[15] Nonetheless, organizations compete for resources, at least at the margin. In any given field or population, for instance, there is a finite amount of money that can be raised by donations, which then limits the number of PGOs that can survive on that revenue stream. At this limit, PGOs will either disappear or innovate in some way to raise money from another finite revenue source, which may require a different strategy or fulfilling some alternative function. In this way, resource scarcity defines the carrying capacity of any environment.

Resource scarcity leads ecologists to emphasize "niches" or specific environments in which different types of organizations can prosper.[16] The more niches, the more types of organizations (populations) we can expect to find in a field. As new niches arise, new populations will form or existing organizations will adapt to the resources opened-up by that specific environment. For GOs, niches are usually created by the demand for new rules and regulations, such as those that arise from market integration or technological change. Entrepreneurial organizations may create niches for themselves that no one else previously recognized – the equivalent of Apple developing the "smartphone." The first mass membership-based advocacy organizations like Amnesty International may be the PGO equivalent.[17] Even entrepreneurial organizations can survive, however, only if a demand for rules exists and the "consumers" are willing to support organizations that set those rules. This is especially true for GOs that cannot mandate contributions from the community they regulate; even when organizations can invest resources in ways that enhance their capabilities for the future, some other actor – an "angel investor" – must be willing to provide the initial "stake." In the case of

PGOs, the "startup funds" have often been provided by some philanthropic foundation, but PGOs are expected to become self-supporting.[18]

New niches may also create additional niches and, thus, synergies between populations. The rise of publicly traded firms, for instance, created a demand for auditors and credit-rating agencies that were not necessary for family-owned businesses.[19] One organizational form spawned a need for other organizations – or in the language of organizational ecology, created additional niches filled by new populations. With new niches, organizations differentiate, rendering the field more heterogeneous and often more complex. Where organizations compete within populations and sometimes across if they share the same resource, niches encourage specialization, oftentimes leading to entirely new populations. Competition and synergies can occur at the same time.

Recognizing the importance of resource scarcity and niches, an ecological approach theorizes regulatory processes, or principles that describe how populations within a field interact.[20] Three regulatory processes are of interest for organizational ecology:

- *Positive Regulation*: A is complementary to B. A classic example is the relationship between food sources and species that eat that food. Similarly, more states after 1945 with more potential conflicts of interest led to the (at least initial) growth of IGOs to improve cooperation. In similar ways, state action in the Kyoto Protocol acted as "coral reef" that attracted PGOs into what became a larger regime complex.[21] Positive regulation is often produced by new niches that encourage specialization.
- *Negative Regulation*: A blocks B. With negative regulation, similar to Daase and Deitelhoff's notion of resistance (this volume), two populations will be inversely related to one another or, perhaps, in equilibrium until one experiences some exogenous change. Outbreaks of the rinderpest virus cause reductions in the population of Wildebeest. Likewise, once a PGO issues a standard and that standard becomes widely adopted (becomes a focal institution), that governance niche is "filled" and the rules become hard (but not impossible) to displace. As discussed further in the section "The Ecology of Global Governance," even states can be shut out of a niche by PGOs meeting the demand for rules.
- *Double-Negative Regulation*: A negatively regulates B, which negatively regulates C. Double-negative regulation is especially likely in fields with a "keystone" population.[22] Examples include sea otters, which eat sea urchins, which eat kelp; the recovery of the sea otter population along the West coast of the United States has led to a thickening

of kelp beds. In this same way, states, desirous of maintaining their sovereignty and autonomy, block the creation of IGOs to regulate, say, environmental emissions (negative regulation), which then leaves open a niche to be filled by PGOs.

Finally, due to regulation and feedback effects, organizational ecologies may experience cascades that produce more extreme populations within fields. Cascades are more likely if keystone populations are present. In a natural system, the elimination of a "top predator" may cause dramatic changes in the system: farmers killed off wolves in North America, leading to an explosion of deer populations that led to the disappearance of several varieties of trees on which deer feed. As below, domestic political systems may also tip toward failure or tyranny through similar cascades. In an organizational ecology it may be difficult to anticipate the effects of one's actions; outcomes are, then, the unintended by-product of many independent decisions. In a dynamic and complex system, exogenous technological change may open niches of governance that organizations race to fill. In this way, an exogenous change may cascade through the field. An ecological approach is at least open to the possibility of complex systems dynamics that are ruled out by functionalist approaches to governance. In Section "Biased Rule in the Global Ecology," I raise the question of whether the current global governance field may be at such a tipping point.

Global Governance: Concepts, Definitions, and Populations

Governance is the exercise of rule by an actor over some limited community. As the Introduction to this volume by Daase, Deitelhoff, and Witt makes clear, rule is ubiquitous and can be wielded by a variety of actors, not just states. Governance is thus broader than mere government, a characteristic on which nearly all definitions agree.[23] Global or transnational governance, in turn, is the exercise of rule across national borders, including by IGOs that possess authority over their member states and PGOs that propagate rules governing communities located in two or more states.

Governance comprises three main functions: making (including attempting to influence), monitoring, and enforcing rules. Rules can be formal laws or informal social norms.[24] Enforcement is often but mistakenly limited to the legitimate use of coercive force, which Weber took to be the defining characteristic of the state. But rules can also be enforced by a variety of means, including ostracism or expulsion from the community and its benefits. Hunter-gatherer societies ostracize individuals who will not obey the elders. Parents threaten to disown their unruly children. Religions excommunicate sinners. Professional associations ban incompetents and transgressors. Indeed, the famous *Lex Mercatoria* that governed trade at the medieval Champagne fairs worked entirely by the threat of denying merchants the opportunity to trade at future fairs.[25] Even states deport "undesirables." Exclusion can be an enforcement mechanism equal in power to the legitimate violence wielded by a state.

Different agents may specialize in one or the other of these governance functions, though many include all three. Some standards setting organizations may simply issue a standard that is then self-enforcing, requiring little monitoring. Other organizations, like Amnesty International, may influence norms and focus on monitoring state behavior. In an organizational ecology approach, the governance field comprises populations of organizations that perform at least one governance function.

Central to the literature on global governance is the idea that many different types of organizations govern. States, of course, assert a claim to rule that is compulsory within a given territory. At the same time, other governors exist alongside states. They include families, where parental authority wanes as children mature; clans, tribes, or other lineage groups, in which elders are recognized to speak for the group and enforce standards of behavior; and religions, which propagate rules governing social, sexual, and dietary practices. In these examples, members are often "born" into the community, though they may choose to exit and are governed by their rules regardless of their place of residence. Other GOs that individuals may choose to join are corporations, which govern work and allow for gains from specialization within integrated production systems, unions, which negotiate wage contracts and other terms of employment for their members, and professional associations, which set standards of practice (the bar association for lawyers), many of which are now transnational in scope. The range of GOs is large.

States have not in principle, and certainly not in practice, displaced other GOs, even within the territories over which they claim jurisdiction. The compromise embodied in notions of Westphalian sovereignty, which are often understood to define the triumph of the modern state over alternative GOs, is subtle.[26] Westphalian sovereignty does not imply that state authority is the only type of rule – even at the national level. Instead, it establishes only the supremacy of state authority when it conflicts with rules issued by other actors.[27] Non-state rule, in other words, can and often is more restrictive than state authority, but it cannot directly contradict it. Rabbis can require that food labeled Kosher meet their more restrictive standards, for instance, but they cannot require Jews to consume food that violates public health and safety standards. The Westphalian compromise does not obviate other forms of rule; it just nests them inside the authority of the state. When facing compelling demands for action and the absence of institutional veto players or affected interests that seek to block change, states can enact laws that trump other governance initiatives. In this sense, states remain the ultimate authorities within their jurisdictions. Nonetheless, the balance between the types of GOs within a society varies dramatically, as we shall see in the section "Governance Organizations and State Structure."

What holds within a single jurisdiction, in turn, holds even more so at the global level, where states cannot even claim to be ultimate authorities.[28] If anarchy means anything at the international level, it means that there is no single authority, but this does not preclude the existence of multiple rulers governing different territories (states) or, more interestingly, different issue areas. Anarchy suggests a broad range of GOs will always be at play.

Both within states and at the global level, the balance between various types of GOs is important because who makes rules matters. Though rules may be functional and move communities closer to the Pareto-frontier, they can have distributional implications that favor some individuals or communities over others. Rules made by a democratic state responsive to all citizens might well differ from the rules made by a business or professional association that leaps into an open governance niche. Environmental organizations make rules based on scientific principles, whereas religious authorities make rules according to God's will. The organizational ecology, and the competition between GOs within it, determine who gets to make the rules over what, which in turn determines the policies and practices we observe. Political outcomes are, in this sense, a product of the organizational ecology.

Governance Organizations and State Structure

In a relatively simple form of negative regulation, it is the rich array of GOs that checks and balances liberal states. As James Madison wrote, "in framing a government, which is to be administered by men over men, the great difficulty lies in this: you must first enable the government to control the governed, and in the next place oblige it to control itself."[29] This is almost a truism. As Daase and Deitelhoff show in their focus on resistance, governing the governor is a necessary part of any stable political system of rule. Yet, effective checks and balances are by no means guaranteed, with the balance between too many and too few GOs of different types easily tipped toward extremes. A rich ecology of GOs appears necessary to sustain limited government, especially in the face of determined minorities seeking to overthrow the system or popular movements spurred by the passions of the moment. But even a rich ecology is no guarantee of stability. As recent trends in the United States and Europe demonstrate, leaders and groups can undermine the "guardrails" embedded in constitutions and enforced by GOs.[30] A balanced ecology may be a necessary but not a sufficient condition for stability.

In limited states, GOs check and balance one another in a rough equilibrium. This helps produce stability or, by definition, state consolidation. Some believe that Madison's dilemma is solved by institutionalized checks and balances within the government, perhaps by a legislature separate from the executive and both monitored by an independent judiciary. Madison himself believed that a more varied society would divide along more dimensions and prevent one faction from dominating others. These solutions to Madison's dilemma are no doubt important. But there are many liberal democracies that lack a separation of powers or that are smaller and less heterogeneous than the United States. The array of GOs of varying types is a third and, in ecological approach, equally important way of limiting state power.

In virtually all societies, a range of GOs existed prior to states in their Westphalian form, and then coevolved with those states. In the United States, for instance, many GOs existed alongside early colonial administrations. Indeed, religious authorities were prevalent in colonial America – even dominant in some areas, notably New England – with many communities founded by religious dissenters. Other "societies" as they were often called ruled functionally defined communities (such as merchants, tradespeople, etc.).[31] The American states were formed around these preexisting entities.

Concerned with maintaining their autonomy and rule over their communities, these diverse GOs resisted state authority. The protections for religious freedom in the federal Constitution were not unintentional. Churches of all denominations were forceful advocates of the separation of church and state. By advocating for their autonomous rights, these religious authorities built restrictions over their affairs into their state. The U.S. government, in other words, was born limited *without* certain powers it might otherwise have claimed. With their authority preserved, in turn, churches continued to be important GOs, pushing back against subsequent efforts by the state to infringe on their rights. In more modern form, large corporations use their financial muscle and ability to mobilize their many employees to restrict the regulatory powers of the state.[32]

Civil society organizations sometimes offset the power of corporations, more often not, but are also in a constant battle of checking and balancing the rule of others and their efforts to capture the state. Reformers rue the immobilism that results from this continual struggle of "vested interests," but this is a natural product of a relatively balanced ecology.

The Ecology of Global Governance

The global political system is a rich ecology of different GOs, perhaps not as dense as some domestic systems, as in limited states, but richer than some other systems. The field includes states themselves, of course, as primary actors. It also includes IGOs and PGOs that set, monitor, and enforce rules in defined spheres. Although we do not have any inventory of GOs at the global level, just as we have no inventory of GOs within countries, the global ecology appears by all accounts to be growing in number and diversity.[33] In an economically, politically, and environmentally integrated world, new demands for global governance are rapidly creating new governance niches, and organizations are rising to meet the demand for rules, with some national organizations going transnational, early transnational organizations broadening their scope, and entirely new organizations sprouting up.

One striking fact of the early twenty-first century is the stagnation of IGOs and the growth of PGOs. While IGOs and their emanations grew rapidly in the early postwar period, by the 1970s momentum had waned. In the case of corporate social responsibility, for instance, there were numerous attempts to establish IGO codes of conduct through the United Nations, OECD, and International Labor Organization, all of which were stillborn.[34] Only in the 1990s did private initiatives take off at the national level followed by the more successful global initiatives.[35] The failure of states to act either on their own or through some IGO is often noted in narratives of PGO development but typically as a passing aside without seeming theoretical import.[36] This is crucial to the approach here in which it is the actions of one population of GOs that create opportunities for other populations and in which the absence of action is as meaningful as its presence. Where in domestic political systems PGOs negatively regulate states, in global governance states negatively regulate IGOs which, in turn, leave open governance niches that are then filled by PGOs. It is not that states are intentionally transferring authority to PGOs. Rather, by providing rules and acquiring stakeholders and, thus, legitimacy in the making of those rules, PGOs gain what Sending (this volume) calls auto-authority despite the best intentions of states.[37] PGOs govern, as a result, not because they are "better" than states or IGOs, but because an open governance niche draws in PGOs that, once established, raise the bar for other GOs. In some cases, rules formulated by PGOs are then taken up by states if only because they are the ones available, further legitimating the role of the PGOs. This creates a highly interdependent ecology in which states, IGOs, and PGOs both compete against and complement one another.

The global ecology of GOs evolved differently than many domestic ecologies. Where PGOs sometimes preceded the formation of states and limited their authority, states preceded the creation of IGOs almost by definition – certainly so in the North, perhaps less so in the Global South where independence came later. Jealous of their sovereign powers, states – and, it should be stressed, their citizens as well – have typically limited IGOs to the role of "orchestrators" rather than independent authorities.[38] Instead of transferring or delegating authority to IGOs, founding states limit IGOs to the role of agenda setters and perhaps negotiating forums. In guarding their prerogatives, states can block IGOs but not the consequences of that negative regulation – unless they are willing and able to fulfill the demand for rules themselves. This is the "opening" or niche into which PGOs have moved and survived because of the governance services they provide.

As long recognized, states are still the primary GOs in the world today. Although they may be in retreat in the face of market pressures and PGOs, as argued by Susan Strange, they remain dominant actors when they choose to exert their authority. Yet, policy disagreements between states make the creation of new institutions to solve problems of global concern difficult. For this reason, some see the condition of international anarchy as immutable.[39] Importantly, states actively inhibit the rise of GOs that might usurp their authority. Even though checks and balances might be necessary for a healthy political system, they are the product of political struggle and resistance, not the goal of any actor. States often aim to block the formation of competing GOs or negatively regulate alternative populations. Negative regulation is likely to be especially prevalent in the case of IGOs, which are legal emanations of states themselves. States may delegate technical tasks to IGOs but are seldom willing to transfer rule-making power to organizations that they cannot control, with the European Union being an important exception. In turn, few IGOs have succeeded in building constituencies independent of their member states to support the construction of authority at the global level.[40] With international business deeply dependent on the free flow of goods and capital around the world, the World Trade Organization is a rare example of an IGO that has developed some independent authority,[41] though it too has been ineffective in the emerging tariff war between the United States and China.

Negative regulation of IGOs is common. Even in the case of the European Union – which has acquired more independent authority than any other IGO – growing opposition focuses on its intrusiveness.[42] A major force behind Brexit, for example, was the desire by many British conservatives to reclaim sovereignty from Brussels. Precisely because they often disagree on how to address issues of common concern, states refuse to transfer significant powers to IGOs that might otherwise respond to global challenges. Nonetheless, and illustrating the potential of IGOs, when interests in the EU are sufficiently aligned that it can adopt regulations, its large internal market can create a cascading "Brussels effect" that then sets a world standard.[43] Nonetheless, we should be careful in generalizing from cases where an IGO has acted successfully to cases where conflicting interests between states block action.[44]

By negatively regulating IGOs, states leave open governance niches that are then filled by PGOs. The advantage shared by PGOs is that they do not require permission or support from states to formulate and disseminate rules. As long as there is some demand for rules – either because those who should follow the rules prefer a common standard rather than multiple standards or consumers want to purchase goods that are produced ethically – PGOs can seize upon the absence of IGO authority and offer a set of private regulations. PGOs cannot require anyone to accept their rules, of course, but if they are subsequently taken up by producers or consumers these private regulations can acquire significant force. Once adopted, in turn, rules by PGOs are hard to displace even by states. Filling an open niche can be relatively easy, as some rules are often better than no rules. To displace one set of rules with another, however, requires new PGOs or even states to offer rules that attract more adherents than the existing rules. For states in particular, this will likely provoke the distributional battles that prevented them from adopting rules in the first place.[45] Once private rules are established, states often simply adopt them as their own. In this way, the absence or at least slower growth of IGOs is leading, perhaps ironically, to the growth of new PGOs with broad rule setting powers. Two well understood and documented cases illustrate this double-negative regulatory process.

As recounted by Büthe and Mattli, problems with the absence of any international accounting standards slowly became evident as finance became more internationalized. In 2002, a study by *Forbes* magazine found twenty-six different accounting standards in use by the top 500 non-U.S. international companies. Most dramatically, the listing of

Daimler-Benz on the New York Stock Exchange produced wildly different views of the company's balance sheet as its $375 million profit under German accounting rules was converted into a $1.1 billion loss under U.S. rules. Because different accounting methods matter, especially for politically powerful business constituents, states were unable to harmonize rules on their own. In the aftermath of the Asian Financial Crisis of 1997–98, the G-7 states turned to the International Accounting Standards Committee (IASC) to promote an international standard, a PGO founded in 1973 by sixteen accountancy bodies from nine countries.[46] In this move, a small group of relatively similar states turned not to an IGO that might be blocked by differing national interests but to a PGO already occupying a governance niche, if ineffectively. In this double-negative regulatory process, states forewent the option of an IGO which, in turn, created the potential for the growth of a PGO. Stymied by the potential veto of members, the problem states foresaw, the IASC transformed itself in the IASB in 1999, which operated under rules that allowed for more effective decision-making. The IASB quickly issued the International Financial Reporting Standards (IFRS), which were then formally adopted by the European Union in 2002 and later the United States.[47] This uptake by key states then served to legitimate the IFRS as the de facto global standard even as it continued to have important distributional implications for other countries and firms.

The FSC is a prime example of non-state market driven (NSMD) regulation.[48] The FSC first emerged from conversations among various environmental groups and gained momentum with support from the World Wide Fund for Nature (WWF).[49] With the failure of the Earth Summit in 1993 to reach a global forest convention, environmental activists along with the WWF created the FSC the following year.[50] Once again, the failure of states to agree to more universal or binding regulations created an opportunity for a PGO to enter and fill an open niche. Fearing blockage by the vested interests that undermined agreement in Rio, the FSC sought to balance the influence of environmental, business, and other interests, creating three equal "chambers" of environmental, economic, and social interests, each with members from the North and Global South. In 2009, the FSC had 833 voting members from 92 countries.[51] Decision-making is by deliberation and supermajority voting in all three chambers.[52] The FSC eventually articulated ten principles governing forest products, including land tenure and use rights, community relations, worker's rights, environmental impact, management plans, monitoring, and preservation of old growth forests.[53] To receive an FSC label, producers must demonstrate control over the entire supply chain.[54]

The FSC was quickly challenged by a number of industry-led certification programs that emphasize procedures over outcomes and "best management practices."[55] Various national industry groups were organized into the Programme for the Endorsement of Forest Certification (PEFC) in 1999. Originally a bottom-up industry association, PEFC did not include other stakeholders or mandate third-party monitoring of performance and left considerable discretion to each member firm and country. Competing with the FSC, the PEFC was eventually forced to upgrade its standards and procedures. Since 2003, the PEFC has applied a set of minimum standards, which have been periodically upgraded. Importantly, public procurement policies have been an important driver of changes in the PEFC. Under discussion for years, the European Commission proposed in 2008 that all timber imported into the EU be certified as sustainably produced. The regulation was approved by the European Parliament and Council in 2010 and entered into force in 2013. This regulation requires that all timber be "legally" harvested, with FSC certification being taken as evidence of this status. This move led PEFC to upgrade its standards and procedures and, since 2008, some but not all EU countries accept its national-level certifications as evidence of legality as well.[56] Competing against the PEFC, however, the FSC also had to be attentive to its producers. This created as Tim Bartley writes, a "race to the middle … as industry-driven initiatives made reforms to increase their credibility and the FSC revised its labeling rules to increase its market share."[57] The impact of certification on forest cover appears to be positive but limited,[58] and in any case interacts with local state governance structures to produce differential outcomes.[59] As in accounting standards, uptake by national governments of the rules set by PGOs both legitimates those rules and facilitates their diffusion through noncoercive means.[60]

NSMD regulations have also been adopted in fisheries and other environmental issues.[61] When consumer demand for sustainably produced goods is sufficiently high, and production assets are sufficiently generic that buyers can change suppliers without great cost, PGOs can promote sustainable practices that cascade through global supply chains. Of course, there are cases in which consumer demand for sustainable products is insufficient for NSMD certification, consumers are ignorant and accept weak certification regimes, or producers are concentrated and self-certify or even seek to mislead consumers. But in the best cases, the absence of legally enforceable standards can open space for PGOs to play important roles in setting standards and certifying products.

In NSMD regulation, we can also see important synergies at work. In all of these instances, uptake of private standards by governments was important to their success. Once a standard is formulated and a critical mass of actors adhere to that standard, states can avoid nasty political battles by simply signing onto existing rules. In this incremental process of diffusion, private standards become focal solutions that are hard, though not impossible, to displace with a more or less restrictive public law. Equally important, the rise of new GOs creates incentives for other organizations to form as well. This is not just emulation, with fisheries following forests – though that is important. Rather, private standards setting bodies need complements. To be credible, PGOs cannot both write and monitor their rules. This is not the case for public bodies, like banking regulators. Public regulators often set rules, inspect facilities or processes, and penalize violators all within the same organization. But because private standards are entirely voluntary, and PGOs work closely with the regulated entities to induce their cooperation, there is the potential for rules to lack credibility.[62] This has led to the rise of independent auditors who monitor production and identify problems that, if not corrected, may lead to decertification. Like other exemplary NSMD programs, the FSC separated rule setting from monitoring by delegating inspections to independent auditors (accredited to the FSC) who must publish summaries of their reports on public websites.[63] Based on these audits, the FSC issues corrective action requests to resolve deficiencies required for continued certification.[64] In a classic case of synergy, one type of PGO (rule setters) has led to the growth of complementary PGOs (monitors), with each being dependent on the other. This synergistic specialization and differentiation has led to a richer organizational ecology and system of global governance. GOs are clearly growing at the international level, but it is not just for functional reasons or because private standards are somehow more efficient. Rather, the growing presence and role of PGOs is the result of complex interactions within the organizational field.

Biased Rule in the Global Ecology

While growing and more diverse overall, this emerging global ecology of GOs is potentially skewed toward a pro-business, free market neoliberalism that promotes yet further globalization. Although attributing greater intentionality to governments than is necessary in an ecological frame, Tim Bartley captures this concern. "As governments offloaded regulation to the private sector to promote a neoliberal model of governance...," he writes, a system has emerged that "generally accepts rather than challenges the power of northern transnational corporations and NGOs."[65] This is especially likely for PGOs dependent on income from those who are subject to the standards and regulations they promote. Without doubt, many PGOs are founded, led, and staffed by individuals who are motivated by strong ethical beliefs. Yet, PGOs are also typically more dependent on those whom they seek to regulate than states and, thus, possibly more sensitive to their interests. The concern here is not that business-affiliated PGOs are necessarily biased. Rather, as in any ecological approach, the questions are about the field of GOs and the balance between populations of organizations fulfilling different roles in different niches. What is missing here – or possibly missing – are civic PGOs representing broader interests in global society.

Governance niches can only be filled when there is some organization able and willing to produce the rules demanded by a community. The advantage of PGOs that allow them to fill governance niches that states or their IGO emanations cannot themselves agree to enter nonetheless limits their freedom of action. PGOs, like all organizations, must survive and function in a world of scarce resources. They must meet a payroll, fund their activities, and fight for their "product" (rules) in the face of competition from other GOs. To survive requires resources. Although foundations have been critical in funding PGOs in their nascent stages,[66] in many cases resources must be provided over the long run by the beneficiaries of the new rules, the only group that can be reliably expected to "pay" for those rules in some voluntary but reliable fashion.

With business willing to provide funding for organizations setting standards they want or find tolerable, the voluntary nature of PGOs appears to be producing rules possibly skewed toward those they seek to regulate.[67] The neoliberalism of the current system of global governance is not so much a question of numbers of organizations, though that may be important, but rather of bias introduced by the need for PGOs to raise scarce resources from voluntary contributions or by "selling" their rules. For businesses and trade associations that believe they can profit from rules formulated in acceptable ways, solving the collective action problem may be relatively easy. For consumers, workers, or the poor, collective action problems are daunting. It appears, for instance, that the profit motives from seeking single standards that businesses can then use across the globe is favoring the creation of new authorities in areas of concern to business and, within those areas and practices, organizations that favor further global economic integration.[68] Even in eco-conscious consumer standards, for example, PGOs are typically dependent on licensing fees paid by the firms they are designed to regulate and, thus, walk a fine line between business profits and meeting consumer demands for sustainably produced goods. In examining the incentives of GOs, we see at least the potential for funding from self-interested parties to skew rules in a neoliberal direction. With states and IGOs thwarted by distributional battles,[69] and consumer and civic organizations facing larger collective action problems, the ecology appears to be tipping toward pro-business PGOs and neoliberal regulations.

To see this problem at work, consider the cases discussed above. The IASB is funded by a mix of public and private sources.[70] Approximately 28 percent of all revenue derives from selling licenses, training, and online services.[71] The remainder comes almost entirely from members, with the major international accounting firms being the largest contributors (24 percent), followed by the European Commission (19 percent) and China (11 percent, from a mix of government agencies and state-owned enterprises). In the case of the national contributions from Germany and the United States, these are derived almost entirely from major multinational firms – including Daimler AG. While the European Commission and central bank contributors are partially insulated from private interests, the majority of the revenue directly and indirectly comes from business firms. Although the standards are merely "technical," the Daimler-Benz case nicely demonstrates that standards matter not only for the companies whose value may vary under different accounting rules but also for investors, consumers, tax authorities, and others. With most contributors businesses and large economies of scale in adoption, the IASB has an incentive to create minimally acceptable rules for the broadest possible user pool. And with the rules now widely in use, it would be hard for states, if they were so inclined, to recapture the authority they have yielded to the PGO. The net effect of this regulatory move has been to facilitate and deepen global financial integration, furthering the neoliberal project under the private authority of the beneficiaries of that authority.

NSMD regulation works differently but with similar effect. Counting on consumers to pay higher prices for sustainably produced goods, producers buy certification from PGOs, such as the FSI and its accredited auditors. It is the willingness of producers to pay for certification that drives the ecology. Indeed, 78 percent of FSC's revenue comes from fees paid by certification holders, with the rest coming from donations, commercial services, and memberships.[72] The PEFC receives 74 percent of its revenue from its national bodies, which are themselves comprised mostly of firms within the industry. The remainder of its revenue is listed as "sponsorship income," which, if the list of "stakeholder members" equates to sponsors, is almost entirely major logging, lumber, and paper companies.[73] Producers want not the highest standards, or even standards that will ensure goods really are sustainable, but standards that will convince consumers to pay more for their products than the increased costs of producing sustainably entails. This same calculus holds for lead firms, often seen as driving this process in cases like fisheries. The higher the standard, the greater the costs of production (usually), and the higher the price that must be charged to consumers. When goods are easily substitutable, there are strict limits on how high the standards on any product can be within any voluntary system of governance. In the case of Rugmark, which intended to certify that handmade rugs are produced without child labor, for instance, limited resources from sales of certification constrained the number of inspectors, who were able to visit looms no more than once every three years, suggesting that the certification system was extremely porous and the certification itself lacking in credibility.[74] With voluntary standards and PGOs financially dependent on income from certification itself, competition from the uncertified fringe restricts just how high standards can reach.

We should be cautious in generalizing from a few examples. Even as certification schemes are heavily dependent on the companies whose practices they seek to regulate, environmental organizations that rely more on individual members like the WWF or Greenpeace have very different incentives yet are important elements of the ecology. The WWF, for instance, derives the majority of its revenues from individuals, in-kind contributions, and government grants with only 4 percent of its income coming from corporations.[75] Such membership-driven PGOs provide a useful civic corrective, but of course they typically face significant collective action problems. Overall, the private structure of PGOs and the collective action problems of global civil society suggest that the field of GOs today may be tipping in a neoliberal direction.

The consequence of this skew, of course, also depends on the relevant counterfactual.[76] Suppose that states did not block the creation of an IGO, thereby inhibiting the rise of a PGO. What might be the policy outcome? An optimistic model comes from the Brussels effect noted earlier, where distributional conflicts have been relatively small and the EU has been able to set global standards in some areas.[77] Where distributional conflicts are more salient, however, businesses would still have an incentive to lobby any IGO for regulations they prefer while the collective action problems facing consumers, labor, and global civil society would remain. The question, then, is whether an IGO with state members would be more inclusive in its representation and decision-making than PGOs now in play. There is likely to be considerable variation here. In more "technical" standard setting, where the effects of one standard over another are somewhat removed from the experience of consumers or global civil society, the intense interests of business are likely to produce a similar result under either form of governance.

Even if states through their IGO were to be more directly involved in setting standards, they are likely to be "captured" by business interests and, thus, to favor neoliberal policies. In the case of child labor, indeed, Rugmark was ultimately undermined by an Indian-government-led certification program (Kaleen) that was captured by industry and competed against Rugmark's attempt to capitalize on its "brand."[78] It is not obvious that public regulation by an IGO would necessarily be better than standards promoted by a PGO. Indeed, many IGOs might look more like the PEFC in its early years, which upgraded its standards only in competition with the FSC. We should be careful in using successful cases of public regulation as a benchmark to compare private regulations that emerge precisely when states and IGOs have been unable to act effectively.

On the other hand, where consumers and labor are mobilized as, say, voters, states and their IGO emanations might be more attentive to civil society interests than the multi-stakeholder models currently used by many PGOs. To the extent that resource scarcity is a driving force in the global governance ecology and who provides the necessary resources matters for the rules produced by PGOs, states and IGOs able to tax producers, consumers, or populations in general would likely produce somewhat less biased policies than at least some of the PGOs that have emerged in recent decades. Where consumer demand for, say, eco-conscious goods can drive some NSMD programs, it is the resource constraints that limit PGOs and their inability to tax beneficiaries that suggests public standards might be preferred to private standards.

The possible skew toward neoliberal rules in private governance is worrisome not because the organizations themselves are normatively questionable, but because the ecology and the rules it produces may be tipping in a single substantive direction that needs to be checked and balanced by other GOs embodying broader social interests. Yet, as states and others adopt the standards issued by PGOs, the skewed ecology appears increasingly hard to overcome. The risk is that through a path-dependent process of double negative regulation, PGOs will build a neoliberal bias into the system of global governance. There is a certain triumphalism in the literature on PGOs, an enthusiasm for private governance over the stale hands of states or the ineffectiveness of IGOs. An ecological perspective opens the question, however, of alternatives to PGOs, why those alternatives do not exist, and what – if they existed – they might look like. PGOs are clearly better than no governance at all. Whether they are always and everywhere preferred over the regulations that might otherwise be produced by states or IGOs is a question that demands attention. All rules contain bias. The question is whose interests are represented in making the rules. While the evidence presented here is admittedly only suggestive – even speculative – the trend is concerning.

Conclusion

Charles Roger and Peter Dauvergne identify two schools in the literature: one, a structural perspective that highlights, following Strange, the diffusion of power in the world system and two, a more functionalist approach that explains the rise of PGOs by the tasks they perform.[79] In treating global governance as a field and, more specifically, a social ecology of diverse populations, this chapter falls somewhat between these approaches. On the one hand, states are complicit in their own "retreat," to borrow Strange's description.[80] In protecting their sovereign prerogatives, coupled with an inability to agree among themselves on rules governing globalization, states have blocked the creation of potentially effective IGOs, leaving open new niches that PGOs have arisen to fill. Other scholars have, of course, noted the failure of states to adopt sufficient regulations has spurred the growth of PGOs, but thinking of the field of global governance as an ecology of resource constrained and competing organizations highlights the complex conditions and interactions that have led to the rise of PGOs in many issue areas.

On the other hand, PGOs do emerge to satisfy needs within the system, but an organizational ecology approach focuses attention on the broad array of possible GOs and especially on the missing IGOs that challenge a simple functionalism. Most important, organizational ecology opens the possibility that any field of GOs might not be socially optimal. Self-interested organizations in a complex system regulate each other and, thereby, configure their environment, opening and closing possibilities. Once a niche is filled, this changes the opportunities for other organizations, creating a path-dependent system. PGOs may be functional, in this view, but we should not assume they are optimal even for the narrow task they perform.

Rules matter. They privilege some actors and harm others, especially when there are distributional implications from alternative outcomes. Who fills a governance niche or who makes which rules is critically important. Although it remains an open question without any clear answer, an ecological approach prompts us to at least ask if the rules emerging at the global level are biased and, if so, whether they are biased in normatively desirable or objectionable ways. The independence that allows PGOs to occupy governance niches that states otherwise block is the main worry. Their dependence for survival on the voluntary participation of those they regulate is a potential source of bias in the rules governing globalization – and given who is being regulated and how resources are channeled to the PGOs, the bias is likely to be in a neoliberal direction. Too little attention, in my view, has been paid to this possibility. The answer is likely to vary considerably across organizations, issue areas, and sets of rules, depending on how the PGOs are themselves structured and the nature of the functions they perform. But as PGOs proliferate, even as populist movements react to the free movement of goods, finance, and people across national borders, it would behoove analysts to inquire into the neoliberal bias that might just possibly undergird both globalization itself and the opposition to globalization.

References

Abbott, Kenneth W., Philipp Genschel, Duncan Snidal, and Bernhard Zangl (eds.). 2015. *International Organizations as Orchestrators*. New York: Cambridge University Press.

Abbott, Kenneth W., Jessica F. Green, and Robert O. Keohane. 2016. "Organizational Ecology and Institutional Change in Global Governance." *International Organization* 70(2): 247–277.

Andonova, Liliana B., Thomas N. Hale, and Charles B. Roger. 2017. "National Policy and Transnational Governance of Climate Change: Substitutes or Complements?" *International Studies Quarterly* 61(2): 253–268.

Avant, Deborah D., Martha Finnemore, and Susan K. Sell (eds.). 2010. *Who Governs the Globe?* New York: Cambridge University Press.

Bartley, Tim. 2003. "Certifying Forests and Factories: States, Social Movements, and the Rise of Private Regulation in the Apparel and Forest Products Fields." *Politics and Society* 31(3): 433–464.

Bartley, Tim. 2007. "How Foundations Shape Social Movements: The Construction of an Organizational Field and the Rise of Forest Certification." *Social Problems* 54(3): 229–255.

Bartley, Tim. 2014. "Transnational Governance and the Re-Centered State: Sustainability or Legality?" *Regulation and Governance* 8(1): 93–109.

Bartley, Tim. 2018. *Rules without Rights: Land, Labor, and Private Authority in the Global Economy*. New York: Oxford University Press.

Barton, John H., Judith L. Goldstein, Timothy E. Josling, and Richard H. Steinberg. 2006. *The Evolution of the Trade Regime: Politics, Law, and Economics of the GATT and the WTO*. Princeton: Princeton University Press.

Bradford, Anu. 2020. *The Brussels Effect: How the European Union Rules the World*. New York: Oxford University Press.

Büthe, Tim and Walter Mattli. 2011. *The New Global Rulers: The Privatization of Regulation in the World Economy*. Princeton: Princeton University Press.

Carroll, Sean B. 2016. *The Serengeti Rules: The Quest to Discover How Life Works and Why It Matters*. Princeton: Princeton University Press.

Cashore, Benjamin. 2002. "Legitimacy and the Privatization of Environmental Governance: How Non-State Market Driven (NSMD) Governance Systems

Gain Rule-Making Authority." *Governance: An International Journal of Policy, Administration, and Institutions* 15(4): 503–529.

Cashore, Benjamin, and Michael W. Stone. 2012. "Can Legality Verification Rescue Global Forest Governance? Analyzing the Potential of Public and Private Policy Intersection to Ameliorate Forest Challenges in Southeast Asia." *Forest Policy and Economics* 18(3): 13–22.

Cashore, Benjamin, Greame Auld, and Deanna Newsom. 2004. *Governing through Markets: Forest Certification and the Emergence of Non-State Authority.* New Haven: Yale University Press.

Dauvergne, Peter, and Jane Lister. 2013. *Eco-Business: A Big-Brand Takeover of Sustainability.* Cambridge: MIT Press.

David, Paul A. 1985. "Clio and the Economics of Qwerty." *American Economic Review* 75(2): 332–337.

DiMaggio, Paul J., and Walter W. Powell. 1983. "The Iron Cage Revisited: Institutional Isomorphism and Collective Rationality in Organizational Fields." *American Sociological Review* 48: 147–160.

Dingwerth, Klaus, and Philipp Pattberg. 2009. "World Politics and Organizational Fields: The Case of Transnational Sustainability Governance." *European Journal of International Relations* 15(4): 707–744.

Eriksen, Stein S., and Ole J. Sending. 2013. "There Is No Global Public: The Idea of the Public and the Legitimation of Governance." *International Theory* 5(2): 213–237.

Fligstein, Neil, and Doug McAdam. 2012. *A Theory of Fields.* New York: Oxford University Press.

FSC. 2018. Annual Report 2018, https://annual-reports.fsc.org/en#downloads (last access July 25, 2022).

Gourevitch, Peter A., David A. Lake, and Janice G. Stein. 2012. *The Credibility of Transnational NGOs: When Virtue Is Not Enough.* New York: Cambridge University Press.

Green, Jessica F. 2013. "Order out of Chaos: Public and Private Rules for Managing Carbon." *Global Environmental Politics* 13(2): 1–15.

Green, Jessica F. 2014. *Rethinking Private Authority: Agents and Entrepreneurs in Global Environmental Governance.* Princeton: Princeton University Press.

Gulbrandsen, Lars H. 2005. "Sustainable Forestry in Sweden: The Effect of Competition Among Private Certification Schemes." *The Journal of Environment and Development* 14(3): 338–355.

Gulbrandsen, Lars H. 2014. "Dynamic Governance Interactions: Evolutionary Effects of State Responses to Non-State Certification Programs." *Regulation and Governance* 8(1): 74–92.

Hacker, Jacob S., and Paul Pierson. 2020. *Let Them Eat Tweets: How The Right Rules in an Age of Extreme Inequality.* New York: Liveright.

Hall, Rodney B., and Thomas J. Biersteker. 2002. "The Emergence of Private Authority in the International System." In: Rodney B. Hall and Thomas J. Biersteker (eds.), *The Emergence of Private Authority in Global Governance.* New York: Cambridge University Press, pp. 3–22.

Hamilton, Alexander, John Jay, and James Madison. 1961. *The Federalist Papers (1787–88).* New York: Penguin.

Hannan, Michael T., and John Freeman. 1989. *Organizational Ecology.* Cambridge: Harvard University Press.

IFRS Foundation. 2019. *Annual Report 2018*, www.ifrs.org/content/dam/ifrs/about-us/funding/2018/annual-report-2018.pdf (last access July 25, 2022).

Jung, Danielle, and David A. Lake. 2011. "Markets, Hierarchies, and Networks: An Agent-Based Organizational Ecology." *American Journal of Political Science* 55(4): 972–990.

Johnson, Tara. 2014. *Organizational Progeny: Why Governments Are Losing Control over the Proliferating Structures of Global Governance*. New York: Oxford University Press.

Kinderman, Daniel. 2015. "Explaining the Rise of National Corporate Social Responsibility: The Role of Global Frameworks, World Culture, and Corporate Interests." In: Kiyoteru Tsutsui and Alwyn Lim (eds.), *Corporate Social Responsibility in a Globalizing World*. New York: Cambridge University Press, pp. 107–146.

Kinderman, Daniel. 2019. "The Challenges of Upward Regulatory Harmonization: The Case of Sustainability Reporting in the European Union." *Regulation and Governance* 14(4): 674–697.

Krasner, Stephen D. 1999. *Sovereignty: Organized Hypocrisy*. Princeton: Princeton University Press.

Levitsky, Steven, and Daniel Ziblatt. 2018. *How Democracies Die*. New York: Crown.

Lim, Alwyn, and Kiyoteru Tsutsui. 2015. "The Social Regulation of the Economy in the Global Context." In: Kiyoteru Tsutsui and Alwyn Lim (eds.), *Corporate Social Responsibility in a Globalizing World*. New York: Cambridge University Press, pp. 1–24.

Locke, Richard M. 2013. *The Promise and Limits of Private Power: Promoting Labor Standards in a Global Economy*. New York: Cambridge University Press.

Loconto, Allison, and Eve Fouilleux. 2014. "Politics of Private Regulation: ISEAL and the Shaping of Transnational Sustainability Governance." *Regulation and Governance* 8(2): 166–185.

Marx, Axel, and Dieter Cuypers. 2010. "Forest Certification as a Global Environmental Governance Tool: What Is the Macro-Effectiveness of the Forest Stewardship Council?" *Regulation and Governance* 4(4): 408–434.

Milgrom, Paul R., Douglass C. North, and Barry R. Weingast. 1990. "The Role of Institutions in the Revival of Trade: The Law Merchant, Private Judges, and the Champagne Fairs." *Economics and Politics* 2(1): 1–23.

Nooruddin, Irfan, and Sarah W. Sokhey. 2012. "Credible Certification of Child Labor Free Production." In: Peter A. Gourevitch, David A. Lake, and Janice G. Stein (eds.), *The Credibility of Transnational NGOs: When Virtue Is Not Enough*. New York: Cambridge University Press, pp. 62–85.

Olegario, Rowena. 2003. "Credit Reporting Agencies: A Historical Perspective." In: Magaret J. Miller (ed.), *Credit Reporting Systems and the International Economy*. Cambridge: MIT Press, pp. 115–159.

Osiander, Andreas. 2001. "Sovereignty, International Relations, and the Westphalian Myth." *International Organization* 55(2): 251–287.

Overdevest, Christine. 2010. "Comparing Forest Certification Schemes: The Case of Ratcheting Standards in the Forest Sector." *Socio-Economic Review* 8(1): 47–76.

Overdevest, Christine, and Jonathan Zeitlin. 2014. "Assembling an Experimental Regime: Transnational Governance Interactions in the Forest Sector." *Regulation and Governance* 8(1): 22–48.

PEFC. 2020. *PEFC Annual Review 2019*, https://cdn.pefc.org/pefc.org/media/2020-04/428b28a8-8f04-45c0-af1c-d911bc0039b5/430e50ab-6653-50a6-875b-449823c04679.pdf (last access July 25, 2022).

Philpott, Daniel. 2001. *Revolutions in Sovereignty: How Ideas Shaped Modern International Relations*. Princeton: Princeton University Press.

Roger, Charles, and Peter Dauvergne. 2016. "The Rise of Transnational Governance as a Field of Study." *International Studies Review* 18(3): 415–437.

Rosenau, James N. 2002. "Governance in a New Global Order." In: David Held and Anthony McGrew (eds.), *Governing Globalization: Power, Authority and Global Governance*. Malden: Polity Press, pp. 70–86.

Scott, W. Richard, and Gerald F. Davis. 2007. *Organizations and Organizing: Rational, Natural, and Open System Perspectives*. Upper Saddle River: Pearson/Prentice Hall.

Strange, Susan. 1996. *The Retreat of the State: The Diffusion of Power in the World Economy*. New York: Cambridge University Press.

Stroup, Sarah S. and Wendy H. Wong. 2017. *The Authority Trap*. Ithaca: Cornell University Press.

Taylor, Alan. 2001. *American Colonies: The Settling of North America*. New York: Penguin.

Van der Ven, Hamish, Steven Bernstein, and Matthw Hoffmann. 2017. "Valuing the Contributions of Nonstate and Subnational Actors to Climate Governance." *Global Environmental Politics* 17(1): 1–20.

Waltz, Kenneth N. 1979. *Theory of International Politics*. Reading: Addison-Wesley.

Wilks, Stephen. 2013. *The Political Power of the Business Corporation*. Cheltenham: Edward Elgar.

Wong, Wendy H. 2012. *Internal Affairs: How the Structure of NGOs Transforms Human Rights*. Ithaca: Cornell University Press.

WWF-US. 2019. *2019 WWF-US Annual Report*, http://assets.worldwildlife.org/financial_reports/37/reports/original/WWF-AR2019-FINALPAGES.pdf?1582917951&_ga=2.172903979.926075631.1592436566-1025158361.1592436566 (last access July 25, 2022).

Young, Oran R. 1994. *International Governance: Protecting the Environment in a Stateless Society*. Ithaca: Cornell University Press.

Zürn, Michael. 2018. *A Theory of Global Governance: Authority, Legitimacy, and Contestation*. New York: Oxford University Press.

Notes

1 A related version of this chapter originally appeared in the *European Journal of International Relations* 27(2): 345–368. I would like to thank the editors and reviewers of that journal, the editors and participants in this volume, and Peter Gourevitch, Jessica Green, Danielle Jung, Miles Kahler, Robert Keohane, and Wendy Wong for helpful comments.

2 There are continuing differences over what to call these organizations. Roger and Dauvergne (2016) call the entire subject transnational governance, but

here I emphasize organizations as the unit of analysis. Abbott, Green, and Keohane (2016) refer to Private Transnational Regulatory Organizations, which limits the domain to regulation. At the risk of further confusion, I use PGOs.

3 There have been many appeals to field theory in the literature on private transnational governance, but most studies nonetheless focus on a single population, e.g., Dingwerth and Pattberg (2009) and Loconto and Fouilleux (2014). Bartley (2003) confines his study to states and PGOs and Bartley (2007) focuses on the relationship between foundations and PGOs.
4 Locke 2013: 15–16.
5 On early global governance, see Young (1994). On private organizations in global governance, see among others Avant et al. (2010), Büthe and Mattli (2010), Green (2014), and Hall and Biersteker (2002).
6 For exceptions, see Abbott, Green, and Keohane (2016) and Jung and Lake (2011). See also Sending, this volume.
7 Hannan and Freeman 1989.
8 Hannan and Freeman 1989: 166.
9 Scott and Davis 2007: 116.
10 Hannan and Freeman 1989: 45
11 DiMaggio and Powell 1983: 143.
12 Fligstein and McAdam 2012.
13 Stroup and Wong 2017.
14 Hannan and Freeman 1989: 17–23 and 35–40.
15 David 1985.
16 Hannan and Freeman 1989: chapter 5.
17 Wong 2012.
18 Bartley 2007.
19 Olegario 2003.
20 Carroll 2016.
21 Green 2013.
22 Carroll 2016: 120–127.
23 Rosenau 2002; Young 1994: 15–16.
24 On the different kinds of rules, see Onuf, this volume. On law, see chapters by Hurd and Alter, this volume, and Witt, this volume.
25 Milgrom et al. 1990.
26 Krasner 1999.
27 Osiander 2001; Philpott 2001.
28 Eriksen and Sending 2013.
29 Hamilton et al. 1961: 246.
30 Hacker and Pierson 2020; Levitsky and Ziblatt 2018.
31 Taylor 2001.
32 Wilks 2013.
33 For a possible method of assessing organizations by "value," see van der Ven et al. 2017.
34 Lim and Tsutsui 2015: 2.
35 Kinderman 2015.
36 Bartley (2003, 2018: 4) argues this negative regulation is, in part, a function of the neoliberal political context prevailing in the 1990s.
37 Cashore 2002.

38 Abbott et al. 2015.
39 Strange 1996; Waltz 1979.
40 For a contrary view, see Johnson 2014.
41 Barton et al. 2006.
42 Zürn 2018.
43 Bradford 2020.
44 Locke 2013.
45 Locke 2013.
46 Büthe and Mattli 2011: 68.
47 Büthe and Mattli 2011: 71–72.
48 Cashore et al. 2004.
49 Bartley 2003: 440.
50 Overdevest 2010: 53; Overdevest and Zeitlin 2014: 30.
51 Overdevest 2010: 54.
52 Overdevest and Zeitlin 2014: 30.
53 Cashore 2002: 507.
54 Overdevest and Zeitlin 2014: 31.
55 Cashore 2002: 508.
56 Gulbrandsen 2005: 79.
57 Bartley 2018: 17. On the limits of upward harmonization, see Kinderman 2019.
58 Marx and Cuypers 2010.
59 Bartley 2018.
60 On the interaction of states and PGOs, see Gulbrandsen 2014 and Andonova et al. 2017.
61 Dauvergne and Lister 2013.
62 Gourevitch et al. 2012.
63 Cashore 2002: 513.
64 Overdevest 2010: 55.
65 Bartley 2018: 4.
66 Bartley 2007.
67 Bartley 2018: 260.
68 Büthe and Mattli 2011.
69 Locke 2013.
70 Büthe and Mattli 2011: 74–75.
71 IFRS Foundation 2019: 26, 38–41.
72 FSC 2018: 56–57.
73 PEFC 2020: 20–21.
74 Nooruddin and Sokhey 2012: 72.
75 See WWF-US 2019: 32.
76 Evaluating counterfactuals in this area is difficult. In assessing the long-term impact of certification regimes vs. legal rules on forestry management, for instance, see Bartley 2014; Cashore and Stone 2012; Gulbrandsen 2005; Overdevest and Zeitlin 2014.
77 Bradford 2020.
78 Nooruddin and Sokhey 2012.
79 Roger and Dauvergne 2016.
80 Strange 1996.

4 Anarchy, Authority, Rule: Reconsidered

Nicholas Onuf[1]

Thirty-some years ago, Frank Klink and I wrote a paper that we called "Anarchy, Authority, Rule." In due course, that paper appeared in a major journal.[2] Bearing the title "Political Society," it made up most of a chapter in my book, *World of Our Making: Rules and Rule in International Relations*, published in 1989. At the time, scholars in the field of International Relations (IR) had little to say about *authority*, except in the context of European regional institutions. They had even less to say about *rule* – the condition of rule in any political society, including international society. Only some of those scholars would even concede that states in their relations constitute a society in any meaningful sense of the term. They had a good deal to say about *anarchy* in international relations – a condition generally construed to be the absence of rule such as we find within states – even to the extent of calling international society anarchical.[3]

Anarchy remains a deeply embedded assumption, still serving to define IR as an autonomous scholarly concern. Nevertheless, as this volume attests, intimations of authority and rule have seeped into the field's margins. Given the opportunity to reconsider what Klink and I put forward years ago, I see no need to repudiate or significantly revise what we said then. Instead I review and sharpen our major claims. Then I take the opportunity to consider briefly conditions of rule as they have revealed themselves in the time since. My frame of reference is *not* IR as conventionally defined by reference to anarchy. Rather, it is the current state of the modern world, now half a millennium old. In the space available, I can do no more than sketch its major features and point to the evidence of pervasive rule in modernity writ large.

Beyond Anarchy

"Anarchy, Authority, Rule" sought to make short work of the assumption that anarchy prevails in international relations. Friedrich Kratochwil, whose *Rules, Norms, and Decisions* also appeared in 1989, also undertook "a refutation of the 'anarchy' argument," if more elliptically.[4] Judging from two papers appearing in 1992, anarchy's conceptual hegemony would not be ended so easily. Helen Milner's "The Assumption of Anarchy in International Relations Theory" engages in conceptual clarification, as Klink and I had, only to conclude that "anarchy is an important condition of world politics," but "it is not the only one."[5] Alexander Wendt's "Anarchy Is What States Make of It," would seem, by its very title, to treat anarchy as a description of how things look when states act as they so often have reasons to do, the result being "a Hobbesian world of their own making."[6] By Wendt's reckoning, such a world is neither epiphenomenal nor inescapable. States' agents are free to act within the limits imposed by the "anarchic structure" of their relations; anarchy is a permissive cause of competitive behavior.[7]

In effect, Milner and Wendt saved the concept of anarchy from the charge of irrelevance and the threat of displacement, if indeed this threat was even noticed. Their papers are much cited – Wendt's strikingly so. Neither paper cites "Anarchy, Authority, Rule" or the relevant chapter of *World of Our Making*. Nor did these papers cite Kratochwil's book. Since then relatively few scholars have shown any great interest in eliminating anarchy from the field's conceptual repertory. For the field to find its way "beyond anarchy" may not even be possible, for anarchy's conceptual demise would deprive IR of its slender rationale for treating international relations as a distinctive subject deserving its own field of study. The assumption that anarchy prevails in international relations *still* defines IR.

Kenneth Waltz offered the most obvious reason why this should be so: "The enduring anarchic character of international politics accounts for the striking sameness in the quality of international life through the millennia, a statement that will meet with wide assent."[8] As stated, Waltz's empirical generalization may seem to be obviously true to a casual observer (hence, wide assent), but it is, needless to say, overly inclusive (millennia) and insufficiently specific (sameness, quality of life) – far too much so to suit contemporary scholarly standards. Nor is it obvious that anarchy explains (accounts for) sameness so much as describes (counts as) this condition. Nevertheless, Waltz articulated a commonplace in IR, in the process lending it his authority as the field's leading theorist. If Waltz's stature were not enough, scholars had other reasons to assert that international relations constitute a condition of anarchy.

Waltz himself provided one by drawing a sharp distinction between hierarchic and anarchic "political orders" on structural grounds. "Hierarchy entails relations of super- and subordination among a system's parts, and that implies their differentiation."[9] While all states are hierarchies, not all hierarchies are states; sovereignty is also required;[10] "Anarchy entails relations of coordination among a system's units, and that implies their sameness."[11] System units, or states, are the same in possessing sovereignty, there being no sovereign over them. Waltz's structural binary hinges on an utterly conventional conceptualization of internal and external sovereignty, one that goes back to Vattel. Its appeal lies in its stripped-down clarity, greatly aided by the use of a term – *hierarchy* – belonging to the same genus as the term *anarchy*. Hierarchy and anarchy are conditions of *rule*: Rule by some over others, rule by none over others.

Waltz's binary opposition is omnipresent but not just in the terms in which he chose to express it. Looming behind it and looming over three and a half centuries of political thought is Thomas Hobbes, and, with Hobbes, the stark alternatives of "the Soveraigne Power of the Common-wealth" and "the naturall condition of Warre."[12] Oddly perhaps, Waltz did not trouble to trace his binary back to Hobbes. Other scholars give credit where it is due almost reflexively; recall Wendt's "Hobbesian world" (quoted above). Milner for her part quoted Hedley Bull's characterization of "the Hobbesian Tradition."[13] Later Wendt devoted many pages to "the logic of Hobbesian anarchy" in a book directly challenging Waltz's structural theorizing.[14]

In *Leviathan*, Hobbes spoke of anarchy only three times. One passage is worth quoting:

> That the condition of meer Nature, that is to say, of absolute liberty, such as is theirs, that neither are Sovereigns nor Subjects, is anarchy, and the condition of warre: That the praecepts, by which men are guided to avoyd that condition, are the Lawes of Nature: that a Common-wealth without Soveraign power is but a word, without substance, and cannot stand: That Subjects owe to Soveraigns, simple Obedience, in all things, wherein their obedience is not repugnant to the Lawes of God, I have sufficiently proved, in that which I have already written.[15]

It is hard to imagine a more eloquent summary of what Hobbes had said in earlier chapters of his monumental book. Or a more authoritative statement of anarchy's "logical" relation to unconstrained action, or liberty, on the one hand and unbridled competition, or war, on the other. So much for Waltz's "relations of coordination"; his reluctance to invoke Hobbes may not be so odd after all. If there is coordination or cooperation, it can only be "under anarchy," however conditionally or ephemerally, and not entailed by it.[16]

In *Leviathan*, Hobbes spoke of hierarchy only once, in a slashing attack on the Papacy – in his words, "The Kingdome of Darkness."[17] Nevertheless, the passage quoted earlier neatly supports Waltz's structural binary. Where, in Hobbes's words, there is a sovereign power and obedient subjects, there are, in Waltz's words, relations of super- and subordination. Where there is neither sovereign nor subject, and thus anarchy, there are system-units in side-by-side relations. Hierarchy is a vertical structure, anarchy a horizontal one.

Subjects having surrendered a broad range of their powers, Hobbes's sovereign is a "person" (indeed an "artificial person" perhaps embodied in a single individual) upon whom great powers have been conferred.[18] By implication, Hobbes's commonwealth consists of just two units in a vertical relation. Yet Hobbes gave his sovereign the power to delegate powers to "Counsellours, Ministers, Magistrates, and Officers, both in Peace and War."[19] Delegation constitutes a stable hierarchy of as many units as the sovereign sees fit to designate, always in a vertical relation. Anarchy never permits the delegation of powers except as a temporary and dangerous expedient or in a constitutive act of the whole. As an alternative, adding side-by-side system-units could increase opportunities for units to engage in local or occasional coordination. For an observer, anarchical structure is stable – this is Waltz's sameness or, borrowing Michel Foucault's words, an "anarchy of minor differences."[20] For units, it is anything but.

According to Hobbes, the sovereign possesses "the whole power of prescribing the Rules whereby every man may know what Goods he may enjoy, and what Actions he may doe, without being molested by any of his fellow Subjects."[21] In practical terms, the sovereign issues commands. Some commands are directed to subordinates whose delegated powers enable them to act; once acted on, such commands are discharged. Other commands variously directed to subjects, including subordinates, stand until the sovereign rescinds them; these commands are rules. Hobbes argued at length that subordinates wielding "the sword of the Common-wealth" could enforce the sovereign's commands – both kinds, so to speak, on command.[22] "Law, properly, is the word of him that by right hath command over others."[23]

Although Waltz the structuralist avoided the language of agency and thus of powers, he alluded to "the difference between politics conducted in a condition of settled rules and politics conducted in a condition of anarchy."[24] This is not the place for an extended discussion of rules – how they become "settled," the degree to which they may be informal, when they are "properly" legal, what happens to them when they are not followed, whether international society has settled rules properly understood as law.[25] Whether anarchy is lawless depends on one's definition of law (and we may assume that Waltz held to Hobbes' conception – laws must be formally stated and subject to enforcement). Absence of law by this or any other definition does not imply an absence of rules.

Agents' relations are never ruleless. Putting people in a state of nature is a theatrical contrivance.[26]

As persons capable of acting, people are agents. They have powers, however limited, conferred by the rules of the society in which they exercise their powers. Elsewhere I have argued that rules are linguistic phenomena and that distinctive kinds of speech acts (assertive, directive, and commissive) eventuate in, or serve as a model for, three kinds of rules.[27] Assertions convey beliefs, typically expressed in declarative sentences; directives convey wishes, typically formulated as commands, demands, orders, or requests; and commissives, or promises, offer to effectuate future events. Once accepted, promises are generally taken to be binding. Directives are intended to obligate addressees (this is so, at least in some degree, even with requests[28]); uncontested assertions typically acquire normative weight over time. Insofar as language makes obligation a relative condition, a matter of degree, then rules enhance obligation – within limits.

Like recipes in a cookbook, *instruction-rules* tell us how to proceed if we are to get the result that we are hoping for. If we do not follow rules of this kind, it will be harder for us to accomplish what we had hoped to and people will remind us of the value of doing what these rules tell us to; we are likely to feel ashamed when we are reminded. *Directive-rules* are the kind of rules that Hobbes associated with law; fear motivates people to obey the law. *Commitment-rules* are like contracts reciprocally undertaken to assure a mutually desired result. When generalized to the society as a whole, they create what we ordinarily call rights and duties; failure to perform one's duties can elicit a feeling of guilt.

Linked sets of rules form institutions; the three kinds of rules constitute functionally analogous kinds of institutions.[29] Rules, institutions, and constitutive acts need not be formal in order to be effective – to perform their regulative function effectively. If we think of agency as the condition of someone or something acting on behalf of someone or something, including one's self or itself, then institutions can and frequently do function as agents. Rules regulate behavior – this is what we *see* rules doing. At the same time, the very same rules establish conditions for what people (as agents) *can* do in society (as an ensemble of institutions).[30] All rules do this in one of three ways; some rules (powers, of which there must be three kinds) do so a greater degree than others. Briefly, here's how it works:

(1) Instruction rules confer *statuses* on people and institutions by drawing and assigning value to distinctions that define status groups or cohorts. Status cohorts are layered as networks, thereby constituting

a status order. As network nodes, members of status cohorts are laterally linked. They occupy a single plane or level, which makes them status equals; multiple networks must occupy multiple planes and are therefore stratified.[31]

Status arises most directly from the value that members of any society assign to expressions of deference, such as titles, honors, prizes, exemptions, and courtesies. Thus Hobbes associated "the Value we set upon one another" with honor and "the publique worth of a man" with dignity.[32] For Marcel Proust, status is the "*coefficient social*" by which everyone is measured.[33] Max Weber associated "status" (*Stand*) with social esteem (*sozialen Schätzung*) in *Wirtschaft und Gesellschaft*.[34] Given the values at stake and the ease with which they can be attached to a variety of objects subject to ranking, status competition is pervasive and often intense.[35]

(2) Directive rules confer *offices* (recall Hobbes's use of this term), arranged in descending order, thereby constituting an organization. As with status cohorts, officers within organizations occupy multiple planes, often formally designated as ranks or, less often, echelons, and these ranks may hold for many similar organizations. The term *rank* is also routinely applied to the position of a status cohort in a status-order. For expository clarity, I distinguish between *status-rank* and *office-rank*.

While the number of cohort members tends to decrease from any given status-rank to the next higher one, that number is rarely fixed and bears no functional relation to adjacent ranks. By contrast, office-ranks are routinely fixed in number and functionally related to adjacent ranks. As Weber pointed out, vacant offices must be filled for organizations to function effectively, and "a new incumbent will be appointed if a vacancy occurs."[36] For the incumbent, being an officer is a vocation and not an honor or reward.

(3) Commitment rules confer *roles*, such as actors assume in a theatrical performance. A role differs from a status or office by being voluntarily assumed and arranged on a horizontal plane (contrary to Talcott Parsons' inclusive, implicitly liberal conception of role as "the most significant unit" in a social structure[37]). Actors on that plane are members of a single status cohort and therefore status equals. However much their roles differ (following Wendt, they may be allies, rivals, or enemies[38]), they constitute an association or generalized partnership.[39]

Taken together, the rules conferring statuses, offices and roles constitute agency for people as well as institutions acting on their behalf. Every agent is thus in a position to act in and on the world, but always within the limits specified by those rules. No agent has the same aggregate of statuses, offices, and roles as any other agent; every agent is a unique social being. While different societies favor one or another kind of rule in the constitution of agency, the result is to make people "egocentric" but not necessarily "individualistic."[40] How agents act in society also depends on their purposes (goals and motivations) and available means for achieving them.

Rule

In their regulative function, rules are tools for social control. There would seem to be an obvious relation between rules as regulative instruments and rule as a system for the distribution of privilege to the benefit of some over the many. The editors of this volume define rule more elaborately as "constellations of formally or informally institutionalized sub- and superordination with the aim of affecting the distribution of basic goods and influence and of stabilizing expectations ..." (Daase et al., this volume). Their "constellations" are vertically ordered, as the prefixes "sub-" and "super-" indicate. My "systems" are variously arranged (as I will go on to explain), with the common result of distributing privilege (goods, influence, and stability) asymmetrically.

The editors avoid defining rule by reference to rules. They are in good company. Liberal thinkers and legal scholars who emphasize the relation between law and order construe rules too narrowly and privilege as secondary to order – even a just order. Decades ago, a variety of Western Marxists, elite theorists, and renegade sociologists gave their attention to domination and exploitation, and this remains a central concern for critical scholars.[41] Rarely do these writers use the language of rules and rule. One might think that at least some of their predecessors did. Among them Karl Marx and Gaetano Mosca stand out. After all, Marx and Engels eloquently indicted "the ruling class" in *The German Ideology* and Mosca's great work is called *The Ruling Class*. Yet appearances can be deceiving.

The words that Marx and Engel actually used are "*herrschenden Klasse*"; they also made frequent use of the term *Herrschaft*, rendered "domination" or, less often and rather figuratively, "rule," as in "the rule of religion." At no point in this text do they concern themselves with rules. In Italian, Mosca's book bears the title, *Elementi di scienza politica* (1896); his key concern is "*la classe politica*," and not "the ruling class." As Arthur Livingston observed in his Introduction to the English translation, this is "the group of people who actually and directly participate in government or influence it."[42] They rule in the most conventional sense of the term.

Ideology aside, Marx and Mosca held a common point of view. Some few people in any society have the means to exercise control over everyone else; the few benefits systematically from doing so; they are subject to resistance from others as they do so. Even if proponents of this point of view are reluctant to use the language of rules and rule, the necessary transpositions come readily to mind:

(1) *source* of social control (privilege) = unequal resources;
(2) *mode* of social control (power) = violence, wealth, symbols (by way of rules);
(3) *exercise* of social control (domination) = subjection (legitimated as a condition of rule);
(4) *effect* of social control (exploitation) = unequal benefits (privilege: benefits = resources).

In making these transpositions, I added something as important as it is neglected. Rules *are* normative statements, and this makes rule – let me emphasize – a *normative* condition.[43] When Daase and Deitelhoff (this volume) point out that rule "is mostly conceptualized in terms of obedience and compliance rather than in terms of resistance or contestation," I am pretty sure they are pointing at me – and making a political point. I could (*should*) point out that obedience and resistance are the two sides of the same coin. Rules tell people what they *should* do and what they should expect if they fail to do as they are told.

Daase and Deitelhoff might reply: The coin is biased, the compliance-resistance binary is ideologically freighted, and that is why we avoid conceptualizing rule by reference to rules as such (and speak of "sub- and superordination" instead of "super- and subordination"). I concede the point – it does matter whether we put resistance or compliance first (or consider rule bottom-up instead of top-down) – but I suggest that the political implications of our respective conceptual choices are more complicated than this. Whether we feel obligated to follow rules or indeed to defy them, or we follow them, or not, on prudential grounds, or we follow them merely out of habit, the empirics are incontestable: most rules work most of the time, most likely for some combination of all three reasons. That this is the case makes rule effective – far more effective than domination over any extended time and for any significant number of people.

Here I use the term *domination* to suggest direct, physical coercion or, as we so often say, naked power (see also the introduction to this volume). Despite the Latin roots of the term (*domus*, house) and many of its cognates, this is today the standard sense of the term in IR (and throughout this volume). Yet "naked power is the exception, not the rule."[44] As Marx and Mosca knew full well, the rule is never naked, by definition and in practice. How power gets dressed, what clothes the emperor wears: this is another matter. The power of the sovereign, however achieved and consecrated, is top-down; popular sovereignty is bottom-up. Either way, *what* matters is the distribution of privilege: such is *my* politics.

If there are three kinds of rules, then it should be possible to identify three kinds of rule on functional grounds. Naming two kinds of rule *hegemony* and *hierarchy* is reasonably straightforward. The third kind of rule has no obvious name. While international society may exhibit elements or episodes of hegemony and hierarchy, it is more generally characterized by a condition of rule here named *heteronomy*. As such, it would seem to pose a direct challenge to the assumption that anarchy prevails in international relations or, more abstractly, that international society is self-ordering.

Hegemony has long been a familiar term, appropriately connoting leadership (here again, see the introduction to this volume).[45] Many scholars use the term specifically to describe the overwhelmingly important position of the United States in the post–Cold War world.[46] Thanks to Antonio Gramsci, there has developed a sense of hegemony as a system of rule. With Gramsci in mind, Klink and I used the term to identify the kind of rule in which instruction rules are paramount, status yields deference, leaders lead by example, and the legitimacy of rule is a fiction in which everyone is complicit (I take up the question of legitimacy below). Looking back, I would emphasize that hegemonial rule produces a status-order from top to bottom, stratification is a straightjacket, and thus hegemony also produces resistance at multiple points in the status-order.[47]

Where directive rules are paramount, rule depends on a rank-order of offices assuring that these rules are carried out whenever and wherever they are ignored, resisted, or subverted. Directives pass down from rank to rank, office to office, and information moves up. *Hierarchy* describes the familiar Weberian model of an organization as a chain of command.[48] In the same year that our "Anarchy, Authority, Rule" appeared, Ian Clark published a book called *The Hierarchy of States.*[49] Before launching into an historical survey of international order since 1815, Clark defined hierarchy as "a social arrangement characterized by stratification in which, like the angels, there are orders of power and glory and the society is classified in successively subordinate grades." In effect, he conflated hierarchy as the order of power and hegemony as the order of glory. It is no wonder, then, that he urged his readers to think "in terms of disparities of power" and warned against trying to be any more precise than this.[50]

That Clark used the term hierarchy indiscriminately for the "orders of power and glory" and their symbiotic relation is hardly unusual. Even philosophers elide them.[51] The very term *hierarchy* combines the Greek words for *sacred* (*hieros*, perhaps better translated as *ritualized*) and *rule* (*archē*) and found an important place in Christianity's celestial imagery.[52] Clark's reference to angels is no coincidence. More telling is the importance of ecclesiastical hierarchy in the Western Church. Max Weber distinguished between "compulsory political organization" – "the 'state'" – characterized by a "monopoly of the legitimate use of physical force" and "hierocratic organization" – "a 'church'" – which relies on "psychic coercion."[53] As an institution, the Papacy forged the status derived from sacred warrant and a formalized chain of command into a co-constitutive relation.

Any such relation is contingently probable for obvious reasons: status justifies office; office protects status. Weber understood this dynamic. "Whether he is in a private office or a public bureau, the modern official … always strives for and usually attains a distinctly elevated *social esteem* vis-à-vis the governed. His social position is protected by prescription about rank order."[54] To the extent that "rank order" supports status-ordering, institutionalization makes hegemony look like hierarchy, and conversely. Yet hegemony and hierarchy, status order and chain of command, are not *always* conjoined in practice. Indeed they are occasionally at odds, and this is sufficient reason to consider them separately.

Over the years, interest in hierarchy has grown in IR and International Law.[55] Throughout this body of work, the relation between hegemony and hierarchy, status and office, gets almost no attention. Nor does the large literature on empire help us here. For good reason, its authors grant the importance of directive-rules in relations between states and their colonies, which are then implicitly contrasted with the anarchical relations of states.

The third kind of rule presents the most direct challenge to the assumption that anarchy prevails in international relations. If we take anarchy to be rule by no one in particular, then anarchy is perhaps just another term for the condition of rule that has the appearance of a spontaneous order. In this case, everyone's insistence on their rights compels everyone to perform all those duties corresponding to the rights of others. This is rule as I defined it earlier – a system of rules for the distribution of privilege to the benefit of some few over the many. This is the kind of rule to which liberals are most susceptible, take to be just and fair, and are least likely to resist. It is, on their account, the rule *of* law, not just rule *by* law. As the editors of this volume say, "even though the international rule of law is a 'fiction', it is an effective fiction ..." (Daase et al., this volume; see also chapters by Hurd and Alter, this volume).

Borrowing from Immanuel Kant (but not Weber), Klink and I called this kind of rule *heteronomy*.[56] We may not have made the case sufficiently for heteronomy as the form of rule. To strengthen the case, I draw on Michael Tomasello's "shared intentionality theory" of human development.[57] Children are born demanding. Soon they are "acting in parallel" with others, often mimicking them. They learn to make requests (first by pointing and then by speaking) to satisfy needs. Finally they come to appreciate the implications of making promises at about three years of age.

By making promises, children work together to achieve common goals (collective intentionality). The result is "joint commitment."[58] They *recognize* their parity in doing so: autonomy yields to "self-other equivalence." A "sense of obligation" ensues, and collaboration displaces autonomy within a jointly framed space for ongoing conduct. This condition *is* heteronomy; it *rules* ongoing conduct by mutual agreement (see also Sending, this volume).

In recent work, I have argued that the ruled practice of state recognition is striking evidence of international society's heteronomous character.[59] Recognition connotes reciprocity predicated on equality (self-other equivalence). As such, it confers access to a determinate set of relations understood as freely chosen exchanges of values broadly defined. States seek recognition and thus the right to participate in these relations because, on balance, it benefits them to do so. How much they benefit is something else.

Whatever the evidence that international relations are heteronomous in the first instance, and not anarchical, scholars in IR will always be skeptical. Adopting some other term would change nothing. Jack Donnelly has muddied these waters even further by advocating the term *heterarchy* to describe an international system "composed of multiple heterogeneous units organized in varying types of relations on varying scales," with "divergent (and often tangled) hierarchies" resulting.[60] Lest anyone take Donnelly's heterarchy to be roughly comparable to heteronomy as I have used the term, his further claim that heterarchy is "fundamentally *non-territorial*" (that is, functionally differentiated) decisively negates the possibility.[61] Heteronomy may start with heterogeneous units, but it makes them alike for the limited purpose of their relations – they are equivalent, however nominally. Waltz's "sameness" prevails, at least as an "ordering principle."[62] And this is so even if those relations produce divergent and tangled hierarchies.[63]

Authority as Legitimate Rule

The term *authority*, often qualified as "central authority," pops up in IR whenever anarchy and hierarchy are conceptualized in opposition. Just for example, Waltz considered the risks involved in "moving from a situation of coordinate action to one of super- and subordination, that is, by erecting agencies with effective authority and extending a system of rules."[64] Agencies with "effective authority" constitute a government, which "ruling by some standard of legitimacy, arrogates to itself the right to use force – that is, to apply a variety of sanctions to control the use of force by its subjects."[65]

Granting the Weberian state as a frame of reference, Waltz reduced effectiveness to the use of force, which is nevertheless accepted as legitimate; were it not accepted, it would not be effective for long. Authority, then, is the use of force accepted as legitimate and (we should surmise) institutionalized in or as rule. To the same effect, Harold Lasswell and Abraham Kaplan defined *power* as "the process of affecting the policies of others with the help of (actual or threatened) severe deprivations," *authority* as "the expected and legitimate possession of power," *agency* as "an authority structure," and *office* as "a position of authority."[66] Deriving from the Latin verb *legitimare*, to make lawful, legitimacy is taken for granted as the source of or basis for law. In effect, a human disposition akin to Weber's "*Fügsamkeit*" or "willingness to obey" makes law, indeed normativity, possible.[67]

Clearly implied is the sense that authority is "'subjective': its existence depends on someone's think-so, though not, to be sure, simply on the think-so of the person having authority."[68] In Thomas Franck's influential definition, *legitimacy* is "that quality of a rule *which derives from a perception on the part of those to whom it is addressed that it has come into being in accordance with right process.* Right process includes the notion of valid sources but also encompasses literary, socio-anthropological and philosophical insights."[69] Ian Hurd has taken a similar stance: "*Legitimacy,* as I use it here, refers to the normative belief by an actor that a rule or institution ought to be obeyed. It is a subjective quality, relational between actor and institution, and defined by the actor's *perception* of the institution."[70]

Any such line of thought comes very close to a Hobbesian position on the social contract as the foundation for the state and its internal arrangements. For Hobbes, actions have authors.[71] The act of constituting sovereign authority (supreme authority, sovereign power: for Hobbes, these were interchangeable terms) is more than Consent, or Concord; it is a real Unitie of them all in one and the same Person, made by Covenant of every man with every man, in such manner as if every man should say to every man: *I Authorise and give up my Right of Governing myself, to this Man, or to this Assembly of men, on this condition; that thou give up, thy Right to him, and Authorise all his Actions in like manner.* This done, the Multitude so united in one Person, is called a Common-wealth.[72]

The Hobbesian Covenant may be a singular constitutive event, but the many, as actors, continue to have powers accorded them by the rules and accepted by them as legitimate.

Despite Hobbes's authorial authority and perhaps because he only used the term *legitimate* in passing (for children),[73] scholars today are disposed to invoke Weber's authority in discussing power, legitimacy, and authority.[74] And for good reason: the English translation of *Wirtschaft und Gesellschaft* is replete with these terms, often used in close association. The trouble here is the German term *Herrschaft*, which has a central place in Weber's text. Yet for his English-language translators, *Herrschaft* was an interpretive puzzle, which they solved by using either *domination* or *authority* in its place. Both choices are misleading. As I said earlier, domination implies the exercise of naked power. When Weber qualified *Herrschaft* as legitimate, the resulting near-oxymoron, "legitimate domination" is laughably inappropriate.[75] As for substituting authority for *Herrschaft*, I should acknowledge that Weber himself authorized this transposition.[76] Moreover, he used the Latinate term *Autorität* extensively to mean *Herrschaft* when, in my view, he ought not to have.

In Weber's hands, *Herrschaft* is a general term for rule in any form.[77] It does not refer to the state as a product of Hobbesian consent, to the modern state as a vehicle for rule, or to the internal arrangements of any particular state. The effect of translating *Herrschaft* as *authority* is to authorize the democratic, republican state or union of states as the paradigmatic, indeed normative condition of rule in the modern world. Any political society not conforming to this model is subject to criticism as "authoritarian" (in its ambiguous relation to authority, an exceedingly odd term), "undemocratic" or, in the case of international society, unruled.

It is not, however, Weber's story. Rule is a general social phenomenon. Wherever manifest, *Herrschaft* (not "authority," as in translation) depends on belief, *Glaube* – a willingness to be ruled.[78] Weber seems never to have defined "legitimacy" ("*Legitimität*" emphasized, his scare marks) – at least in *Wirtschaft und Gesellschaft*. Rather he associated it with "validity" ("*Geltung*," again his scare marks).[79] Perhaps to emphasize the relation between rule and the willingness to be ruled, Weber specifically if redundantly claimed that there are three pure types of legitimate rule ("*Es gibt drei reine Typen legitimer Herrschaft*"): rational, traditional, and charismatic.[80] The first rests on "belief in enacted rules," the second "on belief in the sanctity of immemorial traditions," and the third on "devotion to the exceptional sanctity, heroism or exemplary character of an individual person, and of the normative pattern or order revealed or ordained by him."[81]

It should be obvious that there is not a complete one-to-one correspondence between the three kinds of rules that I have put forward and Weber's three types of rules. Hegemony may find its legitimacy – better to say, its source of normativity – in tradition or in the presence and activities of a charismatic individual. Insofar as charisma lends itself to myth and becomes enveloped in tradition, hegemony has two, entwined sources of normativity. Hierarchy is legitimate when everyone accepts formalized relations of super- and subordination, and their enforcement, for good, practical reasons.[82] Offices are assigned, bureaucratization ensues, and administration is impersonal, accountable, and efficient – at least ideally. Here the correspondence is direct and exclusive; Hobbes and Weber join forces in conceptualizing the Weberian state.

In striking contrast, Weber's typology says almost nothing about heteronomy in the sense that I have stipulated. If Weber largely ignored the legitimation of heteronomous rule, he more than adequately set out the grounds for hegemonial and hierarchical rule, wherever found. Better than any of his contemporaries he identified the hierarchical properties of the modern state and its rational legitimation through, and as, positive law. Most of all, his extended discussion of legitimate rule effectively demonstrates that rule in general (not domination, not just authority) secures its legitimacy through rules, which are themselves normative by definition. If rules did not have a validating source, then they would lack the normative force that makes them what they distinctively are and rule the dominating social condition that it is. In Weber's vocabulary, legitimate rule is an overdetermined concept, a useful pleonasm.

Rule Today

Weber was the first great student of modernity writ large – and this despite his relative indifference to heteronomy. Weber's typology of legitimate forms of rule lends itself to an interpretation of modernity such as we find dominating the second half of the twentieth century. More than this, Weber and his typology are substantially responsible for "modernization theory." There are five main tenets of this influential perspective on what it means to become modern.[83]

(1) Modernity is to be understood as a transformation in the material conditions of life, starting in Europe and North America, broadly associated with capitalism as a mode of production and benefiting ever larger numbers of people. Integral to this transformation is the ideological (intellectual, cultural, and sociopolitical) transformation culminating in the Enlightenment and later associated with liberalism. In short, modernity rewards change.
(2) By definition, tradition resists change; as I pointed out earlier, hegemony diffuses resistance. Modernity must overcome tradition, which supports stratified social relations and legitimates the old regime (whether monarchical or, more rarely, republican). In the old regime, organizational rank and status position coincide in the distribution of privilege, ascription trumps achievement, hegemony and hierarchy converge.
(3) Modernization is the process in which individual autonomy, instrumental rationality and democratic legitimacy go hand-in-hand in changing almost everything from daily life to the production of goods to conditions of rule. Throwing over the old regime is a blow to tradition; discrediting tradition undermines the old regime. Hierarchy and heteronomy complement each other as cause and consequence of modernization.
(4) Once initiated, modernization is inevitable and irreversible; its universalist ideology and the promise of material abundance appeal to the vast majority of the human population. Nevertheless, change may be slow and uneven because the ruling beneficiaries of tradition will use the many resources under their control to resist change or divert material gains to themselves.
(5) Modernization can result in a perverse, ideologically unbalanced form of rule, in which organizational goals exclude individual endeavor, meaningful representation and democratic participation; hierarchy squelches any sign of heteronomy. 20th century totalitarianism exemplifies modernization gone drastically wrong.

After a burst of interest in so-called democratic transitions, modernization theory has fallen out of favor among scholars, mostly for what it overlooks or underestimates. Consider the canny ability of traditionalists to turn modern technologies against modernity; the resilience of traditional beliefs and persistence of local practices; manifold excesses and distortions in the production, distribution and consumption of material goods; the long, hypocritical history of imperial exploitation; post-modern critique of modern hubris. Nevertheless, these limitations do not challenge modernization theory's central claims: modernity defeats tradition by eliminating status, stratification, and hegemony as the basic means for ordering social relations and replacing them with authoritatively arranged offices and roles, hierarchy, and heteronomy. The measure of modernization theory is a growing number of liberal democratic republican states locked in peaceful relations – the so-called democratic peace.

If, however, we consider these claims in the context of globalization, they are subject to qualification. First, status and stratification. In confronting tradition, Enlightenment republicans asked whether, by nature, hereditary aristocrats are the best qualified citizens to rule. If they are not, if indeed privilege has corrupted them (always a republican concern), then the question is how to identify and educate citizens who would be better qualified. Liberal practice and democratic procedures would seem to answer the latter question.

Extending the binary of heritage and competence to social relations in general, modernization theory associates ascription with tradition and achievement with modernity. High status confers access to high office; if stratification is suppressed, talent will rise to the top. In effect, hierarchy is modernized – one might even say, sanitized – by severing its close relation to hegemony and tying it instead to heteronomy as manifest in an open, pluralist society. Ever since the Enlightenment, the sociopolitical revolution has been a conspicuous method by which to abolish or degrade status.

Skeptics would say, even if such revolutions succeed in their own terms, they do not prevent status from reasserting itself in due course. Modern theorists would respond, once liberal democratic societies are established and continuous change is legitimated, these societies endlessly renew themselves by rewarding those whose achievements best serve society. Even if achievement's reward is status, no one's status is assured for long. Stratification is nothing more than the distribution of status rewards at any given moment.

No doubt the actual experience of modern societies falls somewhere between these two poles. There is, however, one trend in the late modern world pointing to the enduring power of ascription, a return to status-ordering and a reunion of hegemony and hierarchy. This is professionalization. In the first instance, the professions themselves have rapidly professionalized. So has an ever-wider range of productive activities.[84] Anyone in professional training learns the overwhelming importance of status position and what Andrew Abbott has called "internal stratification."[85] Even if status is initially earned, it soon fuels itself. Even if status dies with its holder, status-ordering runs rampant.

Professionalization does not take place in a vacuum. It requires great deal of administrative support (itself ever more professionalized) and thus of organization – not just professional associations, but organizations within which professionals find themselves assigned to offices specifying duties, along with training, supervision, and evaluation. As professionalization takes place, organizations confer status through office. Officers of the same rank and profession routinely communicate with each other within and across similar organizations, with the effect of strengthening professional stratification.

Professionalization and stratification cannot be extricated from the proliferation of organizations in and among modern societies. This is, of course, a spectacular trend, widely seen as a major feature of globalization and best understood as an accelerating process of functional differentiation. With the dramatic growth in everything from tweets to landfill, productive activity in the broadest sense depends on ever greater specialization in the tasks that must be performed competently; the "division of expert labor" also produces an ever greater need for administrative support.[86] In my view, this development prompted an epochal transition in modernity as a whole – a transition dating from the last decades of the nineteenth century and perhaps most visible in the arts as *modernism.* My concern here is the effect of specialization and professionalization on conditions of rule.

Mystified by what is going on, scholars and policy specialists talk loosely about *global governance* and associate it with liberalization and democratization. The neoliberal fantasy of deregulation serves mostly to legitimate marginally effective alterations in large-scale organizational arrangements, in the process shifting status and its rewards to large firms, their investors, and their senior officers. The popular fantasy that new constitutions and electoral reforms instantiate democracy serves mostly to legitimate the organizational apparatus of the Weberian state. In both cases, the correlative result is to legitimate stratification within organizations and across a landscape that is densely organized on every scale.

While the professions generally contribute to the legitimation of rule, the legal profession is preeminent in doing so. The legal profession is differentiated into increasingly varied activities. Many lawyers work in large firms. Most of the work they do is organizationally mandated (and merely modern in a Weberian sense); much of it is functionally defined (and therefore also modernist); some of it is oriented to the management of interorganizational relations (modern in a larger sense that includes the negotiation of contracts, litigation, and settlement of disputes – hallmarks of liberal modernity).

Here again scale matters. Even as large, functionally differentiated organizations intrude on the everyday life of ordinary people, legal assistance is rarely sufficiently organized to combat large organizations and their teams of lawyers. At the other extreme, large organizations deal with each other as equals in law. The largest such organizations are states engaged in a wide range of heteronomous relations.

Much is happening in law and to the legal profession. Lately, lawyers have been writing about the fragmentation of international law, global administrative law, judicial governance, functional regimes, global constitutionalism, and legal pluralism. Whatever they say, the state figures centrally. Although not a lawyer, Jens Bartelson has claimed that states are now "embedded within a larger governmental framework, and … their status as actors and bearers of rights and obligations derive from their position within an emergent global legal order rather than from their membership in an international society of sovereign equals."[87] The rise and differentiation of organizations have indeed affected states in a variety of ways. Yet the framework for all of this is *not* new; it is the robust, centuries old framework that Bartelson aptly called the "international society of sovereign equals."

However paradoxical it may seem, organizational agents with their teams of lawyers have assiduously strengthened international society so that it can carry the cumulative weight of all these changes. They are largely unaware that they have done so. When lawyers talk about human rights or ocean resources or small arms or any other global issue, they also talk about treaties (concluded by states), responsibility (of states), standards (applicable to states), and compliance (from states, often enough elicited through measures adopted by states). If they did not, they could not even make sense of any such issue in relation to the global framework.

It might be argued that states are no longer the sovereign equals they once were, and therefore international society no longer functions as a heteronomous system of rule. Conceptually speaking, sovereignty is an early modern invention fusing the power to rule (*imperium*) and the ruler's capacity to inspire awe (*majestas*; *cf.* Weber's charisma). Practically speaking, the sovereign rulers of Europe could never fully consolidate the power to rule or monopolize dignity.[88] Sovereigns delegated power to subordinates; they struck agreements and shared responsibilities with other sovereigns. They also conferred honors, observed courtesies, and participated in ceremonies dignifying others to affirm their own exalted status. As sovereignty shifted from the person of the ruler to the territorial state and the nation unified land, history, and sentiment within the state's boundaries, *majestas* became a permanent feature of the modern state, not (or not just) as an organization but as a member of an international society of sovereign equals.

In short, states are not just nominal or juridical equals. Their majesty has no modern parallel, and in this respect, they are *equivalent* in the way they are set apart from all other sociopolitical arrangements. The heteronomous relations of states continue to matter as much as they do because states collectively have a unique status in today's world, a legitimacy undamaged by the rise of organizations and their functional differentiation. On the contrary, every challenge or threat to the state, whether mounted by other states or deriving from the erosion of authority, has the perverse effect of rallying people to the state in all its majesty.

Thus speaks the global *demos*, even if lawyers who supply organizations with expertise or litigate human rights are reluctant to listen. Scholars in IR might also profit from listening to the *demos*. Realists take for granted what I have been calling heteronomy without the slightest sense that this is a global condition of rule, not anarchy, and that its legitimacy is democratic in the largest, most powerful sense possible. Sovereignty works at two levels: bottoms-up, legitimizing states, and top-down, states having legitimized each other. Liberals and self-styled constructivists talk about norms, law, institutions, and identity, unaware that global governance demands and supports heteronomy as a mighty frame.

Then there is an odd lot of scholars who carry on about emancipatory politics, Foucauldian power, democratic legitimacy, and cosmopolitan ethics. They do so without the slightest sense that hegemony and hierarchy, stratification and organization, work together as a primary feature of sociopolitical life just about everywhere. Or that this unholy alliance is a striking feature of a world that nevertheless depends on a heteronomous framework in the form of a thriving society of sovereign equals. This is not at all what the Enlightenment or its contemporary critics have taught us to expect.

References

Abbott, Andrew. 1988. *The System of Professions: An Essay on the Division of Expert Labor*. Chicago: University of Chicago Press.

Agnew, John. 2005. *Hegemony: The New Shape of Global Power*. Philadelphia: Temple University Press.

Anderson, Perry. 2017. *The H-Word: The Peripeteia of Hegemony*. London: Verso.

Barder, Alexander D. 2015. *Empire Within: International Hierarchy and Its Imperial Laboratories of Governance*. Abingdon: Routledge.

Bartelson, Jens. 2014. *Sovereignty as Symbolic Form*. Abingdon: Routledge.

Bartelson, Jens. 2015. "Sovereignty and the Personality of the State," in Robert Schuett and Peter M. R. Stirk (eds.), *The Concept of the State in International Relations: Philosophy, Sovereignty and Cosmopolitanism*. Edinburgh: Edinburgh University Press, pp. 81–107.

Beaumont, Paul. 2020. The Grammar of Status Competition: International Hierarchies as Domestic Practice. PhD dissertation, Norwegian University of Life Sciences.

Bially Mattern, Janice, and Ayşe Zarakol. 2016. "Hierarchies in World Politics." *International Organization* 70(3): 623–654.

Böröcz, József. 1997. "*Stand* Reconstructed: Contingent Closure and Institutional Change." *Sociological Theory* 15(3): 215–248.

Brumfiel, Elizabeth M. 1995. "Heterarchy and the Analysis of Complex Societies: Comments." *Archeological Papers of the American Anthropological Association* 6(1): 125–131.

Bull, Hedley. 1977. *The Anarchical Society: A Study of Order in World Politics.* New York: Columbia University Press.

Clark, Ian. 1989. *The Hierarchy of States: Reform and Resistance in the International Order.* Cambridge: Cambridge University Press.

Cooley, Alexander. 2005. *Logics of Hierarchy: The Organization of Empires, States, and Military Occupations.* Ithaca: Cornell University Press.

Deudney, Daniel H. 2007. *Bounding Power: Republican Security from the Polis to the Global Village.* Princeton: Princeton University Press.

Donnelly, Jack. 2006. "Sovereign Inequalities and Hierarchy in Anarchy: American Power and International Society." *European Journal of International Relations* 12(2):139–170.

Donnelly, Jack. 2012. "The Elements of the Structures of International Systems." *International Organization* 66(4): 609–643.

Donnelly, Jack. 2016. "The Heterarchic Structure of Twenty-First-Century International Governance." *Korean Journal of International Studies* 14(1):1–29.

Fei, Xiaotong. 1992. *From the Soil: The Foundations of Chinese Society.* Berkeley: University of California Press.

Foucault, Michel. 2003. *Society Must Be Defended: Lectures at the Collège de France, 1975–1976.* New York: Picador.

Franck, Thomas M. 1988. "Legitimacy in the International System." *American Journal of International Law* 82(4): 705–759.

Galtung, Johan. 1971. "A Structural Theory of Imperialism." *Journal of Peace Research* 8(2): 81–117.

Gramsci, Antonio. 1971. *Selections from the Prison Notebooks.* New York: International Publishers.

Hobbes, Thomas. 1991. *Leviathan*, ed. Richard Tuck. Cambridge: Cambridge University Press.

Hobson, John M., and J. C. Sharman. 2005. "The Enduring Place of Hierarchy in World Politics: Tracing the Social Logics of Hierarchy and Political Change." *European Journal of International Relations* 11(1): 63–98.

Hurd, Ian. 1999. "Legitimacy and Authority in International Politics." *International Organization* 53(2): 379–408.

Ikenberry, G. John. 2011. *Liberal Leviathan: The Origins, Crisis, and Transformation of the American World Order.* Princeton: Princeton University Press.

Kang, David C. 2010. *East Asia before the West: Five Centuries of Trade and Tribute.* New York: Columbia University Press.

Kant, Immanuel. 1998. *Groundwork of the Metaphysics of Morals*, trans. Mary Gregor. Cambridge: Cambridge University Press.

Klotz, Audie. 1995. *Norms in International Relations: The Struggle against Apartheid*. Ithaca: Cornell University Press.

Koskenniemi, Martti. 1997. "Hierarchy in International Law: A Sketch." *European Journal of International Law* 8(4): 566–582.

Kratochwil, Friedrich V. 1989. *Rules, Norms, and Decisions: On the Conditions of Practical and Legal Reasoning in International Relations and Domestic Affairs*. Cambridge: Cambridge University Press.

Lake, David A. 2009. *Hierarchy in International Relations*. Ithaca: Cornell University Press.

Lanoszka, Alexander. 2013. "Beyond Consent and Coercion: Using Republican Political Theory to Understand International Hierarchies." *International Theory* 5(3): 382–413.

Larkins, Jeremy. 2010. *From Hierarchy to Anarchy: Territory and Politics before Westphalia*. Basingstoke: Palgrave Macmillan.

Lasswell, Harold D. 1936. *Politics: Who Gets What, When, How*. New York: McGraw-Hill.

Lasswell, Harold D., and Abraham Kaplan. 1950. *Power and Society: A Framework for Political Inquiry*. New Haven: Yale University Press.

Lenski, Gerhard E. 1966. *Power and Privilege: A Theory of Social Stratification*. New York: McGraw-Hill.

Mandel, Ernest. 1975. *Late Capitalism*, trans. Joris de Bres. London: New Left Books.

Marcuse, Herbert. 1964. *One-Dimensional Man: Studies in the Ideology of Advanced Industrial Society*. Boston: Beacon Press.

Milner, Helen. 1992. "The Assumption of Anarchy in International Relations Theory: A Critique." *Review of International Studies* 17(1): 67–85.

Mills, C. Wright. 1956. *The Power Elite*. New York: Oxford University Press.

Mosca, Gaetano. 1939. *The Ruling Class*, trans. Hannah D. Kahn. New York: McGraw-Hill.

Onuf, Nicholas Greenwood. 1989. *World of Our Making: Rules and Rule in Social Theory and International Relations*. Columbia: University of South Carolina Press.

Onuf, Nicholas Greenwood. 1998. *The Republican Legacy in International Thought*. Cambridge: Cambridge University Press.

Onuf, Nicholas. 2008. *International Legal Theory: Essays and Engagements, 1966–2006*. Abingdon: Routledge-Cavendish.

Onuf, Nicholas Greenwood. 2013a. *Making Sense, Making Worlds: Constructivism in Social Theory and International Relations*. Abingdon: Routledge.

Onuf, Nicholas. 2013b. "Recognition and the Constitution of Epochal Change." *International Relations* 27(2): 121–140.

Onuf, Nicholas. 2017. "Center-Periphery Relations: What Kind of Rule, and Does It Matter?" *All Azimuth: A Journal of Foreign Policy and Peace* 6(1): 5–16.

Onuf, Nicholas, and Frank F. Klink. 1989. "Anarchy, Authority, Rule." *International Studies Quarterly* 33(2): 149–173.

Onuf, Nicholas, and Peter Onuf. 2006. *Nations, Markets, and War: Modern History and the American Civil War*. Charlottesville: University of Virginia Press.

Oye, Kenneth A. (ed.). 1986. *Cooperation under Anarchy*. Princeton: Princeton University Press.
Parsons, Talcott, and Edward A. Shils (eds.). 1951. *Toward a General Theory of Action: Theoretical Foundations for the Social Sciences*. Cambridge Harvard University Press.
Proust, Marcel. 1946. *Du côté de chez Swann*. Paris: Gallimard.
Ruggie, John Gerard. 1998. *Constructing the World Polity: Essays in International Institutionalization*. London: Routledge.
Simpson, Gerry. 2004. *Great Powers and Outlaw States: Unequal Sovereigns in the International Legal Order*. Cambridge: Cambridge University Press.
Tomasello, Michael. 2019. *Becoming Human: A Theory of Ontology*. Cambridge: Harvard University Press.
Towns, Ann E. 2010. *Women and States: Norms and Hierarchies in International Society*. Cambridge: Cambridge University Press.
Wallerstein, Immanuel. 1974. "The Rise and Future Demise of the World Capitalist System: Concepts for Comparative Analysis." *Comparative Studies in Society and History* 16(4): 387–415.
Waltz, Kenneth N. 1979. *Theory of International Politics*. Reading: Addison-Wesley.
Weber, Katja. 1997. "Hierarchy amidst Anarchy: A Transaction Costs Approach to International Security Cooperation." *International Studies Quarterly* 41(2): 321–340.
Weber, Max. 1922. *Grundriss der Sozialökonomik, III. Abteilung, Wirtschaft und Gesellschaft*. Tübingen: J. C. B. Mohr.
Weber, Max. 1978. *Economy and Society: An Outline of Interpretive Sociology*, 2 vol., continuous pagination. Berkeley: University of California Press.
Wendt, Alexander. 1992. "Anarchy Is What States Make of It: The Social Construction of Power Politics." *International Organization* 46(2): 391–425.
Wendt, Alexander. 1999. *Social Theory of International Politics*. Cambridge: Cambridge University Press.
Wendt, Alexander, and Daniel Friedheim. 1995. "Hierarchy under Anarchy: Informal Empire and the East German State." *International Organization* 49(4): 689–721.

Notes

1 I am grateful to Christopher Daase, Nicole Deitelhoff, and Antonia Witt for suggesting improvements to this chapter. It substantially revises the paper I presented in the lecture series "Beyond Anarchy: Rule and Authority in the International System," at the Cluster of Excellence: The Formation of Normative Orders, Goethe University Frankfurt/Main, February 5, 2014, and the Erik Castrén Institute of International Law and Human Rights, University of Helsinki, April 24, 2014.
2 Onuf and Klink 1989.
3 Bull 1977.
4 Kratochwil 1989: 250.
5 Milner 1992: 85.
6 Wendt 1992: 412.

7 Wendt 1992: 395, 404; quoting p. 409.
8 Waltz 1979: 80.
9 Waltz 1979: 93.
10 Waltz 1979: 95–96.
11 Hobbes 1991: 93.
12 Hobbes 1991: 68, 100.
13 Milner 1992: 69; Bull 1977: 24–25.
14 Wendt 1999: 264–278.
15 Hobbes 1991: 245.
16 Oye 1986.
17 Hobbes 1991: 480.
18 See Hobbes 1991: chapter xviii for a detailed list; on artificial persons, see Hobbes 1991: chapter xvi.
19 Hobbes 1991: 126.
20 Foucault 2003: 91.
21 Hobbes 1991: 125.
22 Hobbes 1991: 152.
23 Hobbes 1991: 111.
24 Waltz 1979: 60.
25 Instead, see Alter, this volume.
26 Onuf and Onuf 2006: 118–127.
27 Onuf 1989: chapter 2; Onuf 2013a, chapter 1.
28 See Zürn's discussion of requests as indirect demands, this volume.
29 Onuf 1989: chapter 4.
30 Many scholars hold that rules are either regulative or constitutive in function (see, e.g., Klotz 1995: 9, Kratochwil 1989: 26, Ruggie 1998: 22–25). I hold that all rules regulate conduct by definition and, in doing so, constitute the social arrangements within which they function. Onuf 1989: 50–52. Thus, the regulative function of rules – *all* rules – serves to connect agents to an ever-changing world, the structure of which is constantly being remade as those same rules simultaneously perform their constitutive function.
31 Here and for the next several paragraphs, I borrow directly from Onuf: 2017, with some changes and permission from the journal's publisher.
32 Hobbes 1991: 63.
33 Proust 1946: 29.
34 Weber 1978: 305–306; but see Böröcz 1997: 216–222 on "estate" as a better translation of what Weber meant by *Stand* in this context.
35 See Onuf 1989: chapter 8; Beaumont 2020.
36 Weber 1978: 957–958.
37 Parsons and Shils 1951: 23.
38 Wendt 1999: chapter 6.
39 Onuf 2013a: chapter 10.
40 Fei 1992: 67.
41 Illustratively: Lasswell 1936; Mills 1956; Marcuse 1964; Lenski 1966; Galtung 1971; Gramsci 1971; Wallerstein 1974; Mandel 1975.
42 Mosca 1939: xli.
43 See Onuf 2008: chapter 28 for an extended discussion of rules, with particular attention to their normative properties.

44 Lasswell and Kaplan 1950: 99.
45 For an overview, see Anderson 2017.
46 Agnew 2005 and Ikenberry 2011 offer two very different examples.
47 Here again and below, I borrow some material from Onuf 2017.
48 Weber 1978: 956–8. Weber appears not to have used the expression *Befehlskette*, at least in *Wirtschaft und Gesellschaft.*
49 Clark 1989.
50 Clark 1989: 2.
51 See, for example, Jeremy Waldron's important discussion of dignity; 2012: Lecture 1.
52 Larkins 2010: chapter 4.
53 Weber 1978: 54.
54 Weber 1978: 959 (emphasis in translation).
55 Barder 2015; Cooley 2005; Deudney 2007; Donnelly 2006, 2012; Hobson and Sharman 2005; Kang 2010; Koskenniemi 1997; Lake 2009; Lanoszka 2013; Simpson 2004; Towns 2010; Weber 1997; Wendt and Friedheim 1995. Also see Bially and Zarakol 2016 for a helpful review.
56 Kant drew a sharp distinction between autonomy and heteronomy, most clearly in describing the categorical imperative.

> All my actions as only a member of the world of understanding would therefore conform perfectly with the principle of the autonomy of the pure will; as only a part of the world of sense they would have to be taken to conform wholly to the natural law of desires and inclinations, hence to the heteronomy of nature. (Kant 1998: 58)

57 Tomasello 2019, quoted in this and the following paragraph.
58 See Tomasello 2019: chapter 7 for a detailed treatment of joint commitment.
59 Onuf 2013b.
60 Donnelly 2016: 9. See pp. 9–13 for a brief history of the term and Brumfiel 1995: 125 on its vague and inconsistent uses.
61 Quoting Donnelly 2016: 9 (emphasis in original). The archeological literature to which Donnelly adverted emphasizes lateral differentiation (that is, segmentation), not functional differentiation. In this volume, Daase and Deitelhoff skirt the issue with a broad construction of heterarchical rule: "a juxtaposition and superimposition of vertically and horizontally structured partial orders."
62 Waltz 1979: 88–97.
63 Donnelly's conception of heterarchy calls to mind the corporatist model of civil society, visualized as "a lattice formed from ascending levels of association and functionally differentiated forms of activity" and subject to variety of distortions in practice. Onuf 1998: 271; see generally chapter 10. In this volume, Zürn's claim that authority is "a functionally differentiated form of a right to do something" points to the same model.
64 Waltz 1979: 111.
65 Waltz 1979: 103.
66 Lasswell and Kaplan 1950: 76, 133, 198.
67 Quoting Weber 1922: 153, 1978: 263.
68 Lasswell and Kaplan 1950: 133.

69 Franck 1988: 706 (emphasis in original). Franck's definition of legitimacy is all but tautological – if the process is "right," then it is already legitimate.
70 Hurd 1999: 382 (emphasis in original, footnote deleted).
71 Hobbes 1991: chapter xvi.
72 Hobbes 1991: 120 (emphases in original).
73 Hobbes 1991: 477.
74 But see Lake 2009, where, on Hobbes's authority, we find a relational conception of authority, in which the right to rule rests on a social contract. Legitimacy – "a political construct that derives from many sources: tradition, divine revelation, charisma, formal-legal rules" – is key to what makes rule rightful (p. 8), and in this respect Lake's debt to Weber is obvious. In this volume, also see Zürn on "contractual authority," Alter on "contested authority," and Morse on "the loss of freedom."
75 Weber 1922: 124; 1978: 215.
76 Weber 1922: 122; 1978: 212.
77 Onuf and Klink 1989: 152–6; Onuf 1989: 197–205.
78 Weber 1922: 153, 1978: 263.
79 Weber 1922: 16, *cf. Legitimitätsgeltung*, Weber 1922: 124.
80 Weber 1922: 124.
81 Weber 1978: 215.
82 "Super- and subordination" is not Weber's wording. On three occasions, we find "hierarchical subordination" (*hierarchische Unterordnung*).
83 Reformulating Onuf 2013a: 192–194.
84 See Abbott 1988; professionalization has accelerated since the appearance of this hugely influential book, and there is, needless to say, a massive literature.
85 Abbott 1988: 118–121.
86 Abbott 1988, quoting subtitle.
87 Bartelson 2015: 99; see Bartelson 2014: chapter 3 for elaboration.
88 Onuf 1998: chapter 5.

Part II

Practicing Rule

5 How Rule Generates Its Own Authority

Ole Jacob Sending[1]

Two landmark multilateral agreements were reached in 2015. The first was the agreement on the Sustainable Development Goals (SDGs). The other was the Paris Agreement on Climate Change. Both were negotiated by states under the auspices of the United Nations (UN). In contrast to the failure of negotiations in other important issue-areas – such as trade – states were able to agree on seventeen ambitious goals for sustainable development, to be reached by 2030. And they similarly agreed on an ambitious plan for reducing greenhouse emissions to ensure global warming below two degrees celsius. What sets these two agreements apart is nonetheless something else: They are based on nonbinding rules – they contain no legal obligation to change behavior – and only require that signatories submit plans and report on progress on measures taken. Soon after the agreement was reached in Paris in late December 2015, Anne-Marie Slaughter argued that the Paris Agreement "falls woefully short" compared to traditional international treaties, where rules are codified and enforceable, and where there are "sanctions for non-compliance."[2] She went on to argue, however, that precisely because it is based on nonbinding rules, the Paris Agreement might just work. The reasons she offers echo the arguments found in numerous studies about the virtues of global governance, where the mobilization of non-state actors and relying on market-mechanisms and naming and shaming are held up as hallmarks of the increasingly transnational character of global governance.[3]

The SDGs and the Paris Agreement represent a "transnationalization" of international authority, whereby governance arrangements – and political rule – are increasingly reliant on transnational networks that include powerful non-state actors, and on voluntary and market-based mechanisms to induce deference. In this way, the question of political rule concerns more than questions of hierarchy and hegemony in the relations between states. It also depends – and increasingly so – on non-state actors and their involvement in the establishment and conduct of political rule. The upshot of this is that the question of political rule and authority emerges in a slightly different light because it does not only concern how already established political authorities (states) delegate to others or how states may be related in super- and subordinate structures of hierarchy or hegemony. It also concerns how authority is established from scratch by non-state actors to initiate and become involved in political rule at the international or transnational level. I seek to explain this development using the editors' overarching focus on the concept of rule and argue that authority can result from the practice of engaging in rule rather than being the basis for it.[4]

To do so, I suggest that we have to move beyond a Weberian approach where beliefs in legitimacy is what produces deference.[5] The reason for this is partly to do with the fact that authority is here located not in a singular actor or "ruler" but in networks, making it difficult to assess distinct relations of super- and sub-ordination defined by beliefs in legitimacy. But more fundamentally, the issue is whether, in fact, beliefs necessarily produce deference by defining the values against which claimants of authority are assessed. I introduce an alternative view, which tracks close to a social contract model discussed by Lake in this volume but which is nonetheless distinct in stressing that deference is induced by the facticity of rule – of how the very establishment and conduct of political rule can generate its own authority regardless of beliefs in legitimacy and independent of the benefits it may produce for those subject to it. Building on Ilana Feldman's work, I call this "auto-authority."

I situate the argument in the context of this book's key claim – that world politics is not defined by the absence of rule, but by its presence. Political rule run the whole gamut from coercion via rules that are enforced, incentivized, or based on voluntary compliance through beliefs in their legitimacy.[6] As the editors note in their introduction, however, we should not rest content with describing the prevalence of such rules but seek to capture the dynamics by which such rules are formed, enforced, and may be contested.[7] This means trying to capture how hierarchies, as expressed in and through rule, is continually produced and contested.[8] One virtue of this concept of rule is that it allows us to explore the role of non-state actors through a focus on the activity of shaping or contesting rules and engaging in rule.[9] This is important, for as I seek to demonstrate below, there is a tendency to explain the expansion of non-state actors' role and power by reference to who they *are* rather than what they *do*. This tendency to engage in explanation by attribution has limits if we want to explain the prevalence, and contents, of rule in the international and transnational sphere.[10]

Because the explanandum here is rule, authority sits alongside other sources or factors that may explain the contents and effects of such rule: Some rules may be based on beliefs in legitimacy, whereas others may be based on coercion or domination, and our task is to identify the configuration of factors that may help explain the emergence, contents, and changes in political rule. This is important because it allows more nuanced discussion of the line between authority and domination and of the very relationship between authority and the practice of rule.[11] I seek to show that we overlook an important feature of authority, and of rule, if rule is seen as resting on, and as defined by, the beliefs that are said to produce deference. I posit, instead, that the very act of engaging in rule can generate its own authority, regardless of whether or not subordinate actors believe in the legitimacy of the superordinate actors. Drawing on Ilana Feldman's work, I call this "auto-authority," where the practice of rule – of actually governing – has a certain "pull-factor" on those affected by it.[12] This is not necessarily due to ideological misrecognition, or the production of belief,[13] nor what Fritz Scharpf calls "output legitimacy."[14] Rather, it is because once rule has been established, it is a fact to reckon with and its sheer presence alters the calculus of those in its orbit.

This feature of rule is of course most closely associated with sovereign states, where rules are established that others are forced to follow, regardless of beliefs in legitimacy. But the same dynamic is found also in the international realm, but with a twist: it is not because of the already established dominance, coercion, or authority of an actor that others defer. Rather, the *act of engaging in rule is what over time generates authority for the actor in question.* This is the dynamic by which the Gates Foundation is now an authority in global health, why the Forest Stewardship Council (FSC) is an authority on environmental governance, and why the International Accounting Standards Board (IASB) is an authority on key aspects of economic governance. They all provide what Abbott and Faude call "low cost" solutions to thorny issues, as they rely on voluntary measures, on mobilizing market dynamics, and seek to establish metrics to make the issue at hand legible.[15] This is nonetheless "rule" in that it entails acting on certain issues in seeking to produce a particular outcome, whether in terms of reduced emissions, reducing poverty, preventing disease, or standardizing how to put economic value on different assets. Below, I discuss how authority can be a product of the act of engaging in political rule by discussing the "transnationalization" of international authority, whereby non-state actors not only become active in political rule but also provide models and methods that are subsequently appropriated by public actors (states and international organizations).

Transnational and International Authority

Some forms of rule are based on agreements between states, either bilaterally or multilaterally, while other types of rule are best understood as transnational, being based on relations between actors where at least one actor is not a state. As a first approximation, international authority is typically associated with the former, where states make rules or delegate particular tasks to an international organization. Transnational authority, by contrast, is associated with soft law as well as a range of market-based mechanisms, and where non-state actors play an important role. What sets transnational authority apart is not only the fact that non-state actors play an important role, but also that it relies on measures that do not require interstate agreement or the capacity of the state to police or regulate behavior. The FSC is a case in point: It is a private initiative which started to develop guidelines and certification schemes for sustainable forestry management in the early 1990s, around the same time that states sought but failed to agree on a binding convention for the same issue.[16] It is the fact that the FSC relies on voluntary measures, whether in the form of incentives in the marketplace, normative shaming, or simply metrics to make things legible, that make it transnational rather than international.

A central question thus becomes how we are to understand the relationship between these two types of authority? At one level, this can be done through analyses of how states and international organizations forge relations with and cooperate with non-state actors. This has to a significant degree been the focus of the research on global governance. We know that ever more non-state actors are involved in global governance, thereby indicating that the scope and density of transnational relations have increased.[17] This has formed the basis for more detailed explorations of the authority of international organizations, non-governmental organizations, and firms.[18] More recently scholars have explored the evolution of the broader ecology of global governance, which helps explain how and why we see a growth in non-state forms of rule (transnational authority), and a stagnation in intergovernmental rule (international authority). Abbott et al., for example, demonstrate that there has been a marked shift, where the growth in IGOs has stopped, and the rise of what they call private transnational regulatory organizations (PTROs) has increased. These new types of organizations advance a distinct type of rule that is characterized by softer forms of rule, emphasizing marked-mechanisms, voluntary compliance, and best practices or benchmarks.[19] Abbott, Green and Keohane's description of PTROs capture well the hallmarks of transnational authority, noting that these, make different claims to legitimacy, provide different avenues for political participation, and are accountable to different constituencies. They complement IGO norms and programs, multiplying their governance impact ....[20]

This is a structural explanation, focused on organizational density within distinct ecologies.[21] Others have provided a more agent-centered account, exploring the authority of distinct groups. Michael Zürn, for example, has introduced the concept of "reflexive authority" to discuss how expert-based authority may both support and undermine the authority of international organizations.[22] Others have explored the role of advocacy networks, assessing the ways in which such actors may establish authority outside of IGOs and over time change them from within, for example, in terms of increased openness and participation of non-state actors within international organizations.[23] There is nonetheless something of a missing link in this research: While we know a lot about the authority and operations of non-state actors and how they supplement but also supplant states and international organizations, we know much less about how these actors establish authority in the first place or of how increased transnational authority may also work to change the *modus operandi* of international authority. There are thus two distinct issues here. The first concerns the very relationship between authority and rule, where the operations of non-state actors suggest that authority is a product of engaging in rule rather than the other way around. As I will argue below, this is a defining feature of transnational authority, which brings us to the second issue, namely what this means for our understanding of already established international authority. The proposition is thus that the rise of non-state actors and the attendant reliance on voluntary and market-based (low cost) forms of rule may also lead to changes in the modus operandi of established international authorities as manifest in international organizations.

Consider the Global Alliance for Vaccines and Immunization (GAVI) – the alliance between governments, philanthropic organizations, pharmaceutical corporations, and IOs to produce and disseminate vaccines. A public–private partnership, voted "best development actor" in a global review of aid effectiveness in 2015, GAVI has arguably become more important than the World Health Organization (WHO) on some issues.[24] It operates through a range of marked-based mechanisms and is based on nonbinding measures. Similarly, the IASB is the main standard setter for international accounting, shaping firms' operations in different jurisdictions. On climate, the Carbon Disclosure Project (CDP) seek to change the behavior of firms and governments by encouraging and facilitating reporting on carbon footprint.

All of these forms of rule are admittedly different from hard law, but their effects on the behavior of states and non-state actors are increasing in both scope and depth. What is remarkable is that these actors did not first establish authority and then start to engage in political rule. Rather, their authority emerged as a result of them engaging in political rule. This prompts the question of the temporal aspects of how rule is established and of the authority of the actors engaged in establishing it. This is important, because it problematizes the idea that distinct beliefs in legitimacy comes before, and thus explain deference of subordinate actors to a superordinate one. This has arguably been somewhat overlooked because a particular interpretation of Max Weber's analyses of authority (*Herrschaft*) have become dominant among students of world politics, where ideal-typical sources of authority – rational-legal, traditional, charismatic, etc. – are used to explain why an actor has authority, and how such authority condition the type of rule that that actor can engage in. Weber was primarily interested not so much in the sources of legitimacy that could be attributed to a particular actor, however, but in the strategies of legitimation – of efforts to justify and legitimate positions of power and forms of rule *already* established.

The upshot of this is that you do not need to have authority before engaging in rule, and so the question is whether the very fact of engaging in rule may produce its own authority. The history of state formation is full of examples of this dynamic: The state did not emerge because people first believed it was legitimate, but through (principally) coercion, followed by efforts aimed at legitimation, in the form of nation-building and the production of symbols anointing the King with authority to rule.[25] In a nutshell, an actor start to rule others, and then seek to legitimate it. This temporal aspect of the relationship between rule and authority thus leaves open the possibility that the very act or practice of engaging in rule, and of producing and enforcing rules, can generate or at least condition its own authority. I argue that the significant expansion of non-state authority and of the emerging trends toward transnational authority is a good example of how engaging in rule may produce its own type of authority – what Ilana Feldman in a different context has called "auto-authority."[26] To see how, we need a brief discussion of Weber's conceptual apparatus.

Weber on Beliefs and Authority

The dominant view of authority is heavily shaped by Weber, who emphasized that it is based on beliefs in legitimacy: the beliefs held by subordinate actors explain their "interest" in complying with or deferring to a superordinate actor. Weber's discussion of authority differentiates it from power and influence by stressing that subordinate actors have an "interest" in complying. He writes that authority is the chance that "certain specific commands (or all commands) will be obeyed by a given group of persons. It thus does not include every mode of exercising 'power' or 'influence' over other persons. ... Hence every genuine form of domination implies a minimum of voluntary compliance, that is, an *interest* (based on ulterior motives or genuine acceptance) in obedience."[27] Weber notes that the "validity of the claims to legitimacy" from potentially superordinate actors may be based on:

> 1. Rational grounds – resting on a belief in the legality of enacted rules and the right of those elevated to authority under such rules to issue commands (legal authority); 2. Traditional grounds – resting on an established belief in the sanctity of immemorial traditions and the legitimacy of those exercising authority under them (traditional authority); 3. Charismatic grounds – resting on devotion to the exceptional sanctity, heroism or exemplary character of an individual person (charismatic authority).[28]

While charisma is here described not explicitly in terms of beliefs, Weber notes that charismatic authority is characterized by the leader instilling obedience with reference to beliefs.[29] Weber then discusses the types of rule that result in or are associated with these ideal types of authority. Here, too, the beliefs in legitimacy that underwrite authority is of the essence, as it is the belief of subjects that ultimately *explain* type of rule. Spencer notes, for example, that "the basic purpose of Weber's analysis is to demonstrate that beliefs of legitimacy determine the structure of political institutions and the dynamics of political life."[30] And Bendix similarly notes with reference to legal domination (or authority) that it "rests upon a belief in its legitimacy, and every such belief is in a sense question-begging. For example, charismatic authority depends upon a belief in the sanctity of exemplary character of an individual person, but this person loses his authority as soon as those subject to it no longer believe in his extraordinary powers."[31]

This is the basic model that most scholars writing on authority in world politics have adopted, where the difference is mainly in what produces the beliefs that explain deference: some stress beliefs that are linked to broader institutional structures,[32] others are more specific on, say, accountability or performance,[33] and others still add a focus on symbolic power as central to the "production of belief."[34] The problem with the stress on beliefs is a complicated one and concerns the issue of evidence for beliefs and of how beliefs relate to the act of deference or to consent. As Beetham argues,

> The subject of consent is a confusing one, and its relationship with legitimacy makes it doubly so. If by consent to power we mean a condition of voluntary

agreement to it, then what counts as voluntary, and what sort of evidence is needed to demonstrate such agreement? Simply obeying the requirements of the powerful, or keeping to the law is not enough, since obedience can be maintained by coercion. The view that people consent to power if they are not openly protesting against it is therefore quite inadequate.[35]

At heart, the problem concerns not only the problem of evidence for beliefs that actors hold but also how such beliefs factor into actors' decisions or behavior. Weber, it should be stressed, did not in fact focus so much on the beliefs that subordinate actors have. This is rather something that IR scholars have adopted as they have sought a stable footing from which to demonstrate that there is, in fact, authority structures in the realm between states. Weber was equally, if not more, focused on the *legitimation efforts* on the part of superordinate actors, which is what provides the link between source of authority, on the one hand, and forms of rule, on the other, as in Weber's stress on how a tradition as a source of authority structures the form of rule that can be performed on its basis.[36]

In this context, Parkin's analysis of Weber's view of authority and legitimations is important, because he describes how legitimation takes center stage: "Legitimations are the claims that dominant groups make about themselves – claims that they would naturally wish everyone else to accept. Legitimacy, on the other hand, refers to the conditions in which such claims have in fact been accepted and endorsed by subordinate groups."[37] Parkin proceeds to note that

> Weber could have proposed his three types of legitimation while keeping an open mind on the question of whether or not they were accepted by the people to whom they were addressed… Instead of asking questions of this kind, Weber proceeds as though widespread endorsement of all three types of legitimation was typically found among all and sundry. The three different types of "dominant legitimations" have metamorphosed into three different types of "legitimate dominations."[38]

This aspect has been lost in contemporary writings on authority, although Zürn does zoom in on the fact that authority must be understood and explained as a relationship between legitimation on the part of superordinate actors and the legitimacy, or deference, of subordinate actors.[39] What we should take from Weber, then, is the stress on the strategies of rule and its legitimation, and seek to account for how rule and its legitimation strategies are responded to by subordinate actors.

The mistake here is to by-pass this type of analysis by introducing – admittedly from Weber himself – beliefs as that which explain deference.

State actors would, on this view, defer to another actor by virtue of believing in the claims to legitimacy that the latter advanced. This means that claims advanced by, say, the WHO or the World Bank would be accepted because states believed in the source or type of authority they represent, such as expertise and their position as custodian of some legal or political order. It also suggests that states would defer independently of whether or not they agreed with the contents of the expertise and the specific policy prescriptions being advanced. This is so because, as Friedman among others note, the concept of authority gives meaning only to the extent that it explains deference with reference to the relation between the two actors, not the specific *contents* of claims to rule or instruct.[40] The combination of relying on beliefs as that which explains deference and on fixing authority to be about relations between specific actors thus appears problematic: While states can be said to defer to international organizations most of the time, it is more problematic to claim that this is explained by state actors having enduring beliefs in these organizations claims to authority, independent of their substantive claims to rule.

A fruitful way out of this is offered by Beetham's suggestion that "most of these problems disappear once we free ourselves of the mistaken view that legitimacy is to be equated with people's belief in it."[41] Beetham, in fact, proposes a program for assessing the relationship between authority and rules that zooms in on the public manifestations of such authority or deference and on the effects of such public manifestations. He notes that

> what is important about consent is not the condition of voluntary agreement, but the specific actions that publicly express it; and that these are important because they confer legitimacy on the powerful, not because they provide evidence about people's beliefs. They confer legitimacy because they constitute public expressions by the subordinate of their consent to the power relationship and their subordinate position within it.[42]

Indeed, as I suggest below, how and why states may defer to international organizations (and other actors) is arguably better explained by the broader sociopolitical environment from which they can construct more or less coherent strategies of action vis-à-vis these organizations:[43] States (or their leaders) may for sure hold certain beliefs about what is and what is not legitimate but to move from there to explain deference, as if beliefs in legitimacy about particular actors define the ends of action, is to overlook all the other factors that are at work in shaping behavior in specific settings. Rather, we should look for the established modes of acting that are associated with different issue-areas to gauge what may count as public expression of support, deference, ignorance, or contestation of some form of rule. This means that political rule may emerge and become institutionalized because actors become drawn into rules and other governance practices without really assessing their effects, because there are few options to not follow them, or because there are no avenues through which to contest or criticize them. Take, for example, the IASB accounting standards: one may contest them, but it requires a very high level of technical expertise. Moreover, precisely because of their "voluntary" character as standards, there is little space for debate on developing alternative standards. Finally, the real effect of these standards come through market-mechanisms because firms operating in global markets have to use them to comply with US standards.

Auto-authority

Ilana Feldman's work on authority is relevant for this discussion. Based on anthropological fieldwork and archival research on Gaza, she notes that "the authority and tenacity of government in Gaza derived not so much from legitimacy, authenticity, or even "good policy," but from the *form, shape, and habits of daily practice.*"[44] She further observes that "authority is best understood not as an objective achievement, but rather as an ongoing process."[45] This attention to the forms of daily practice shifts the register for analyzing authority away from beliefs, which are hard to capture, to observable behavior and the tools or, again, repertoires available to different actors to both engage in rule and to contest, negotiate, or defer. Feldman proceeds to discuss what she calls "auto-authorization" and notes:

> In the elaboration of authority in Gaza during the Mandate and the Administration, when conditions on the ground offered little stability the capacity of bureaucracy to produce its own authority was crucial. *This auto-authorization was a distinctively circular process, and the extent to which it was successful was owing precisely to its circularity.* While external sources of authority were occasionally drawn upon ... none could provide a stable ground for authority .... Most reliable, in fact, were the *general characteristics of bureaucracy itself* .... To the extent that belief was invoked, people were asked not so much to believe that bureaucracy stood for something else as to believe in it for itself. Perhaps more vital than such belief, though, they were asked to participate in its workings ....[46]

Feldman's observations are of importance, for they touch upon the practical aspects of deference, stressing the circularity of generating authority through the practice of rule itself. Her stress on bureaucracy not as a symbol of something else, but as manifestation of rule itself, is important. So, too, is the idea that it is the participation in the workings of political rule that matter rather than the belief in particular ideals that somehow stand behind or justify political rule. Authority here emerges as something that is rooted in distinct forms of rule, rather than from something external to it.

This is akin to so-called "output legitimacy" formulated by Fritz Scharpf, where authority emerges from the assessment of subordinate actors of the goods and services that the authoritative actor produces.[47] But on closer inspection the idea of "output" legitimacy does not help us in explaining authority as a product of deference: it treats legitimacy not so much about deference – to forego one's own judgement – but about calculation and choice based on assessment of value of the output in question. It tracks closer to a contractual exchange between two parties, where subordinate actors do not so much defer but accept the term of the contract as long as they are happy with the service or product they get.[48] Furthermore, the idea of output legitimacy arguably places too much explanatory focus on the assessments of subordinate actors, as if these always have the option to exit or choose differently. As Barker notes, extant works on legitimacy tend to treat legitimacy as produced by the beliefs held by subordinate actors, thus ignoring the process by which it is claimed, worked on, and managed by those that initially claim it.[49]

Viewed in terms of the strategies of action available to different actors allow us to analyze how private actors, in fact, have constraints that public actors do not. If a set of private actors would like to set up a new set of standards or rules for behavior in a certain issue area, they can just go ahead and do it. They would need technical competence and economic resources, as well as the capacity to mobilize other actors. But they would not need to go through time-consuming multilateral negotiations, with little prospect of reaching agreement. The threshold for engaging in some form of "rule," however limited at first, is low. And because the form of rule is relatively weak, there is less at stake in contesting or challenging it. As several examples of private regulatory authority demonstrate, such initiatives can grow fast, and over time become significant actors.[50]

Rule as Productive of Transnational Authority

I have elsewhere analyzed in some detail the formation of population policy as a case of transnational authority.[51] A set of non-state actors, mostly in the US, set out in the 1950s to advance family planning as a tool to control population growth in the Global South. They could do so with private funding, mostly from the Ford Foundation and the Rockefeller Foundation, which they used to establish research centers, build alliances with elites in key developing countries, and develop contraceptive technology. Seeking approval and support from governments in developing countries – often by-passing health ministries to get approval – they set out to build a vast network of organizations engaged in developing contraceptives, training health professionals, and running family planning programs. The UN had a range of intergovernmental conferences on population policy, but there was no political agreement, much like the contemporary situation where lack of interstate agreement results in voluntary measures and the mobilization of private actors: The key actors involved in designing and managing population control efforts pushed ahead outside of formal multilateral arenas, opting for private rule making and bilaterally agreed upon projects with specific governments.

Over time, this network – managed by a small cluster of non-state actors mainly based in the US – was institutionalized transnationally to such a degree that by the late 1960s they were in a position to establish a new UN agency – the UN Fund for Population Activities (UNFPA) – *in spite of* opposition from key UN member states. This development can of course be analyzed in terms described by the research on advocacy networks or epistemic communities. Here, emphasis would be on this network gradually being seen as more legitimate over time. Indeed, by the mid-1960s, a sufficient number of states had arguably developed beliefs in the legitimacy consistent with population control through family planning programs.[52] But this interpretation overlooks just how much the very establishment of a global infrastructure to act on population growth in *itself* induced deference, in the form of its very presence and the absence of meaningful avenues or arenas to contest or delegitimize it.

However, the challenge to family planning did not initially come from developing countries – those subordinate to this type of rule where family planning projects were established – but from critics within the very same network that had globalized it, as they had access to funding, policy arenas, and knowledge about where to push for change. The point here is not simply that you need resources to contest or change rules and that focusing on legitimacy alone overlooks the extent to which resources are needed to actively engage *already established* rule. It is also that by virtue of this criticism, the authority of this network was, if anything, strengthened, as it now emerged as reflective, adjustable, and attentive to the needs and rights of those subject to it.

A similar trajectory is found in the field of health. The last two decades have seen a fundamental transformation of the global health landscape, with so-called global health initiatives (GHIs) comprised of state donors, private firms, international organizations, and philanthropic organizations that identify and mobilize resources to address specific diseases, bypassing more institutionalized forms of global health work.[53] These include the Global Fund to Fight AIDS, Tuberculosis and Malaria, the GAVI, and the Coalition for Epidemic Preparedness Innovations (CEPI). GAVI was established in 2000 on the initiative of the Bill and Melinda Gates Foundation, which provided initial funding of $750 million.[54] CEPI was launched at the World Economic Forum in Davos in 2017, again with the Gates Foundation, together with the government of Norway, as the main initiators and funders, to develop vaccines against future epidemics in 2017. CEPI and GAVI joined forces with the WHO and UNICEF to form COVAX – also a public–private initiative with considerable participation from pharmaceuticals – to respond to the covid-19 pandemic. Upon establishment, they had little authority on which to engage in rule. Rather, it was by virtue of engaging in rule that authority was established. This entailed not only the mobilization of financial resources and expertise to act on specific diseases but also introducing a new model of governance. Rather than rely on institutional reform, capacity building, and expertise from established international organizations such as the WHO,[55] they introduced new metrics to measure and monitor effectiveness of disease eradication and vaccination. GHIs are in this sense marked by what scholars of global health label a "vertical" approach (sometimes also referred to as the "Gates approach"), focused on technical measures and market solutions to global health.[56] Indeed, because of the importance of the Bill and Melinda Gates Foundation and the role of Bill Gates himself in introducing these new initiatives, the Gates Foundation is now an established authority on global health issues.

This authority, transnational in character, is tied to the process of engaging in actual rule rather than being a precondition for engaging in it. Evidence of such authority is found not only in the fact that the approach pushed by the Gates Foundation is central not only in GAVI, but also in CEPI, established more than a decade later. It is also indicated by the fact that the metrics and methods of rule pushed by Gates have also found their way into broader systems for monitoring and assessing global health issues.[57] The circularity of which Feldman speaks can thus be extended and slightly reformulated, as the authority does not emerge from the form of bureaucracy as it does in her analysis of Gaza. Rather it emerges from the circularity between the specific methods of rule being used and the metrics used to monitor and measure their effects, such that it forms a distinct governance complex that – with a certain degree of success or results to show for it – reflects back on the actor in question in terms of deference from others and thus authority.

On climate, too, we see some of the same dynamic. The Paris Agreement sets a target of reducing emissions, leaving it to each state to choose how to achieve it. But the processes linked to such reporting are mandatory. Like the governance model discussed above, the Paris Agreement also relies heavily on mobilizing private resources, on developing metrics to measure and monitor progress, and on market-mechanisms to generate behavioral change.[58] It is no coincidence that the logic of the Paris Agreement follows the type of rule that non-state actors have been advancing for quite some time. The Forest Stewardship Council, for example, was established already in 1993 with the goal of finding an alternative to the failed interstate negotiations to establish a binding global forest convention. By 2005, it had created a model of rule through extensive consultations and negotiations between different NGOs, firms, and business associations, involving certification of sustainable forestry governance, and covered 53 million hectares of forest in 78 countries.[59] Here, too, there was a shift from compliance linked directly to behavioral change to the development of metrics for assessing and evaluating behavior voluntarily – what Bernstein and Cashore terms "non-state market driven" (NSDM) systems of rule.[60] The FSC is typical of the broader set of governance initiatives on environmental and climate issues, where standard setting and certification by non-state actors have been central in designing, promoting, and demonstrating the relevance of their distinct form of political rule.[61]

This form of rule also involves mobilizing and tweaking established models for reporting and disclosure for firms, such as accounting. The Climate Disclosure Standards Board (CDSB) is a case in point, which was established in 2007 as a partnership between professional accounting organizations and a range of standard setting organizations such as the CDP and the Coalition for Environmentally Responsible Economies (Ceres). Granted, the formation of the CDSB and its subsequent role in shaping global standards for reporting on climate-related issues for firms and organizations draws on the professional authority of accountants. But it is through the act of designing and advancing reporting standards – of engaging in rule setting – that the CDSB become an actor to be reckoned with. It has now merged with the long running International Accounting Standards Board under a new name – the International Sustainable Standards Board – under the umbrella of the International Financial Reporting Standards Foundation (IFRS).

The International Sustainable Standards Board (ISSB) and IFRS were unveiled during the COP 26 in Glasgow in late 2021, following a communique from the finance ministers of the G7 in June that noted, "We welcome the International Financial Reporting Standards Foundation's programme of work to develop this baseline standard under robust governance and public oversight" and that they "encourage further consultation on a final proposal leading to the establishment of an International Sustainability Standards Board ahead of COP26."[62] While this can be seen as a delegation of authority from powerful states, it is important to note that the context for the G7 communique anointing the ISSB/IFRS to a central role in climate-related reporting was that the Financial Stability Board (FSB) of the G20 had in 2016 established the Task force of Climate Related Financial Disclosures, where the core model of rule was precisely the type of reporting according to standards developed by the CDSB/ISSB already from 2007 onward. Again, the dynamic is one whereby engaging in rule establishes a level of transnational authority for particular actors, and the models used for such rule subsequently form the platform on which states and international organizations, like the G20, G7, and the FSB, tag on to widen and deepen political rule.

Conclusion

We can now distil key elements of the logic at work in the relationship between authority and rule, and between international and transnational authority: A group of private actors may come together and establish some form of minimal governance initiatives that may range from new forms of reporting or new measurement metrics, to actually running reform programs or engaging in rule in different countries. They get some type of initial support and consent from some actors – either some states or foundations or firms. As they engage in this activity – performing rule – however small it initially may be, these actors generate authority through this activity by producing new facts on the ground and by making available forms of rule that form part of other actors' action strategies. Above a certain threshold – which is hard to pinpoint empirically – the fact of rule takes on a naturalized character, which reflects back on the actors engaging in rule and induces deference in others, much like Timothy Mitchell observes in the case of states, where stabilizing the state as standing above the society over which it rules depends on a range of big and small forms of rule, thus naturalizing its position.[63]

As regards the relationship between international and transnational authority, the dynamic described above suggests that transnational authority emerges as a resource from which international authority can be established and widened. The Paris Agreement is a case in point: Absent the myriad of initiatives to measure, rank, monitor, and report on climate-related issues, the central feature of the Paris Agreement – the reliance on voluntary measures and the mobilization of private actors – would not be there to build on and use to engage in political rule. In this way, transnational authority, produced through engaging in rule, may morph into and be harnessed to establish more formalized international authority. That authority may emerge from engaging in rule which helps explain the significant growth of what is often called hybrid, public–private, or transnational governance in the past few decades. The explanation dovetails with Zürn's stress on reflexive authority[64] but is distinct from it in that the explanation rest not so much on the rise of different forms of conditional authority but on the practice of rule itself, where authority is inherently linked to, and a product of, the activity of rule itself. This should perhaps not be so surprising: authority is a highly practical matter for those subject to it, as the question of deference does not even come up if there is not already some form of political rule in place and where deference becomes an issue. More broadly, this means that the growth in new forms of rule in global governance – in health, climate change, cyber security, etc. – tells us something about what type of social space the transnational one is: It is a space of low barriers to entry, with no formal constraints of whomever would like to try to establish some form of political rule.

References

Abbott, Kenneth W. and Benjamin Faude. 2022. "Hybrid Institutional Complexes in Global Governance." *The Review of International Organizations* 17: 263–291.

Abbott, Kenneth W., Jennifer F. Green, and Robert O. Keohane. 2016. "Organizational Ecology and Institutional Change in Global Governance." *International Organization* 70(2): 247–277.

Anderson, Benedict. 1983. *Imagined Communities: Reflections on the Origin and Spread of Nationalism.* London: Verso.

Auld, Graeme. 2014. *Constructing Private Governance: The Rise and Evolution of Forest, Coffee, and Fisheries Certification.* New Haven: Yale University Press.

Avant, Deborah. 2005. "Private Security Companies." *New Political Economy* 10(1): 121–131.

Avant, Deborah, Martha Finnemore, and Susan K. Sell (eds.). 2010. *Who Governs the Globe?* Cambridge: Cambridge University Press.

Bäckstrand, Karin. 2006. "Multi-stakeholder Partnerships for Sustainable Development: Rethinking Legitimacy, Accountability and Effectiveness." *Environmental Policy and Governance* 16(5): 290–306.

Bäckstrand, Karin, Jonathan W. Kuyper, Björn-Ola Linnér and Eva Lövbrand. 2017. "Non-state Actors in Global Climate Governance: From Copenhagen to Paris and Beyond." *Environmental Politics* 26(4): 561–579.

Barker, Rodney. 2001. *Legitimating Identities: The Self-presentations of Rulers and Subjects.* Cambridge: Cambridge University Press.

Barnett, Michael N. and Martha Finnemore. 2004. *Rules for the World: International Organizations in Global Politics.* Ithaca: Cornell University Press.

Beetham, David. 2013. *The Legitimation of Power*. 2nd edition. Basingstoke: Palgrave Macmillan.

Bendix, Reinhard. 1960. *Max Weber: An Intellectual Portrait*. Berkeley: University of California Press.

Bernstein, Steven and Benjamin Cashore. 2007. "Can Non-state Global Governance Be Legitimate? An Analytical Framework." *Regulation & Governance* 1(4): 347–371.

Best, Jaqueline and Alexandra Gheciu (eds.). 2014. *The Return of the Public in Global Governance*. Cambridge: Cambridge University Press.

Broome, André, and Joel Quirk. 2015. "Governing the World at a Distance: The Practice of Global Benchmarking." *Review of International Studies* 41(5): 819–841.

Büthe, Tim, and Walter Mattli. 2011. *The New Global Rulers: The Privatization of Regulation in the World Economy*. Princeton, Princeton University Press.

Cashore, Benjamin, Graeme Auld, and Deanna Newsom. 2004. *Governing through Markets: Forest Certification and the Emergence of Non-state Authority*. New Haven: Yale University Press.

Cooley, Alexaner, and Jack Snyner. 2015. *Ranking the World: Grading States as a Tool of Global Governance*. Cambridge: Cambridge University Press.

Cutler, A. Claire. 1999. "Locating 'Authority' in the Global Political Economy." *International Studies Quarterly* 43(1): 59–81.

Cutler, A. Claire. 2003. *Private Power and Global Authority: Transnational Merchant Law in the Global Political Economy*. Cambridge, Cambridge University Press.

Feldman, Ilana. 2008. *Governing Gaza: Bureaucracy, Authority, and the Work of Rule, 1917–1967*. Duke University Press.

Friedman, Lawrence M. 1990. *The Republic of Choice: Law, Authority, and Culture*. Harvard: Harvard University Press.

Green, Jessica F. 2014. *Rethinking Private Authority: Agents, Entrepreneurs and Private Environmental Governance*. Princeton: Princeton University Press.

Group of Seven. 2021. G7 Finance Ministers & Central Bank Governors Communiqué, 5 June 2021, London, United Kingdom, https://assets.publishing.service.gov.uk/government/uploads/system/uploads/attachment_data/file/991640/FMCBGs_communique_-_5_June.pdf (last access July 19, 2022).

Haas, Peter M. 1992. "Introduction: Epistemic Communities and International Policy Coordination." *International Organization* 46(1): 1–35.

Hanrieder, Tine. 2015. *International Organization in Time: Fragmentation and Reform*. Oxford: Oxford University Press.

Haufler, Virginia. 2009. "The Kimberley Process Certification Scheme: An Innovation in Global Governance and Conflict Prevention." *Journal of Business Ethics* 89(4): 403–416.

Hopgood, Stephen. 2006. *Keepers of the Flame: Understanding Amnesty International*. Ithaca: Cornell University Press.

Hurd, Ian. 1999. "Legitimacy and Authority in International Politics." *International Organization* 53(2): 379–408.

Jönsson, Christer, and Jonas Tallberg. (eds.) 2010. *Transnational Actors in Global Governance: Patterns, Explanations and Implications*. Basingstoke: Palgrave Macmillan.

Kahler, Miles (ed.). 2009. *Networked Politics: Agency, Power, and Governance.* Ithaca: Cornell University Press.

Keck, Margaret E., and Kathryn Sikkink. 1998. *Activists beyond Borders: Advocacy Networks in International Politics.* Ithaca: Cornell University Press.

Kentikelenis, Alexander, and Leonard Seabrooke. 2021. "Organising Knowledge to Prevent Global Health Crises: A Comparative Analysis of Pandemic Preparedness Indicators." *BMJ Global Health* 6(8):1–12.

Keohane, Robert O., and Joseph S. Nye. 1977. *Power and Interdependence. World Politics in Transition.* Boston: Little, Brown.

Lake, David A. 2009. *Hierarchy in International Relations.* Ithaca: Cornell University Press.

Macdonald, Kate. 2014. *The Politics of Global Supply Chains.* Cambridge: Polity Press.

Mattli, Walter, and Ngaire Woods (eds.). 2009. *The Politics of Global Regulation.* Princeton: Princeton University Press.

Mattli, Walter, and Tim Büthe. 2005. "Accountability in Accounting? The Politics of Private Rule-Making in the Public Interest." *Governance* 18(3): 399–429.

McConaughey, Megan, Paul Musgrave, and Daniel H. Nexon. 2018. "Beyond Anarchy: Logics of Political Organization, Hierarchy, and International Structure." *International Theory* 10(2): 181–218.

McNeill, Desmond, and Kristin I. Sandberg. 2014. "Trust in Global Health Governance: The GAVI Experience." *Global Governance* 20(2): 325–343.

Mitchell, Timothy. 1991. "The Limits of the State: Beyond Statist Approaches and Their Critics." *American Political Science Review* 85(1): 77–96.

Parkin, Frank. 2002. *Max Weber*, revised edition. New York: Routledge.

Pattberg, Philipp H. 2005. "The Forest Stewardship Council: Risk and Potential of Private Forest Governance." *The Journal of Environment & Development* 14(3): 356–374.

Pouliot, Vincent. 2016. *International Pecking Orders: The Politics and Practice of Multilateral Diplomacy.* Cambridge: Cambridge University Press.

Reus-Smit, Christian. 1999. *The Moral Purpose of the State. Culture, Social Identity, and Institutional Rationality in International Relations.* Princeton: Princeton University Press.

Reus-Smit, Christian. 2018. *On Cultural Diversity. International Theory in a World of Difference.* Cambridge: Cambridge University Press.

Rosenau, James N., and Ernst-Otto Czempiel (eds.). 1992. *Governance without Government: Order and Change in World Politics.* Cambridge: Cambridge University Press.

Scharpf, Fritz W. 1999. *Governing in Europe: Effective and Democratic?.* Oxford: Oxford University Press.

Seabrooke, Leonard, and Ole J. Sending. 2020. "Contracting Development: Managerialism and Consultants in Intergovernmental Organizations." *Review of International Political Economy* 27(4): 802–827.

Sending, Ole J. 2015. *The Politics of Expertise: Competing for Authority in Global Governance.* Ann Arbor: University of Michigan Press.

Sending, Ole J. 2017. "Recognition and Liquid Authority." *International Theory* 9(2): 311–328.

Slaughter, Anne-Marie. 2015. "The Paris Approach to Global Governance." *Project Syndicate*, www.project-syndicate.org/commentary/paris-agreement-model-for-global-governance-by-anne-marie-slaughter-2015-12 (last access July 19, 2022).

Spencer, Martin E. 1970. "Weber on Legitimate Norms and Authority." *The British Journal of Sociology* 21(2): 123–134.

Steffek, Jens. 2015. "The Output Legitimacy of International Organizations and the Global Public Interest." *International Theory* 7(2): 263–293.

Storeng, Katerini T. 2014. "The GAVI Alliance and the 'Gates Approach' to Health System Strengthening." *Global Public Health* 9(8): 865–879.

Swidler, Ann. 1986. "Culture in Action: Symbols and Strategies." *American Sociological Review* 51(2): 273–286

Tilly, Charles. 1978. *From Mobilization to Revolution*. Reading: Addison-Wesley.

Tilly, Charles. 1990. *Coercion, Capital, and European States, AD 990–1990*. Cambridge: Cambridge University Press.

Vogel, David. 2008. "Private Global Business Regulation." *Annual Review of Political Science* 11(1): 261–282.

Wapner, Paul. 1995. "Politics Beyond the State: Environmental Activism and World Civic Politics." *World Politics* 47(3): 311–340.

Weber, Max. 1978. *Economy and Society: An Outline of Interpretive Sociology* (vol. 1). Berkeley: University of California Press.

Zarakol, Ayşe (ed.). 2017. *Hierarchies in World Politics*. Cambridge: Cambridge University Press.

Zürn, Michael, Binder, Martin, and Matthias Ecker-Ehrhardt. 2012. "International Authority and Its Politicization." *International Theory* 4(1): 69–106.

Zürn, Michael. 2018. *A Theory of Global Governance: Authority, Legitimacy, and Contestation*. Oxford: Oxford University Press.

Notes

1 Financial support from the Research Council of Norway, through the project "The Market for Anarchy", project number 274740, is gratefully acknowledged.
2 Slaughter 2015.
3 Seabrooke and Sending 2020.
4 See Daase et al., this volume.
5 On the relationship between authority and legitimacy, see also chapters by Zürn and Alter, this volume.
6 Hurd 1999.
7 Daase et al., this volume.
8 Daase et al., this volume.
9 Lake 2009; Zarakol 2017.
10 Sending 2015, Zürn et al. 2012.
11 See, for example Pouliot 2016; see also Zürn 2018.
12 Feldman 2008.
13 Sending 2015, 2017.

14 Scharpf 1999; see also Steffek 2015.
15 Abbott and Faude 2022.
16 Pattberg 2005.
17 Keck and Sikkink 1998; Keohane and Nye 1972; Mattli and Büthe 2005; Rosenau and Czempiel 1992; Wapner 1995;.
18 Barnett and Finnemore 2004; Cutler 1999; Hopgood 2006.
19 Broome and Quirk 2015; Cooley and Snyner 2015.
20 Abbott et al. 2016: 249.
21 On ecologies, see also Lake, this volume.
22 See Zürn, this volume, and Zürn 2018.
23 Haas 1992; Jönsson and Tallberg 2010; Keck and Sikkink 1998.
24 See Hanrieder 2015; Sending 2017.
25 See, for example Anderson 1983; Tilly 1990.
26 Feldman 2008.
27 Weber 1978: 212
28 Weber 1978: 215.
29 Weber 1978: 216.
30 Spencer 1970: 123.
31 Bendix 1960: 418.
32 Reus-Smit 1999, 2018.
33 Bernstein and Cashore 2007.
34 Sending 2015.
35 Beetham 2013: 90–91, emphasis added.
36 Spencer 1970: 123, emphasis added.
37 Parkin 2002: 77.
38 Parkin 2002: 78.
39 Zürn 2018.
40 Friedman 1990: 60
41 Beetham 2013: 91.
42 Beetham 2013: 91
43 Swidler 1986; cf. Tilly 1978.
44 Feldman 2008:13, emphasis added.
45 Feldman 2008: 15.
46 Feldman 2008: 16, emphasis added.
47 Scharpf 1999.
48 Lake 2009.
49 Barker 2001.
50 Avant 2005; Mattli and Büthe 2005.
51 Sending 2015.
52 My earlier interpretation ran along these lines, stressing the "production of beliefs" via the deployment of symbolic resources.
53 Storeng 2014.
54 McNeill and Sandberg 2014.
55 Hanrieder 2015.
56 Storeng 2014.
57 Kentikelenis and Seabrooke 2021.
58 Slaughter 2015.

59 Pattberg 2005.
60 Bernstein and Cashore 2007.
61 Bäckstrand et al. 2017.
62 Group of Seven 2021.
63 Mitchell 1991.
64 Zürn, this volume.

6 The Region as Site of Rule
Disciplining States, Reconfiguring Orders

Antonia Witt[1]

In July 2000, the Assembly of Heads of State and Government of the Organisation of African Unity (OAU) took a far-reaching decision: in light of a growing number of coups d'état on the African continent, they decided that from that day onward, governments that come to power by extra-constitutional means should not be recognized and consequently be banned from the intergovernmental organization.[2] Moreover, they mandated the organization to work toward reestablishing "constitutional order" as quickly as possible by negotiating with the putschists, mobilizing international support, and, if necessary, imposing economic and political sanctions. With the birth of this African anti-coup norm and as a result of the continental organization's formal authority to decide how and by whom African states should be governed, the region increasingly became a site of rule. In the ensuing years, this formal authority, granted to the organization by its member states, resulted in a number of intervention practices being followed by the OAU and its successor, the African Union (AU). These practices effectively served to enact this authority to influence the conduct of political actors in the states concerned as well as to reorganize politics in those states accordingly.

This chapter explores the connection between international authority and authority in/of states. It does so by analyzing the African Union's authority to define what counts as legitimate statehood on the African continent and the effects this authority has on both the reproduction and the denial of the ideal of the (democratic) state as the locus of legitimate authority. In so doing, the chapter draws attention to the relational and co-constitutive reconfiguration of patterns of rule that is characteristic of what International Relations (IR) scholars describe as the growing authority of international organizations (IOs).[3] With the term authority, I refer to a conception of rule that describes a relationship of super- and subordination where one actor has the right to command and require deference from others (see Daase et al., introduction to this volume). Authority hence denotes a specific relationship of super- and subordination that rests on the general recognition, from both sides of the relationship, of the right of one side to direct the other on specifically defined issues.[4] In this chapter, I approach authority from a dual relational perspective, exploring both the relational aspects between those claiming and those affected by authority but also the relational and co-constitutive character that binds different authorities together.

Although IR scholars consider world regions to be an "increasingly salient unit of analysis"[5] for studying the international, regions have largely been absent from what is now a burgeoning literature on rule and authority in the international system. This is particularly surprising given the fact that regional organizations across the globe have expanded their policy scope as well as their capacity to decide, execute, and adjudicate on behalf of their members and are thus prominent examples of the increasing delegation and pooling of authority in institutions beyond the state.[6] Yet, IR scholars have so far mainly concentrated on international authority as an apparently *global* phenomenon. Scholars working on regionalism, in turn, have largely neglected the fact that regions, too, have become sites of rule, despite the predominant definition of regionalization as a process of institutionalization beyond the nation-state.[7] Nevertheless, the dominant focus in the study of regionalism remains on *governance*, not *government*, by regional institutions and it thus concentrates on the functional outcomes rather than the power effects of regionalization.[8] Against this background, this chapter seeks to introduce a regional perspective to the debate on the international "beyond anarchy," addressing a crucial blind spot in the spatial imagination of rule, which has dominated the existing literature to date.

Second, this chapter shifts the focus of the analysis of rule in international politics away from seeking to understand the sources and means of authority toward scrutinizing its enactment and effects in a specific social setting. The central question in this chapter is not where international authority comes from, but rather, what does international authority do? With this, my contribution to this volume is a "bottom-up" approach to international authority, which aims at understanding international authority as it materializes in very specific local settings and how its enactment shapes subjectivities and affects the material, ideational, and institutional conditions of people's daily lives.[9]

Since the adoption of the anti-coup norm, the OAU, and later its successor, the African Union, have expanded their legal mandates and scope of action with regard to the promotion of governance, democratization, and post-conflict reconstruction within their member states.[10] In this sense, the African continental organizations epitomize what Anne Orford[11] and Ole Jacob Sending[12] argued applied to the United Nations: that claims to serve as a guardian over (legitimate) order in states not only constituted the UN and its staff as international authorities but also normalized and gradually expanded practices of intervention by which peace and order are reconstructed on the basis of norms and knowledge largely defined in terms of the international. According to this argument, not only do the UN and its staff exercise authority over states but also over those who the international claims to represent and speak for.[13] These observations also hold true for the OAU/AU.

In this chapter, I will home in on one specific case in which the AU's authority to define what counts as legitimate statehood has been enacted: the postcoup intervention in Madagascar (2009–2014). Based on this analysis, I argue that the definition and international diffusion of principles of legitimacy aimed at disciplining authority within African states shows how international authority and authority in/of the state are co-constituted. The expansion of authority in the international realm internalizes the state as a default template for political organization, decision-making, and democratic articulation, while, conversely, the state itself is transformed by an increasingly dense network of international norms and corresponding practices of intervention. In short, the ideal of the (democratic) state is constitutive of international authority, while the international is inevitably present in the state and thus also subverts and defers this very ideal. In practice, this has the paradoxical effect of simultaneously legitimating and superseding, actualizing and undermining, and reproducing and denying the state as site of (legitimate) authority.

This co-constitution has two profound implications: on the one hand, it means that efforts to grasp the changing contours of the international should, from an analytical perspective, transgress rather than reify boundaries of "scales" or "levels of analysis" by interrogating the underlying rationalities that establish and reconfigure these boundaries in the first place. This would involve mapping how the dominant configuration of the international, state, and societies are signified and historically changing. This, I attempt to show, also requires more fine-grained empirical analysis, which mainstream IR scholarship has so far rarely recognized. On the other hand, the simultaneous constitution of the state and the expansive international realm has a very practical implication for all those who are currently challenging how they are governed and seeking alternatives. If the state is increasingly transnationalized, resistance to contemporary forms of rule will have to take different forms. It will require revealing and reclaiming those forces that sustain and re-legitimate the statehood and authority that are far beyond the individuals and buildings in which legitimate state authority is claimed and assumed to reside.

To develop this argument, the chapter draws on more than 90 interviews with African and international diplomats, mediators, bureaucrats from numerous regional and international organizations, Malagasy politicians, members of the military, civil society activists, church leaders, and youth activists, conducted between 2011 and 2014 in Addis Ababa (Ethiopia), Antananarivo (Madagascar), Johannesburg and Pretoria (South Africa), Gaborone (Botswana), and Paris (France).

In the remainder of the chapter, I will first explain what it means to view international authority through a relational lens that draws attention to the co-constitutive effects between international authority and authority in/of states. I then explain the emergence and formal sources of the AU's authority to define what counts as legitimate statehood on the African continent before focusing on exploring the effects of this authority in practice. Based on a case study of Madagascar, I show how the enactment of the AU's authority serves, at the same time, to reproduce and deny the state as the locus of (legitimate) authority, thus illustrating the co-constitutive relationship between international and state authority. In the conclusion, I summarize my argument and discuss what it means for the study of international authority more broadly as well as for political struggles in existing states.

International Authority through a Relational Lens

One of the key challenges for IR scholarship today is developing and refining a conceptual vocabulary to grasp "the international" as a distinct realm of politics and rule in which multiple kinds and constellations of sub- and superordination overlap and intersect (see Daase et al., this volume). However, this identification of different forms of rule in the international has been the starting point rather than the conclusion of an ongoing conceptual and theoretical search.[14] This search seeks to detect and theorize the manifold sites, agencies, and consequences of rule in the international realm and has so far also underlined the need for different (and probably multiple) analytics.

International organizations, in particular, have become a key object of inquiry in which this search has been pursued. Like nongovernmental organizations, celebrities, or business actors, IOs have been identified as global governors whose norms, ideas, and policies produce order and structure actors' behavior, not only internationally but also within states (see also contributions by Sending and Alter, this volume).[15] A key question in this body of literature is what makes actors in IOs have or enact authority in the first place. In one strand of research, scholars have paid increasing attention to the growing formal capacity of IOs to take binding decisions on behalf of their membership.[16] Others have seen the growing authority of IOs as a result from their ability to make rules, define problems and adequate solutions, and to allocate responsibilities and thus structure social reality.[17] Still others have emphasized the moral sources of the growing authority of IOs, which stem from these organizations' claims to values such as neutrality and impartiality and their association with the broader "global good."[18]

Overall, this body of research has a key interest in showing the relative power that new authorities in the international realm, like IOs, command vis-à-vis the state, hitherto seen as the only site of authority. The rise, constitution, and role of new authorities are thus often (if only implicitly) defined as alternatives or a challenge to the state.[19] From a liberal perspective, this is also accompanied by the assumption that actors apart from states are in fact somewhat better than the state. It is hoped that they stand for universalism and cosmopolitan values rather than particularism.[20] At the same time, the rise of new authorities is said to pose a challenge to the problems of legitimacy and accountability that the state was still able to accommodate.[21]

The growing international authority of actors other than states is thus often narrated in relation to the state and an assumed (historical) starting point set by the imagined Westphalian system of sovereign states. Change in the structure of the system is seen largely as a zero-sum game. Either in terms of scales – that is, the relative increase of one "level," such as the state and the international, compared to another – or in terms of units – that is, relative power and autonomy between actors. In both the scalar and the unit-based measurement, the state remains the ontological starting point and prism through which change in the international is made visible.

Both narratives follow what Patrick Thaddeus Jackson and Daniel Nexon call a substantialist approach to world politics, according to which changing relations are traced on the premise of an actor's assumed ontology as logically prior.[22] Much of IR theory, they argue, presumes

> that entities precede interaction, or that entities are already entities before they enter into social relations with other entities. … Units come first, then, like billiard balls on the table, they are put into motion and their interactions are the pattern we observe in political life.[23]

An alternative approach, termed processual relational, would inquire how actors are made in the first place through changing ties between them as well as the demarcation of boundaries and points of connection.[24] Translated for the argument presented here, this means that what is missing in the readings of the growing international authority of IOs summarized above is how the political imaginary of the state was part of and became transformed by the claims to as well as the institutionalization and sedimentation of international authority.

Against this background, this chapter takes a different approach to studying transformations in the international realm. Rather than assuming these changes take place vis-à-vis or even against the state, I suggest taking into account how the state itself – as an idea and practice – is reified and reconstituted in these transformations. This builds on a very foundational idea from the constructivist research agenda: that sovereignty is a social practice rather than an essence or property.[25] It requires claim-making and recognition and is therefore best conceived of as a historically contingent, symbolic yet consequential practice.[26] In this regard, historically changing principles of international legitimacy have produced different regimes of sovereignty and thereby defined who is a legitimate agent and what constitutes good conduct in international politics.[27] Yet today, what counts as sovereignty is no longer merely "what some collectivity of state leaders say it is."[28] Rather, international agencies beyond the state are increasingly involved in defining what can be deemed legitimate statehood. Rather than tracing the emergence of international authority in opposition to the state, I propose reading changes in the constitution of the international as altering power relations between the international, the state, and societies. The question is thus not to what extent others possess power *over* the state, but rather how the idea of the state itself is constituted by and constitutive of new claims to and locales of authority. This, I argue, is fed by the international dissemination of ideas and practices that define what counts as legitimate authority, which "licence the organization of power and authority,"[29] both internationally and within states.

Such a perspective on the international follows the above-cited processual relational approach described by Jackson and Nexon, according to which shifting ties, emergence, and co-constitution, rather than relations between ontologically fixed units, are the starting point of empirical inquiry and theorizing.[30] From this perspective, changing notions of statehood and sovereignty have to be seen as corresponding to more fundamental changes in the very essence of both what makes the state and what makes the international. These changes can be mapped out by investigating shifting rationalities and "social epistemes"[31] of authority and order, as well as the corresponding practices of intervention and ordering that aim at realizing and legitimating them. In this vein, Jens Bartelson suggests conceiving of sovereignty as symbolic form, which "not only structures our perception of political reality, but also allows us to shape objects in rough conformity with this form."[32] Sovereignty has thus become a crucial "template for organizing political life."[33] The responsibility for its endurance, however, has been "wrested out of the hands of domestic governments"[34] and given to IOs, experts, and bureaucrats who act on behalf of a global/regional common good. This legitimates interventions from beyond the state, including implementing economic reforms, capacity-building for civil society and the security forces, and combatting corruption.[35] International organizations play an important role in this. Iver Neumann and Ole Jacob Sending therefore argue that IOs have increasingly become "sites for the negotiation and formulation of universal categories and practices of rule,"[36] which define how states ought to be governed. In a similar vein, Anne Orford traces the emergence of the United Nations as an international authority, not on the basis of the organization's capacity to sanction or coerce states, but as resulting from the sedimentation of practices and rules that define the terms for statehood and legitimate authority, as well as by intervening when these standards are under siege.[37] From a relational perspective, the key question is thus not the relative autonomy of IOs vis-à-vis states, but to understand how and with what consequences "sovereignty is part of the episteme within which IOs operate."[38] Understanding change thus requires seeing IOs and their expansive missions not as the antithesis of states and as a challenge to sovereignty, but in their co-constitutive relationship to the latter. The crucial extension of this perspective that this chapter seeks to highlight, however, is that, due to this co-constitutive relationship, the ideal of the state is, paradoxically, both reproduced and denied at the same time.

Outlawing Coups and the Emergence of Regional Authority in Africa

For the first few decades of Africa's postcolonial history, the governance of African states was not a matter of continental concern. With the exception of those territories under colonial or white minority rule, the definition of what counted as a legitimate form of government was the exclusive domain of states. Membership in the OAU was based on geographic, not political criteria. Although the Charter of the Organization of African Unity referred to human rights and the "inalienable right of all people to control their own destiny,"[39] no continental mechanism guaranteed respect of these standards. In 1990, Botswana, Cape Verde, and Mauritius were the only African countries that had been independent for more than 25 years and not experienced one or more coups d'état.[40] For all the others, the irregular was actually the norm.

Since the early 1990s, the African continent has seen a dramatic change in that regard, driven by various efforts to define continental standards for what counts as legitimate authority and what to do if these are transgressed. Defining a continental anti-coup norm that outlaws coups d'état is but one example.[41] These developments did not merely lead to the creation of new norms on how states ought to be governed. They also implied an expansion of authority beyond the state, realized here through the capacities and responsibilities of the continental organization in particular. The African continent thus provides an apt example of the region as a site of rule and the expansion of international authority, which is sustained by the (re-)definition of principles of legitimate authority in African states.

With the adoption of the Lomé Declaration in 2000, African Heads of State and Government defined coups d'état as a threat to the continent's path toward peace, security, and democracy.[42] The OAU Assembly decided henceforth to outlaw any government that comes to power through unconstitutional means. As "unconstitutional change of government" the Assembly defined the following scenarios: "(i) military coup d'état against a democratically elected government; (ii) intervention by mercenaries to replace a democratically elected government; (iii) replacement of democratically elected governments by armed dissident groups and rebel movements; (iv) the refusal by an incumbent government to relinquish power to the winning party after free, fair and regular elections."[43] In 2007, the African Charter on Democracy, Elections and Governance extended this list by adding changes to the constitution in order to prolong an incumbent's term in power to the scenarios categorized as unconstitutional change of government.[44] The Lomé Declaration also mandated the Secretary-General of the OAU to "facilitate the restoration of constitutional order" through mediation, sanctions, and other more coercive means where necessary.[45] The continental anti-coup norm was thus meant to discipline authority within OAU member states and to enshrine peoples' right to choose how and by whom they want to be governed.

This redefinition of continental principles of legitimacy was based on and itself contributed to a (self-)responsibilization of the continental organization. Then OAU Secretary-General Salim Ahmed Salim publicly defended the organization's new role by referring to the shared responsibility of "Africa" of which the OAU was the organizational embodiment. He claimed that coups are a "serious blow to the process of democratization in Africa as a whole,"[46] that "Africa is saying that it is now an age of the ballot and not the bullet,"[47] and that ignoring this would be "contrary to the will of the people ..., Africa and the international community."[48]

The Lomé Declaration, likewise, refers to coups as a "serious setback to the ongoing process of democratization in the Continent" and that "there is a need to provide a solid underpinning in the OAU's agenda of promoting democracy and democratic institutions in Africa."[49] The discursive creation of a shared continental concern thus provided the logical foundation upon which the OAU and its Secretary-General were authorized to serve as new guardians over legitimate authority in African states.[50] It also tied into a more general shift in the UN's and other international donors' Africa policies, which increasingly embraced the narrative of "African solutions to African problems" and thereby assigned the responsibility for conflict resolution, democratization, and economic reforms on Africans themselves and their regional institutions in particular.

This process also implied a gradual expansion and routinization of practices of intervention. The Lomé Declaration defined a threefold response mechanism in cases of unconstitutional changes of government: suspension of the member state from the organization, diplomatic pressure on the perpetrators, and coordination with other international actors, regional groupings, and neighboring states.[51] With the transformation of the OAU into the African Union in 2002, this series of responses now takes place in the more complex and institutionalized African Peace and Security Architecture (APSA), which exemplifies the AU's increasing role in managing issues of peace and security on the African continent.[52] The AU's Constitutive Act reiterated that "governments which shall come to power through unconstitutional means shall not be allowed to participate in the activities of the Union."[53] Likewise, the fifteen-member Peace and Security Council (PSC), whose decisions are binding, was mandated to address issues of unconstitutional changes of government.[54]

The adoption of the Lomé Declaration thus defined new continental standards of legitimate authority in African states, which, in turn, formed the basis upon which the OAU/AU claimed responsibility as guardian over these newly enshrined standards. This claim included a twofold authority: on the one hand, over defining the standards for what exactly counts as legitimate authority, and on the other, over the conduct of all those domestic and international actors threatening to violate these standards.

Since the adoption of the Lomé Declaration, the African anti-coup norm has been invoked in a total of eighteen cases. In all situations, various kinds of political crises of varying degrees of intensity culminated in the ouster of the incumbent government and thus provoked condemnation and intervention by the AU aimed at reestablishing constitutional order. These efforts took divergent paths and led to different results.[55]

They nevertheless exemplify the undeniable rigor with which the Lomé Declaration has been put into practice since its adoption. For some, this shows that the AU is an effective norm entrepreneur[56] and defender of democratic rule.[57] Without wanting to understate the relevance of these developments, I contend that such interpretations fail to grasp and problematize the broader processes of order-making and transformation that are at stake here, particularly how the application of the anti-coup norm affects the relationship between the international realm, states, and societies in Africa. In the remainder of this chapter, I will elaborate on this argument based on a case study on the effects of the AU's authority to define legitimate statehood by homing in on the almost five years of post-coup intervention in Madagascar.

Homing in on the Effects of Regional Authority

In early 2009, several months of public protest had mobilized a broad movement of discontent against the incumbent regime of President Marc Ravalomanana. On March 20, after weeks of demonstrations, Marc Ravalomanana handed over power to a military directorate, which, in turn, installed the head of the protest movement, Andry Rajoelina, as President of the Transition. The AU, the Southern African Development Community (SADC), and most of Madagascar's international donors condemned this act as an unconstitutional change of government.[58] They decided to suspend Madagascar's membership and cut development funds. Several mediators and special envoys were sent to Antananarivo in order to encourage Rajoelina and his government to leave power and organize elections. Despite varying international interpretations of what constituted "la crise malgache," the Malagasy crisis, consensus soon emerged around the demand for a "consensual and inclusive transitional period" and an "inclusive, transparent and credible dialogue."[59] Several rounds of negotiations in Antananarivo, Maputo, Addis Ababa, and Pretoria between the so-called four movements (*quatre mouvances*) – Rajoelina, Ravalomanana, and the two former Presidents Ratsiraka and Zafy – failed to bring about an agreement that all parties were willing to accept and implement. In March 2010, the AU PSC imposed targeted sanctions on 109 members of the putschist government. In September 2011, the *SADC Roadmap for Ending the Crisis* was signed by eight political parties and two of the former Presidents. In December 2013, presidential and legislative elections were held and in January 2014, the AU PSC officially declared that constitutional order had been successfully restored.[60]

In the rest of this chapter, I will elaborate on how these efforts to restore "constitutional order" both reproduced and undermined an ideal image of the state as the locus of legitimate authority. This shows the effective power that stems from the (African) international in setting the terms for legitimate authority today. However, it also shows the persistence of the ideal of the state as the locus of social organization and political articulation that is part of and not superseded by the expansion of international authority. For analytical purposes, I therefore distinguish between modes of reproduction and modes of transformation (or denial), illustrated and discussed in turn in the remainder of this chapter.

Reproducing (Legitimate) State Authority

The almost five years of international efforts to reestablish constitutional order in Madagascar were shaped by and reproduced the ideal of the (democratic) state as the default form of political organization and locus of legitimate authority. This became evident in three dimensions: in the conflation of legitimate order with elected government, in the justification for excluding alternatives, and in who benefitted from the particular manner in which constitutional order was reestablished. I will discuss each of these aspects in the following.

Legitimate Order as Elected Government The persistence of the democratic state as the ideal model of political organization and locus of legitimate authority first became evident in terms of what counted as a viable solution to the Malagasy crisis. From the very beginning, resolving the political crisis was approached as a matter of intra-elite power-sharing aimed at reestablishing an elected government that enjoys both internal and external legitimacy. To achieve this, transitional elections had to be organized that fulfilled the principles of inclusivity and neutrality. Hence, the main mode of conflict resolution was intra-elite negotiations and the integration of key political figures into the postcoup order.[61]

In May 2009, AU special envoy Ablassé Ouédraogo, for instance, opened the negotiations in Antananarivo by remarking that the aim was to sign a consensual charter which (1) guarantees stability and durable peace in Madagascar and (2) leads to transitional elections.[62] In the same vein, in July 2009, SADC appointed the former President of Mozambique, Joaquim Chissano, as lead mediator, stipulating that "the work of the SADC Facilitator should be finalized upon completion of the inclusive dialogue and holding of the general elections in Madagascar."[63]

Initially, this approach to resolving the Malagasy crisis was contested, even among the various international actors that came to "accompany" Madagascar's return to constitutional order. There were diverging views as to who should be included in organizing transitional elections, for how long the transitional period should last, and who should be allowed to run in presidential elections. As the negotiations stalled and consensus among those invited to negotiate Madagascar's postcoup order became increasingly illusive, reaching an agreement to organize elections that allow for the establishment of an internationally recognizable government nevertheless emerged as an undisputable minimal consensus.[64] The standard against which the return to constitutional order was internationally recognized was therefore the organization of a "consensual, inclusive, neutral and transparent transition."[65] Despite the obvious difficulties in meeting this demand, the AU and SADC regularly confirmed its validity.[66]

From the very beginning, the menu of legitimate solutions to the Malagasy crisis was thus restricted. Solving the Malagasy crisis of authority and legitimacy was immediately fused with international norms that conditioned legitimacy on the organization of transitional elections. The essence of the negotiations was thus focused on how (quickly) to organize elections rather than for what purpose. As observed by one of my interviewees, there was an immediate "obsession" with elections, which was soon treated as cure in itself rather than as a path to something else.[67] Moreover, from the very beginning, the path to elections was predetermined as comprising negotiated power-sharing among the Malagasy political elite. Despite the mediator's mandate "to encourage the Malagasy stakeholders to take the lead in the inclusive dialogue and work to ensure that the Malagasy people take full ownership of the process,"[68] reestablishing constitutional order was thus a highly exclusionary and restricted endeavor.

The approach to resolving the political crisis in Madagascar thus immediately focused on the reestablishment of an order understood as a government legitimated by elections. The purpose of crisis resolution was hence the formation of a new, internationally recognizable government. This would result in the state being confirmed as a constituent unit of the international system, while state authority was conditioned on its origins in democratic elections. This, however, was only possible if alternatives were excluded.

Excluding Alternatives As indicated in the above-quoted observation on the international "obsession" with elections, in Madagascar there were different answers to the question of how order ought to be reconstituted. While it might have been a general consensus that any ensuing government would have to be legitimated by democratic elections, it was not at all consensual that the transition should be reduced to the organization of elections. That transition, in other words, *was* the organization of elections. The SADC Roadmap, which ultimately paved the way for the organization of transitional elections, in fact, explicitly turned this into a legal prescription. Paragraph 8 of the Roadmap stipulated that:

> The Transitional Government shall be responsible for administering the day-to-day affairs of the country and creating the necessary conditions for credible, fair, and transparent elections in conjunction with the international community. It shall refrain from making new long-term commitments as such commitments fall within the competences of the future government ....[69]

This meant that questions pertaining to more long-term and structural changes in the organization of Madagascar's political and social life were gradually excluded from the transitional program. In April 2009, the so-called *Assises nationales*, or national conferences, organized by the High Transitional Authority (*Haute autorité de la transition*, HAT) government had, for instance, demanded a human rights charter and a new constitution, the evaluation of the socioeconomic causes of the crisis, and a national conference on reconciliation.[70] In a similar vein, several civil society organizations, as well as participants in the negotiations themselves, repeatedly demanded more attention be paid to the issue of reconciliation as a principle underpinning the search for a new way of organizing politics in Madagascar. Here, reconciliation did not merely refer to confidence-building measures among the political elite, but rather to a process of dialogue to identify the causes of societal exclusion.[71] This was based on the observation that the Malagasy polity was deeply divided along socioeconomic, cultural, and politico-spatial lines, which had functioned as effective mechanisms of marginalization throughout Madagascar's postcolonial history.[72] Another round of regional consultations, organized in June 2010, therefore also demanded that the transition be about the return of sociocultural and moral values in order to establish a society "without pain" as well as sustainable development and a fair distribution of Madagascar's wealth.[73]

That the establishment of peace and order in Madagascar required more than the mere organization of elections was of course not denied by the AU, SADC, or those who had been named as guarantors of the implementation of the Roadmap. As indicated in Paragraph 8 quoted above, however, anything geared toward long-term changes was postponed to the time after the elections as it fell "within the competence of the future government."[74]

Thus, the postponement of what were deemed long-term questions also prepared the ground for re-legitimating and reauthorizing the newly elected government. In their decision to readmit Madagascar to the AU, the AU PSC, for instance, "urges the new President of the Republic of Madagascar and the other Malagasy stakeholders to work towards the promotion of national reconciliation, good governance and respect for human rights."[75] In a similar vein, the SADC Summit "welcomed" the newly inaugurated president's efforts toward "national reconciliation, and social and economic recovery."[76] The International Contact Group on Madagascar (ICG-M), an international forum for consultation and negotiation, in turn, remarked in March 2014 that based on the prescriptions including in the Roadmap, the issue of reconciliation was still pending.[77]

All this serves to underline that the focus solely on elections and the reestablishment of a government was indeed not without alternatives. Even though these alternatives were neither uncontested nor necessarily a radical departure from the ideal of legitimating authority through elections, they nevertheless questioned the conditions on which this ideal was to be reanimated. In this sense, by not denying the need for long-term changes in the organization of political and social life in Madagascar, the AU, SADC, and other guardians of the transition regularly confirmed this necessity, yet simultaneously placed primary responsibility for its realization on the newly established Malagasy government.

Empowerment of Agents of the State Reestablishing constitutional order in Madagascar was by no means driven solely by powerful external demands superimposed on passive Malagasy actors. Rather, creating a new order for postcoup Madagascar effectively empowered certain actors, despite or, in fact, because of its limited focus on the organization of transitional elections.

This empowerment can be illustrated with the rise of a branch of the Malagasy political elite, which appropriated the international demand for an inclusive and consensual transition. Under the umbrella of the so-called *Espace de concertation des organisations et partis politiques* (ESCOPOL), several members of the political elite, who had initially sided with the President of the HAT Andry Rajoelina, used the latter's resistance to bow to international pressure by portraying themselves as a neutral, inclusive, and cooperative alternative. Political parties, they argued, were the ultimate vehicles to resolve a political crisis like this.[78] Until then, the AU and the SADC had officially organized the mediation process among the four former presidents, who were said to represent Madagascar's entire political spectrum.

In contrast, the members of ESCOPOL now claimed that they should be the legitimate drivers of the transition and demanded that SADC and the AU recognize this role. This created a hitherto unprecedented dynamic in the Malagasy party system. In the ensuing months, membership in ESCOPOL rose from nine to more than 100 people, all demanding to be included in the transition.[79] In summer 2010, HAT President Rajoelina signed a deal with more than 160 political parties, including ESCOPOL, who confirmed him as President of the Transition. In return they were guaranteed a seat in the transitional institutions.[80] Between 2010 and 2011, the number of registered parties in Madagascar rose from less than 100 to more than 300.[81] Of those that had signed the deal with Rajoelina, only 15 had existed before.[82] These shifts in the organization of the Malagasy political elite were ultimately also reproduced in the SADC Roadmap: of the ten signatories, one of which was ESCOPOL itself, five parties were established just months before.

The international demand for an inclusive and neutral transition thus first of all prompted the formation of new parties and renewed contestation among the Malagasy political elite. It provided the terms and justification for their claims to authority and legitimacy and served as a mechanism to (auto-)integrate into the organization of the transition. This, however, also meant that the transitional institutions had to be gradually expanded. The legislative grew from 160 to 526 in the final stage of the transition while the number of ministerial portfolios reflects a similar trajectory.[83]

The focus on elections and the formation of a new government thus also empowered a particular branch of the Malagasy elite and provided a new basis for their claims to authority and legitimacy. While overall this also re-legitimated political parties as vehicles for the will of the democratic sovereign, this ideal remained no more than a future prospect.[84] What was upheld, however, was both the ideal that parties are bearers of the will of the people and that politics – that is, contestation and decision-making regarding the distribution of the common good – takes place within the legislative and executive institutions of the Malagasy state.

Denying/Transforming (Legitimate) State Authority

While practices of international intervention served, on the one hand, to reproduce the ideal of the state as the locus of legitimate authority, on the other, they also simultaneously denied it and redefined what this implied in practice. They reproduced and questioned the role of the state as a regulator of social and political organization; they defended, reestablished, and constrained the idea of popular sovereignty. I want to highlight two dimensions of this in-built ambiguity: first, the limitations to popular sovereignty and second, the transnationalization of governance. The result of both is a form of transnationalization that reassembles the international, the state, and society into a novel configuration, which flies in the face of perceptions of them as individual components, as separate locales of power, "scales," or "units" of analysis.

Limits to Popular Sovereignty Although, as mentioned above, SADC mediator Chissano was officially mandated to "encourage the Malagasy stakeholders to take the lead in the inclusive dialogue and work to ensure that the Malagasy people take full ownership of the process,"[85] this ownership, as evident from the aforementioned, was heavily constrained.

From the very beginning, not only did the international provide the overall terms and purpose of what it meant to reestablish constitutional order in Madagascar, it also served as the ultimate arbitrator of the legitimate path this was to take. The international efforts to reestablish constitutional order in Madagascar, therefore, could not evade the paradox of aiming to restore something – popular sovereignty – that was in practice effectively undermined.[86] This inevitably meant pitting international and "local" principles of legitimacy against each other, while the AU and SADC were constantly pressured to mask and deny the illiberalism their intervention was about to produce.

This particularly became evident when Rajoelina's candidacy for the 2013 presidential elections was internationally rejected as "illegitimate"[87] because it was an infringement of the AU's principle that coup leaders should be banned from participating in postcoup transitional elections.[88] In a hitherto unprecedented storm of diplomatic attention, the AU, SADC, and the ICG-M pressured Rajoelina to withdraw his candidacy. Failing to do so, the ICG-M warned, would imply the discontinuation of international money for the organization of elections and the nonrecognition of their final results. In turn, the ICG-M promised that the "restoration of constitutional order would enable Madagascar to benefit from increased support through international cooperation."[89] The concerted diplomatic pressure finally succeeded. The result, however, was that the role of the international in "assisting" the reestablishment of order in Madagascar was increasingly perceived as foreign interference.[90]

In May 2013, the Malagasy Council of Christian Churches (FFKM) organized a national dialogue, which ended in the demand for "another transition" and the complete abandonment of the SADC Roadmap.[91] One of their key demands, once again, was national reconciliation as a condition for free, fair, and credible elections. These demands were initially ignored by SADC and the AU who instead called on the Malagasy parties to place the "interest of their country and the people" before partisan interests and personal ambitions.[92] Subsequently, the ICG-M promised the FFKM a "perspective of national reconciliation" once constitutional order was reestablished.[93] This, however, was dependent on the latter's support for transitional elections and thus contradicted the FFKM's demand that reconciliation was a *precondition* for elections.

The realization of people's right to the ballot as enshrined in the Lomé Declaration was thus also an instruction to take this path. While officially claiming to return sovereignty to the Malagasy people, the "interest of the country and the people," which all those contesting this path were commanded to obey, was something defined from the outside that assumed rather than inquired what (different) Malagasies actually wanted (differently). Popular sovereignty was thus simultaneously reestablished and restricted.

Transnationalization of Governance While the normativity that shaped how and with whom constitutional order was reestablished in Madagascar resulted from a merger between international demands and local agency, its effect, too, was a continuation of this merger.

As elaborated above, even before their actual election, the to-be-inaugurated president and government were already given responsibility for all those aspects of the transition that had been postponed to postelection times. However, the transition produced even more governmental responsibilities, also for actors other than the Malagasy government. Apart from the official Malagasy state institutions, a variety of IOs and bilateral partners also claimed responsibility for henceforth addressing what the transition had identified as being in need of reform. In this sense, the reestablishment of constitutional order not only re-legitimized the Malagasy government to carry out more comprehensive interventions in society but also assigned new roles and responsibilities to international actors, including other states and international organizations that were charged with supporting the government's efforts. The transnationalization of governance is hence also a reflection of the proliferation of authorities through self-responsibilization (on "auto-authority," see Sending, this volume; see also Lake, this volume).

In March 2014, the ICG-M therefore decided to transform itself into an international support group (GIS-M) with the aim of supporting the Malagasy government, particularly in the area of socioeconomic development and governance.[94] Concretely, this meant, for instance, that experts from the South African government were contracted to counsel the Malagasy government on matters of national reconciliation.

Similarly, the SADC Summit reaffirmed, in 2014, its "commitment to support Madagascar in the context of dialogue, national reconciliation and national building process [sic]."[95] The AU, in turn, also selected reconciliation as a priority area for the work of the AU Liaison Office in Antananarivo, which continued to operate as a peacebuilding office even after the official return to "constitutional order."[96] The defunct Malagasy security forces, a key driver behind the fall of President Ravalomanana, were identified as an equally important area for more long-term Malagasy continental/regional cooperation.[97]

The reproduction of the Malagasy state was thus both an effect and a source of the reorganization of the international, so neither the nature of the government nor the nature of international actors can be made sense of without the other. The (re)definition of governmental responsibilities for reconciliation and security sector reform resulted from the excluded and postponed aspects of the transition, which had nevertheless been internationally sanctioned as necessary and legitimate areas for greater governmental involvement. The more expansive international engagements in these areas, in turn, can only be legitimated as being in support of the effective reestablishment of Malagasy governmental responsibilities. That the newly established GIS-M is coheaded by "Madagascar" and the African Union is more than a rhetorical commitment to "ownership." It epitomizes a hybrid and transnationalized order that weaves together the international, the state, and society into novel figurations.

In summary, five years of reestablishing constitutional order in Madagascar have both re-legitimated and subverted the ideal of the (democratic) state as a default form of social organization, decision-making, and democratic articulation and as constituent unit of international society. This was made possible through the terms and modes of crisis resolution that equated order with the establishment of an elected government. On the one hand, this meant excluding alternatives while, on the other, empowering those actors able to claim legitimacy and responsibility in the order to be established. Yet, this ideal of political organization was subverted and deferred at the same time: There were clear limits to the extent to which Malagasies were actually exercising their right to choose how they wanted to be governed, while the transition produced new governmental responsibilities that are defined and fulfilled in concert with a variety of international actors.

Order in Madagascar was thus the result of the internationalization of principles of legitimacy and corresponding claims made by a variety of international actors to the authority to intervene for their protection. The simultaneous reproduction and denial of the state as the locus of legitimate authority meant that the legitimacy of the newly established government was compromised and, at the same time, it was faced with rising expectations that resulted from the additional responsibilities defined during the transition. In early 2013, more than 80 percent of the respondents to the Afrobarometer survey, for instance, reported having had no contact at all with a party official over the past 12 months, while more than 70 percent had never seen a representative from any of the executive or legislative institutions of the transition.[98] At the same time, however, 54 percent of the respondents answered that it was "very likely" that the newly elected government would resolve the island's main problems within the coming five years.[99] While not based on substantive everyday experiences, the state was thus nevertheless effectively revived as a projection screen for high expectations and as a potential agent of social and political change.

Conclusion

When the OAU Assembly adopted the Lomé Declaration in 2000, it was supposed to make state authority subject to shared principles and to enshrine people's right to choose how and by whom they want to be governed. The more than eighteen cases of unconstitutional changes of government since then suggest that this vision is not yet fully attained. But the ensuing concerted efforts to reestablish constitutional order, of which Madagascar's experience is but one example, testify to the tangible effects this vision had. It authorized the continental organization to intervene in its member states with the aim of reestablishing constitutional order and this – as shown above – has consequences for how, led by whom, and what kind of authority is reestablished in the countries concerned.

Using these observations, I sought to show that by taking a relationalist perspective on transformations in the international realm, the African continent indeed offers apt experiences for theorizing rule in international politics. The fate of the continental anti-coup norm illustrates how the dissemination of principles of international legitimacy – of what counts as legitimate authority – feeds the expansion of international authority and reproduces the ideal of the state as the locus of legitimate authority. Yet, when translated into practice, this co-constitution means that the state as the locus of legitimate authority is both reproduced and denied. In Madagascar, this led to a transnationalized order that is sustained by both the ideal of the state as a locale of political organization and democratic articulation as well as by the norms, practices, and interventions of a variety of international actors who claim responsibility for addressing the obvious shortcomings this state in reality still has.

These insights have both scholarly and practical consequences: for how we conceive of the fabric of the international realm and how we study it, as well as for how and to what extent it is possible to change the way people are governed. With regard to the first, the chapter demonstrates the value added of describing transformations "beyond anarchy" through a relationalist lens that interrogates how, by what means, and with what consequences rule in/of the international and rule in/of states hang together, rather than taking units of rule as an ontological starting point. As argued throughout this chapter, the state is a fundamental, constitutive element of these transformations, which increasingly sediment forms of rule in the international. For students of rule and authority in international politics, the chapter thus demonstrates that the expansion of international authority both internalizes and reproduces an ideal image of the democratic state as a default "template of political organization,"[100] while at the same time deferring its full realization.

With regard to the prospects for change, these observations mean that the international dissemination of principles of legitimacy not only internationalizes rights, but also restricts what kind of change is imaginable. Thus, the international enshrinement of the democratic state as the locus of legitimate authority may not only make (more) radical change more difficult; it also means rethinking the locale for contesting authority in states. Under conditions of increasingly transnationalized orders, such contestations may have to address and demand another, less paternalistic and prescriptive international rather than seeking change either by reforming the state or by expanding the authority and practice of the international to address persisting shortcomings in these states.

References

AFP. 1996. *Burundi Coup Is "Illegal, Unacceptable": OAU Chief*, https://global.factiva.com/ha/default.aspx#./!?&_suid=14486221851160980090620694682 (last access November 17, 2015).

AU. 2002. *Protocol Relating to the Establishment of the Peace and Security Council of the African Union*. Durban: African Union.

AU. 2007. *African Charter for Democracy, Elections, and Governance*. Addis Ababa: African Union.

AU Assembly. 2010. Decision on the Prevention of Unconstitutional Changes of Government and Strengthening the Capacity of the African Union to Manage Such Situations. Assembly/AU/Dec.269(XIV) Rev.1. Addis Ababa: African Union.

AU PSC. 2009a. *Communiqué of the 181st Meeting of the Peace and Security Council*. PSC/PR/COMM.(CLXXXI). Addis Ababa: African Union.

AU PSC. 2009b. Press Statement of the 202nd Meeting of the Peace and Security Council. PSC/PR/BR/(CCII). Addis Ababa: African Union.

AU PSC. 2010. Press Statement of the 237th Meeting of the Peace and Security Council. PSC/PR/(COMM-2(CCXXXVII). Kampala: African Union.

AU PSC. 2011. *Communiqué of the 303rd Meeting of the Peace and Security Council.* PSC/PR/COMM.1 (CCCIII). Addis Ababa: African Union.

AU PSC. 2013. *Communiqué of the 376th Meeting of the Peace and Security Council.* PSC/PR/COMM.(CCCLXXVI). Addis Ababa: African Union.

AU PSC. 2014. *Communiqué of the 415th Meeting of the Peace and Security Council.* PSC/PR/COMM.(CDXV). Addis Ababa: African Union.

Avant, Deborah D., Martha Finnemore, and Susan K. Sell (eds.). 2010. *Who Governs the Globe?* Cambridge: Cambridge University Press.

Barnett, Michael, and Martha Finnemore. 2004. *Rules for the World: International Organizations in Global Politics.* Ithaca: Cornell University Press.

Bartelson, Jens 2014. *Sovereignty as Symbolic Form.* Abingdon: Routledge.

BBC. 1993. *OAU Secretary-General in Rwanda, Says that Something Has to Be Done for Burundi.* https://global.factiva.com/ha/default.aspx#./!?&_suid=144862194405803351135831326246 (last access November 17, 2015).

Biersteker, Thomas J., and Cynthia Weber. 1996. "The Social Construction of State Sovereignty," in Thomas J. Biersteker, and Cynthia Weber (eds.), *State Sovereignty as Social Construct.* Cambridge: Cambridge University Press, pp. 1–21.

Buchanan, Allen, and Robert O. Keohane, 2006. "The Legitimacy of Global Governance Institutions." *Ethics & International Affairs* 20(4): 405–437.

Butedi, Nzolani François. 2018. "The Work of the African Union Liaison Office in Building Peace on the Ground: A Case Study of Madagascar." *South African Journal of International Affairs* 25(1): 99–116.

Châtaigner, Jean-Marc. 2014. "Madagascar: le développement contrarié." *Afrique contemporaine* 251: 107–124.

Chesterman, Simon. 2004. *You, the People: The United Nations, Transitional Administration, and State-Building.* Oxford: Oxford University Press.

COSC. 2010. *Résultats du Dinika Santatra.* Antananarivo: Coalition des organisations de la société civile.

Daase, Christopher, and Nicole Deitelhoff. 2019. "Opposition and Dissidence." *Journal of International Political Theory* 15(1): 11–30.

Dalichau, Oliver, and Jean-Aimé Raveloson. 2009. *Machtkampf in Madagaskar: Erste Ergebnisse der nationalen Tagung.* Antananarivo: Friedrich-Ebert Stiftung.

Day, John. 1963. "Authority." *Political Studies* 11(3): 257–271.

Engel, Ulf, and João Gomes Porto (eds.). 2010. *Africa's New Peace and Security Architecture: Promoting Norms, Institutionalizing Solutions.* Farnham: Ashgate.

Engel, Ulf, and João Gomes Porto (eds.). 2013. *Towards an African Peace and Security Regime. Continental Embeddedness, Transnational Linkages, Strategic Relevance.* Farnham: Ashgate.

Engel, Ulf. 2012. "The African Union and Mediation in Cases of Unconstitutional Changes of Government, 2008–2011," in Ulf Engel (ed.), *New Mediation Practices in African Conflicts.* Leipzig: Leipziger Universitätsverlag, pp. 55–82.

Eriksen, Stein Sundstøl, and Ole Jacob Sending. 2013. "There is No Global Public: The Idea of the Public in the Legitimation of Governance." *International Theory* 5(2): 213–37.

ESCOPOL. 2011. *Espace de concertation des organisations et partis politiques: Documentation du travail.* Antananarivo: mimeo.

Fawn, Rick. 2009. "'Regions' and the Study: Wherefrom, What for and Where to?" *Review of International Studies* 35(S1): 5–34.

Grovogui, Siba N'Zatioula. 1996. *Sovereigns, Quasi Sovereigns, and Africans. Race and Self-Determination in International Law.* Minneapolis; London: University of Minnesota Press.

Grund, Constantin. 2010. *Auf der Suche nach Kontrolle: Die Politische Krise in Madagaskar 2009/2010.* Antananarivo: Friedrich-Ebert-Stiftung.

Haftel, Yoram Z., and Stephanie C. Hofmann. 2017. "Institutional Authority and Security Cooperation within Regional Economic Organizations." *Journal of Peace Research* 54(4): 484–498.

Hooghe, Lisbeth, and Gary Marks. 2015. "Delegation and Pooling in International Organizations." *Review of International Organizations* 10(3): 305–328.

Hooghe, Lisbeth, Gary Marks, Tobias Lenz, Jeanine Bezuijen, Besir Ceka, and Svet Derderyan. 2017. *Measuring International Authority: A Postfunctionalist Theory of Governance,* Volume III. Oxford: Oxford University Press.

ICG-M. 2013a. *Aide-Mémoire: plan en sept points pour sortir le processus électoral à Madagascar de l'impasse.* Addis Ababa: African Union.

ICG-M. 2013b. *Communiqué of the 7th Meeting of the International Contact Group on Madagascar (ICG-M).* Addis Ababa: African Union.

ICG-M. 2014a. *9ème Réunion consultative du Groupe international de contact sur Madagascar (GIC-M).* Antananarivo: mimeo.

ICG-M. 2014b. *Joint Press Statement: AU and Partners End Joint Security Sector Assessment Mission to Madagascar.* Antananarivo: mimeo.

Ikome, Francis. 2007. "Good Coups and Bad Coups: The Limits of the AU's Injunction on Unconstitutional Changes of Government." *Occasional Paper (55).* Johannesburg: Institute for Global Dialogue.

Imbiki, Anaclet. 2015. *La réconciliation nationale à Madagascar: une perspective complexe et difficile.* Paris: L'Harmattan.

Jackson, Thaddeus P., and Daniel Nexon. 1999. "Relations before States: Substance, Process and the Study of World Politics." *European Journal of International Relations* 5(3): 291–332.

Jayasuriya, Kanishka (ed.). 2003. *Governing the Asia Pacific. Beyond the "New Regionalism."* London: Palgrave Macmillan.

Karbo, Tony, and Tim Murithi (eds.). 2018. *The African Union: Autocracy, Diplomacy and Peacebuilding in Africa.* London, and New York: I.B. Tauris.

Kustermans, Jorg, and Rikkert Horemans. 2022. "Four Conceptions of Authority in International Relations." *International Organization* 76(1): 204–228.

Lake, David A. 2009. "Regional Hierarchy: Authority and Local International Order." *Review of International Studies* 35(S1): 35–58.

Lake, David A. 2010. "Rightful Rules: Authority, Order, and the Foundations of Global Governance." *International Studies Quarterly* 54(3): 587–613.

Lawson, George, and Luca Tardelli 2013. "The Past, Present, and Future of Intervention." *Review of International Studies* 39(5): 1233–1253.

Leininger, Julia. 2014. *A Strong Norm for Democratic Governance in Africa.* Stockholm: International IDEA.

Lukes, Steven. 1987. "Perspectives on Authority." *Nomos* 29: 59–75.

Madagascar Tribune. 2013a. *Pour un gouvernment neutre et une autre transition*. www.madagascar-tribune.com/Pour-un-gouvernement-neutre-et-une,18687.html (last access July 26, 2022).

Madagascar Tribune. 2013b. *La souveraineté illusoire d'un pays à genoux*. www.madagascar-tribune.com/La-souverainete-illusoire-d-un,18329.html, (last access July 26, 2022).

Malmvig, Helle. 2001. "The Reproduction of Sovereignties: Between Man and State during Practices of Intervention." *Cooperation and Conflict* 36(3): 251–272.

McGowan, Patrick J. 2003. "African Military Coups d'état 1956–2001: Frequency, Trends and Distribution." *Journal of Modern African Studies* 41(3): 339–370.

Migdal, Joel, and Klaus Schlichte. 2005. "Rethinking the State," in Klaus Schlichte (ed.), *The Dynamics of States: The Formation and Crises of State Domination*. Aldershot: Ashgate, pp. 1–40.

Mouvance Zafy. 2009. *Procès verbal des résultats des pourparlers du Carlton, Antananarivo, 20–22 mai 2009*. Antananarivo: mimeo.

Mouvance Zafy. 2010. *Mémorandum par la Mouvance Albert Zafy pour une délégation de parlementaires UE-ACP sur la situation de la crise, juillet 2010*. Antananarivo: mimeo.

Neumann, Iver B., and Ole Jacob Sending. 2010. *Governing the Global Polity: Practice, Mentality, Rationality*. Ann Arbor: University of Michigan Press.

OAU. 1963. *Charter of the Organisation of African Unity*. Addis Ababa: Organisation of African Unity.

OAU. 2000a. *Declaration on the Framework for an OAU Response to Unconstitutional Changes of Government*, AHG/Decl.5 (XXXVI). Lomé: Organisation of African Unity.

OAU. 2000b. *Constitutive Act of the African Union*. Lomé: Organisation of African Unity.

Orford, Anne. 2011. *International Authority and the Responsibility to Protect*. Cambridge: Cambridge University Press.

Philpott, Daniel. 2001. *Revolutions in Sovereignty: How Ideas Shaped Modern International Relations*. Princeton: Princeton University Press.

Rajerison, Olivia. 2013. *La légitimation démocratique du pouvoir à Madagascar*. Antananarivo: Friedrich-Ebert-Stiftung.

Rakotomamonjy, Joël, Laetitia Razafimamonjy, Mireille Razafrindrakoto, Désiré Razafindrazaka, François Roubaud, and Jean-Michel Wachsberger. 2014. "Redevabilité sociale et attentes des Malgaches envers leurs dirigeants." *Afrobarometer Briefing Papers* 141. Accra: Afrobarometer.

Razafindrakoto, Mireille, François Roubaud, and Jean-Michel Wachsberger. 2014. "Élites, pouvoir et régulation à Madagascar: Une lecture de l'histoire à l'aune de l'économie politique." *Afrique contemporaine* 251: 25–50.

République de Madagascar. 2010. *Ordonnance No. 2010-010 relative à la mise ne place du Parlement de la Transition*. Antananarivo: mimeo.

Reus-Smit, Christian. 2001. "Human Rights and the Social Construction of Sovereignty." *Review of International Studies* 27(4): 519–538.

Reuters. 1993. *OAU Condemns Coup in Burundi.* https://global.factiva.com/ha/default.aspx#./!?&_suid=1448621191464010041779675520957 (last access July 22, 2022).

Roth, Brad R. 1999. *Governmental Illegitimacy in International Law.* Oxford: Claredon Press.

Ruggie, John G. 1993. "Territoriality and Beyond: Problematizing Modernity in International Relations." *International Organization* 47(1): 139–174.

SADC. 2009a. *Communiqué Summit of SADC Heads of State and Government.* Sandton: Southern African Development Community.

SADC. 2009b. *SADC Mediation Efforts in Madagascar: Draft Report 7 July-10 August 2009.* SC-A87.3. Gaborone: Southern African Development Community.

SADC. 2010a. *Double Troika Summit Communiqué.* Maputo: Southern African Development Community.

SADC. 2010b. *Communiqué of the Extra-Ordinary Summit of SADC Heads of State and Government.* Gaborone: Southern African Development Community.

SADC. 2011. *SADC Roadmap for Ending the Crisis in Madagascar.* Antananarivo: Southern African Development Community.

SADC. 2014a. *Extraordinary Summit of SADC Heads of State and Government.* Addis Ababa: Southern African Development Community.

SADC. 2014b. *Communiqué of the 34th Summit of SADC Heads of State and Government.* Victoria Falls: Southern African Development Community.

Sending, Ole J. 2014. "The International Civil Servant." *International Political Sociology* 8(3): 338–340.

Sending, Ole J. 2015. *The Politics of Expertise: Competing Authority in Global Governance.* Ann Arbor: University of Michigan Press.

Sending, Ole J., and Jon Harald Sande Lie 2015. "The Limits of Global Authority: World Bank Benchmarks in Ethiopia and Malawi." *Review of International Studies* 41(5): 993–1010.

Souaré, Issaka K. 2014. "The African Union as a Norm Entrepreneur on Military Coups d'Etat in Africa (1952–2012): An Empirical Assessment." *Journal of Modern African Studies* 52(1): 69–94.

Thomson, Janice E. 1995. "State Sovereignty in International Relations: Bridging the Gap between Theory and Empirical Research." *International Studies Quarterly* 39(2): 213–233.

Tieku, Thomas K. 2009. "Multilateralization of Democracy Promotion and Defense in Africa." *Africa Today* 56(2): 75–91.

Tieku, Thomas K. 2017. *Governing Africa: 3D Analysis of the African Union's Performance.* New York: Rowman & Littlefield.

Various. 2009: *Assises nationales 2–3 avril 2009.* Antananarivo: mimeo.

Walker, R. B. J. 1993. *Inside/Outside: International Relations as Political Theory.* Cambridge: Cambridge University Press.

Walters, William, and Jens Henrik Haahr. 2005. *Governing Europe: Discourse, Governmentality and European Integration.* New York: Routledge.

Weber, Max. [1921/22] 1968. *Wirtschaft und Gesellschaft.* Tübingen: Mohr Siebeck.

Witt, Antonia. 2020. *Undoing Coups: The African Union and Post-coup Intervention in Madagascar*. London: Zed Books.

Witt, Antonia. 2022. "Beyond Formal Powers: Understanding the African Union's Authority on the Ground." *Review of International Studies* 48(4): 626–645.

Zanotti, Laura. 2011. *Governing Disorder: UN Peace Operations, International Security, and Democratization in the Post-Cold War Era*. University Park: Pennsylvania State University Press.

Zarakol, Ayşe (ed.). 2017. *Hierarchies in World Politics*. Cambridge: Cambridge University Press.

Zaum, Dominik. 2007. *The Sovereignty Paradox: The Norms and Politics of International Statebuilding*. Oxford: Oxford University Press.

Zürn, Michael. 2018. *A Theory of Global Governance. Authority, Legitimacy, and Contestation*. Oxford: Oxford University Press.

Zürn, Michael, Alexandros Tokhi, and Martin Binder. 2021. "The International Authority Database." *Global Policy* 12(4): 430–442.

Zürn, Michael, Martin Binder, and Matthias Ecker-Erhardt. 2012. "International Authority and its Politicization." *International Theory* 4(1):69–106.

Notes

1 I would like to thank the participants of the 2017 workshop "Beyond Anarchy: Rule and Authority in the International System," in particular Ole Jacob Sending, for their invaluable feedback on an earlier version of this chapter, as well as Felix Anderl for his very helpful comments on the final draft.

2 OAU 2000a.

3 Hooghe et al. 2017; Zürn 2018; Zürn et al. 2021.

4 Day 1963; Lukes 1987; Weber [1921/22] 1968: §16.

5 Lake 2009: 57.

6 Haftel and Hofmann 2017; Hooghe and Marks 2015: 322; Zürn 2018; Zürn et al. 2021.

7 Fawn 2009: 12.

8 For exceptions, see, for instance, Walters and Haahr (2005) on the European Union (EU) and Jayasuriya (2003) on the Asia-Pacific region.

9 For a more detailed discussion, see Witt 2022; see also Sending and Lie 2015.

10 See, for instance, Engel and Porto 2010; Tieku 2017.

11 Orford 2011.

12 Sending 2015.

13 Orford 2011: 192; Sending 2015: 130.

14 See, for instance, Daase and Deitelhoff 2019; Lake 2009; Zarakol 2017; Zürn 2018.

15 Avant et al. 2010; Barnett and Finnemore 2004.

16 Hooghe and Marks 2015; Hooghe et al. 2017.

17 Barnett and Finnemore 2004: 3.

18 Avant et al. 2010; Sending 2014.

19 Kustermans and Horemans 2022: 220; Lake 2010: 600; Zürn et al. 2012: 70.

20 For a critical discussion, see Eriksen and Sending 2013.
21 See Buchanan and Keohane 2006; Zürn 2018.
22 Jackson and Nexon 1999: 291.
23 Jackson and Nexon 1999: 293.
24 Jackson and Nexon 1999: 308; see also Walker 1993.
25 Biersteker and Weber 1996: 3.
26 See Bartelson 2014; Malmvig 2001: 254; Migdal and Schlichte 2005: 15.
27 See, for instance, Grovogui 1996; Philpott 2001; Roth 1999.
28 Thomson 1995: 218.
29 Reus-Smit 2001: 520.
30 Jackson and Nexon 1999: 318.
31 Ruggie 1993: 157.
32 Bartelson 2014: 15.
33 Bartelson 2014: 17.
34 Bartelson 2014: 87.
35 See generally Lawson and Tardelli 2013.
36 Neumann and Sending 2010: 136.
37 Orford 2011, see also Zanotti 2011.
38 Neumann and Sending 2010: 145.
39 OAU 1963: Preamble.
40 McGowan 2003: 345.
41 See generally AU 2007; Tieku 2009; Witt 2020: Chapter 2.
42 OAU 2000a.
43 OAU 2000a.
44 AU 2007.
45 OAU 2000a.
46 Reuters 1993.
47 BBC 1993.
48 AFP 1996.
49 OAU 2000a.
50 See also AU Assembly 2010.
51 OAU 2000a.
52 See generally Engel and Porto 2010, 2013; Karbo and Murithi 2018.
53 OAU 2000b: Art. 30.
54 AU 2002: Art. 7(g).
55 See generally Engel 2012; Ikome 2007; Souaré 2014; Witt 2020.
56 Souaré 2014.
57 Leininger 2014; Tieku 2009.
58 AU PSC 2009a; SADC 2009a.
59 AU PSC 2010; SADC 2010a.
60 AU PSC 2014.
61 AU PSC 2009b; SADC 2009a.
62 Mouvance Zafy 2009.
63 SADC 2009b: 3.
64 See Châtaigner 2014: 119.
65 SADC 2010a.
66 SADC 2010b; AU PSC 2011.
67 Author's interview with member of CNOSC, Antananarivo, 24 March 2014.

68 SADC 2009b: 3.
69 SADC 2011: Art. 8.
70 Dalichau and Raveloson 2009: 2–3; Various 2009.
71 Mouvance Zafy 2010.
72 Mouvance Zafy 2010; see also Imbiki 2015.
73 COSC 2010: 16.
74 SADC 2011: Art. 8.
75 AU PSC 2014.
76 SADC 2014a.
77 ICG-M 2014a: 2.
78 ESCOPOL 2011: 4–5.
79 ESCOPOL 2011: 40–41.
80 République de Madagascar 2010.
81 Rajerison 2013: 14.
82 Grund 2010: 4.
83 Razafindrakoto et al. 2014: 45.
84 Rajerison 2013.
85 SADC 2009b: 3.
86 See generally Chesterman 2004: 1; Zaum 2007: 5.
87 AU PSC 2013.
88 AU Assembly 2010; AU 2007: Art. 25(4).
89 ICG-M 2013b.
90 Madagascar Tribune 2013b.
91 Madagascar Tribune 2013a.
92 AU PSC 2013.
93 ICG-M 2013a.
94 ICG-M 2014a.
95 SADC 2014b.
96 Butedi 2018.
97 ICG-M 2014b.
98 Rakotomamonjy et al. 2014: 3.
99 Rakotomamonjy et al. 2014: 4.
100 Bartelson 2014: 87.

7 Law, Anarchy, and Rule

The Authority of the International Rule of Law

Ian Hurd[1]

Two basic propositions of International Relations (IR) theory contradict each other. The idea that international politics takes place in "international anarchy" is contradicted by the idea of the international rule of law. The former posits the absence of any institutions of authority over states while the latter finds one in the obligation on governments to comply with their international obligations. Both sides claim to be speaking an empirical truth and to derive from it conceptual and behavioral implications. But both cannot be right. This essay unravels the assumptions behind the ideology of the rule of law and finds its practices to be so pervasive, and so fundamental, in world affairs that it overwhelms the suggestion that international politics takes place in "anarchy." In the face of convincing evidence against the "anarchy problematique," I find that the international rule of law exemplifies the world of rule "beyond anarchy" that is described by Daase, Deitelhoff, and Witt in this volume.

The idea that international relations takes place within a framework of law is widely taken for granted. A "rules-based international order" is commonly assumed to be both a descriptive fact and a normative goal. John H. Jackson, the trade-law expert, expresses a broad version of this view: "to a large degree the history of civilization may be described as a gradual evolution from a power oriented approach, in the state of nature, towards a rule oriented approach."[2] Debates among social scientists and legal scholars over the effects of international law take place largely within the intellectual and political confines of a shared commitment to a progressive view of the rule of law, as do policy debates about particular pieces of "global governance."[3] Rather than take them as given, I examine these commitments and find the conventional assumptions about the international rule of law to be conceptually inconsistent and empirically unrealistic.[4] In their place, I draw on Daase, Deitelhoff, and Witt to make sense of law's contribution to "constellations of sub- and subordination" in the international.[5]

A world in which governments see themselves as, and act as if they are, subordinate to a legal system is not a system of anarchy. We live in a world of rules and of rule, not anarchy.[6] The rule of law ideology in world politics is compelling evidence against the anarchy problematique and in favor of an authority problematique. But what kind of authority is it? This chapter takes a conceptual look at the rule of law in order to better understand what its international variant is, both on its own and in relation to the more commonly examined domestic variant. Throughout, I am interested in the international rule of law as a system of global authority in which governments are subordinate to global legal forms. My macro view of international law steps back from specific pieces of international legal regulation such as a treaty on landmines, a trade rule against dumping, or membership in an international organization. At the microlevel, governments often act in ways that violate legal commitments that they have made in the past. At the macro-level however, it is almost unheard of for a government to deny the desirability of a rule-of-law system for global affairs. Thus, this chapter presents the international rule of law as a political structure and asks "what does it mean" and "what kind of world does it make?"

The rule of law is central to both the conception of the modern state and to the study of international politics. The international and domestic versions of the rule of law were invented as solutions to very different political problems. In domestic society, the rule of law addresses the dilemmas of centralized authority. It places limits on the exercise of state power by setting it within a stable set of known rules that apply equally to all citizens. In international affairs, the rule of law is a response to the absence of such centralized authority and to the externalities, inefficiencies, and other implications that this implies.[7] The two are commonly united by a shared commitment to a liberal view of politics and society. This includes the assumptions that the rule of law naturally generates valuable goods that are under-supplied in the absence of the rule of law; that the rule of law is an alternative to the arbitrary exercise of power; and that the ultimate product of a rule-of-law system is the choice by the law's subjects to *comply* with the rules.

Once one recognizes the structural authority of the international rule of law, it becomes clearer that its politics are not so unidirectional. Legal justifications are powerful tools for governments. They help legitimize policies that they favor and contest those that they oppose, evident in the competition over legal interpretation and application that is a familiar part of contemporary international politics.[8] Governments are continually fighting over the application of international rules, and the prize that they seek is to authorize their preferred outcomes as legally permitted or required (see also Alter, this volume). This dynamic depends on the shared belief that acting lawfully is more legitimate than acting unlawfully. Shirley Scott has called this the ideology of the international rule of law.[9] This power to legitimize state policies means that international law is both enabling and constraining for governments – it adds to as well as limits state capacity, and so its relation with power is much more nuanced than liberal theorists suppose.[10]

I set out next the domestic rule of law and examine three key elements that define its structure of political authority. I then turn to the international context and find that none of the three suits the unique conditions of international politics. This inapplicability has often been used as support for the anarchy problematique in international relations, but I find that it points in the opposite direction: the international rule of law is a structure of political authority that governs states from above as it were.

The Rule of Law and Domestic Politics

The rule of law is a social system that organizes authority among potentially competing institutions of society including government, leaders, and citizens within a framework of law. Stable rules exist and are binding on the citizens and the government alike, with the overall objective to "prevent the misuse and abuse of political power."[11] This can be understood and institutionalized in a variety of ways, leading to vigorous debates in political philosophy, sociology, legal theory, and comparative politics about what it is and where it exists or doesn't.[12]

From these debates, a conventional core is often identified that centers on three essential requirements:

(1) that society should be governed by stable, public, and certain rules;
(2) that these rules should apply equally to the governed and to the rulers; and
(3) that these rules should be applied equally and dispassionately across cases and people.

These three appear in various ways in the scholarship of legal philosophers. Brian Tamanaha labels them "formal legality," "government limited by law," and "rule of law, not man."[13] Simon Chesterman, following A. V. Dicey, sees the three as "regulating government power, implying equality before the law, and privileging judicial process."[14] Lon Fuller expands his list to eight principles of the "internal morality of law."[15] The World Justice Project Rule of Law Index sees them as four.[16] The differences are minor because there is a great deal of overlap in the core propositions: (1) stable public rules that are (2) applied equally among citizens and (3) equally between citizens and the government. The three components are more than procedural requirements: they require a substantive commitment to dividing political power in a certain way. But they fall short of constituting a full theory of society because they provide only a framework in which other goals are pursued, not the goals themselves. I examine each in its domestic setting before turning to how they do or do not translate to the interstate context.

Public, Stable Rules

Formal legality describes the sense in which rules must be made such that individuals can distinguish between legal and illegal actions. The rules must be clear and public, they must be forward-looking, they must be written in language that is sufficiently specific, yet they must be designed for general categories of behavior rather than particular incidents. Unless the rules are public, prospective, and somewhat stable, the citizen cannot meaningfully take them into account when acting. As Raz says, "the law should be such that people will be able to be guided by it. … The law must be capable of being obeyed. … It must be such that they can find out what it is and act on it."[17] This underpins Hayek's point that predictability in the law is essential for its contribution to human liberty.[18] The ability to differentiate the lawful from the unlawful undergirds law's capacity to influence decisions, to organize society, and to predict general patterns of mass behavior.

The goal of fixed and known rules is in perpetual tension with the possibility of making changes in the law. Law should be stable, but it must be also open to change and amendment – thus, for instance, when Joseph Raz discusses the stability of the law, he couches it as "relative stability."[19] This is managed in the theory of the rule of law by constructing nontrivial institutional requirements that govern the process for changing laws: Parliamentary approval, for instance, or a plebiscite. The procedural rules on law-making exist to make it more difficult for the state to change existing law, but their existence in some form is necessary to accommodate the possibility of change. Of course, this generates the very real danger that the capacity of the government to change the law will undo the benefits thought to come from "relatively" stable law in the first place, and as a consequence it leads to the second component of the rule of law: subordination of the government itself to the body of law.

Government Limited by Laws

Knowability and stability of the law is not enough. The doctrine of the rule of law also insists on certain forms of equality. One of these is represented by what Tamanaha calls "government limited by law," which is the requirement "the state and its officials are limited by the law" just as are regular citizens (the second is described below as equality of application across cases).[20] The law is binding on all citizens, and all operate in the context of the law. In Dicey's words, this means "not only that with us no man is above the law, but … that here, every man, whatever be his rank or condition, is subject to the ordinary law of the realm and amenable to the jurisdiction of the ordinary tribunals."[21] This is the idea behind the view that "diminishing the absolute power of governments is, of course, the objective of the rule of law."[22] This provision subordinates the government to the law and equalizes individuals and government as subjects of the law. Its absence in a legal system is often described as "rule by law," in which "authoritarian rulers … capitalize on the regime-supporting roles that courts perform while minimizing their utility to the political opposition."[23] As we shall see below, the application of this aspect of the rule of law to the international context is problematic due to the very different nature of governance in the interstate realm.

Rules Applied Consistently across Cases

Finally, the rule of law requires that the law be applied across cases in a particular manner – that judges and government officials follow or apply the relevant body of rules to the situation before them in accordance with laws (or norms) of procedure.[24] This is usually seen as being in distinction to the arbitrary exercise of power of some individuals over others, or to decisions taken based on the particular character or identity of the parties. As Raz has noted, this does not prevent laws that treat different groups or people unequally.[25] Inequalities created by law are inevitable.[26] The rule of law requires only that the terms and categories created by law be applied equally across the cases to which they apply. This element of the concept produces the independent judiciary. Courts, "with the duty of applying the law to cases brought before them and whose judgments and conclusions as to the legal merits of those cases are final,"[27] are a device to implement the dispassionate adjudication of disputes arising in and from law. Other institutions may well serve this purpose as well, or instead, but the independent judiciary is its leading institutional form in domestic societies today.

These three elements combine to constitute a conventional account of the rule of law as an amalgamated concept.[28] Its various components represent answers to different political problems and come from distinct historical processes of contestation.[29] These can be combined in different ways, giving rise to the comparative study of legal systems within the rule-of-law family. They are usually seen as mutually reinforcing and as constituting together a distinct and coherent mode of governance, law, and society. It is this form of society that is often taken to characterize a "normal," modern state: This is the system that the historian Paul Johnson calls it "the greatest public achievement of the second millennium";[30] that the United Nations and others strive to create in post-conflict societies and elsewhere;[31] and that conservatives see themselves as defending against the "creeping instrumentalism" of law unmoored from a consensus over the common good.[32]

Two important consequences are often said to follow from this bundle that give it its normative appeal. First, the rule of law is sometimes said to be the source of citizens' obligation to follow the law. People are required to obey the law as a legal matter in the sense that it is compulsory; they are politically forced to obey by the institutions of the state; and they are morally obligated in that the rule-of-law criteria produce an ethical imperative – if the rules were produced legitimately, it is said, there is a moral obligation on the individual to comply.[33] The rule of law is thus intrinsically linked to the idea of compliance on the part of the subjects and with a particular theory of social order and modern governance. Indeed, the threat of Donald Trump's Presidency to modern society was often framed in terms of damage to the rule of law.[34] As a domestic structure of authority, the rule of law means that everyone is expected to comply with the rules and should be able to trust that others will generally comply.

Second, various good things are assumed to follow from having the legal–political arrangement described above. These might include respect for human rights and dignity, a free press, anti-corruption, private property and transactions, individual autonomy, the capacity to plan in advance, and more. These outcomes give the rule of law its political appeal since it is often thought that it is more likely than other arrangements to produce a good society. This is what Lon Fuller sought to capture with the claim that the rule of law has an "affinity with the good."[35]

The relation between the rule of law and these substantive goals provides the basis for a schism in the rule-of-law literature between thick and thin versions. The thin version sees the concept in institutional/procedural terms as a set of rules and practices that give shape and structure to society and set incentives for individuals. A competing view says that a rule-of-law system cannot exist unless it is substantively devoted to goals like human rights, equality, or justice. This is a "substantive" or "thick" approach to the rule of law and requires that the rules enshrine particular social ends, such as equality or liberty or justice. As an example, the UN Secretary-General in 2004 defined the rule of law as "a principle of governance in which all persons … are accountable to laws that are [among other things] consistent with international human rights norms and standards."[36] A commitment to human rights norms is thereby defined into the very concept of the rule of law. Similarly, Tom Bingham explains the contribution made by the rule of law by describing society as it would exist in its absence:

> [T]he hallmarks of a regime which flouts the rule of law are, alas, all too familiar: the midnight knock on the door, the sudden disappearance, the show trial, the subjection of prisoners to genetic experiment, the confession extracted by torture, the gulag and the concentration camp, the gas chamber, the practice of genocide or ethnic cleansing, the waging of aggressive war. The list is endless.[37]

To produce this list, Bingham assumes that the things he finds abhorrent are illegal, with the result that a perfectly faithful adherence to the rule of law will lead to a world in which these bad things do not happen.

I adopt a thin, formalist model of the rule of law here. This position is agnostic about whether important social goods do or do not follow from the rule of law but insists that they cannot be constitutive of its existence. As Joseph Raz says, it is a mistake to equate "the rule of law with the rule of the *good* law."[38] He is critical of the common tendency to mix the theory of the rule of law with theories of substantive social and political goods. The thick model assumes too much: It suggests that the question to ask about a legal system is how well it institutionalizes a particular set of goals. Not only does this subordinate the rule of law to a prior theory of what those goals are (and presume prior agreement on that theory), but it also makes it hard to ask questions about how a legal system is different from other kinds of governance or morality or politics.

These are some common elements of the rule of law in domestic legal theory. Next, I bring these to bear to think about the rule of law in interstate relations. The domestic materials do not travel well, and the reasons reveal both the differences between domestic and international institutions and also of hidden political life of the rule of law as a concept. This points toward an account of the rule of law for world politics that is built on foundations that are unique to the arrangement of political power and institutions that exist in the international domain.

The Domestic Rule of Law in the International System

The three components of the domestic rule of law encounter difficulties when applied to the international system, each for its own reasons. This section examines these difficulties and uses them to produce a more realistic account of the authority of law in world affairs. The international version of the rule of law cannot be simply inferred from the domestic version. The domestic and international variants developed separately, in response to different political needs and challenges and they are premised on different arrangements of political power.

Public, Stable Laws?

The first component of the domestic rule of law (i.e., that rules be public and stable and forward-looking) has a simple international analogue in the form of the interstate treaty, and more generally in the codification movement from the nineteenth century through the post–World War II period. This roughly overlaps with what Koskenniemi has called the "heroic period" for international law from 1870 to 1960.[39]

Treaties are thought to be valuable because they incorporate both the fixity that is presumed to be required for the rule of law and the consent of the subjects (i.e., states) through ratification by domestic political institutions. These two values are promoted by the legal positivist school into the very definition of international law: in the words of the Permanent Court of International Justice in the *Lotus* case "International law governs relations between independent States. The rules of law binding upon States therefore emanate from their own free will."[40] Consent to a formal text is, for Reinold and Zürn, the most direct means by which international law can achieve its "core objective," which they summarize as to "stabilize actors' normative expectations in an otherwise volatile world and shield them from … the vicissitudes of politics."[41] To do so, it is required "that legal rules display certain features, such as transparency, clarity, non-retroactivity, etc."[42] Treaties are widely assumed to embody these characteristics and therefore the codification of international law is often equated with its "progressive development."[43]

The drive for codified law enacts the first piece of the rule-of-law ideology described above, on the desirability of clear and stable rules. Explicit well-written law is believed to make a particularly powerful contribution to international order. This is reflected in the modern "legalization" project among scholars of law and political science: Goldstein, Kahler, Keohane, and Slaughter suggest that "fully legalized institutions bind states through law: their behavior is subject to scrutiny under general rules, procedures, and discourse of international law and, often, domestic law. Legalized institutions also demonstrate a high degree of precision, meaning that their rules unambiguously define the conduct they require, authorize, or proscribe."[44]

The stability and clarity of the rules are essential in the move to law. Legalization changes the calculations of actors because it specifies whether an action is permitted or not. "The more determinate a standard, the most difficult it is to justify non-compliance," said Thomas Franck.[45]

This idea runs into problems in the international system where individuals – in this case states – have capacity to determine their own legal environment. States choose which legal rules will apply to them and they choose as individuals motivated by their own goals and desires. As a result, a clear rule does not mean a clear obligation on all players. The curious status of unratified treaties reflects the fact that it is state consent to the treaty, rather than the treaty itself, that activates its legal effect.[46] This is different in the domestic version where a law on the books is by definition compelling on citizens (and on their government). The residual autonomy of sovereign states to opt in and out of treaties means that they can tailor their legal obligations to suit their needs and interests: states decline to sign or ratify treaties they disagree with, and they write reservations and understandings that limit or explain their obligations under the treaties that they do ratify. They exit treaties that come to impinge on their decisions in ways that they dislike (see also the contributions by Alter and Morse, this volume).[47]

This is neatly illustrated by Canada's "adjustment" of its relationship with the International Court of Justice (ICJ) in 1994. In the preceding months, Canada had embarked on an activist position toward protecting North Atlantic fish stocks that looked legally dubious in light of multilateral agreements with European fishing states. To pre-empt the possibility of a complaint to the ICJ, Canada revised its optional-clause declaration under Article 36(2) of the ICJ Statute such that it would no longer include any "dispute arising out of or concerning conservation and management measures taken by Canada with respect to vessels fishing in the NAFO [Northwest Atlantic Fisheries Organization] Regulatory Area."[48] With that, its conduct was outside of the jurisdiction of the ICJ and rested instead in the domain of unfettered sovereignty, a fact that the Court affirmed shortly thereafter in the *Etsai* case.[49]

Much of international law is devoted to managing the degrees of freedom that states enjoy in tailoring their legal obligations. The Vienna Convention on the Law of Treaties includes rules on denunciation of and withdrawing from treaties, adding or changing reservations, fundamental changes in circumstances, obligations and government succession, the relation of subsequent treaties to prior treaties on the same subject, etc.[50] These rules limit how states might use the autonomy that they possess to redefine their legal obligations – but they do not eliminate the autonomy of states to remove themselves from unwelcome legal constraints.

In sum, the international legal system cannot satisfy the standard expectation in a rule-of-law society that law be clear and stable and known in advance.[51] No matter how clearly it is written, it cannot indicate whether an action is legal or illegal independent of the identity of the state in question. Because states are free to tailor their commitments to suit their needs and interests, the bundle of laws that attach to each state are unique to that state and the legality of an act may not be determinable as a general matter. What it means to "comply" with international law depends on who is doing it, and what that state has done and said about the rule in the past and what it might do and say in the present case. The same act may be legal when committed by one state but illegal when committed by another; it may be legal when committed toward one state but illegal toward another. The legality of an act is endogenous to the choices of the state in question, rather than independent of it as it is in the domestic setting.

Government Limited by Law?

The second component of the domestic rule of law is the requirement that law apply to the government as well as to the citizens. This is a solution to the problem of despotic leaders. It implies that the legal system should be an instrument for limiting the government's authority over citizens and perhaps subjecting it to the will of the people, somehow defined. It can be seen as preserving the autonomy of the legal sphere from the political,[52] or as ensuring that law is superordinate over government,[53] or as protecting individuals from the state.[54] The international analogue to this is difficult to find: if the international rule of law is understood with reference to how the government is made accountable under law, then what is the international "government"?

The most popular answer may be to say that there is none, on the theory that the interstate political space is missing the central political institution and is therefore an anarchy in a very specific sense. This accords the standard model of "international anarchy" that is represented in international relations theory in various forms by Kenneth Waltz, Hedley Bull, Alexander Wendt, and others. This is the anarchy problematique discussed by the editors of this volume.[55]

This framing of the problem of international law may be sustainable if one takes the narrowest view of what constitutes "government" – a centralized, authoritative, coercive institution kept in power by the twin forces of legitimacy and coercion. This is the thought behind Kant's Second Article for Perpetual Peace: "As nations, peoples can be regarded as single individuals who injure one another through their close proximity while living in the state of nature ... For the sake of its own security, each nation can and should demand that the others enter into a contract resembling the civil one and guaranteeing the rights of each."[56]

However, few scholars today subscribe to this view of international anarchy. Across the range of IR theory perspectives, it is widely accepted that various forms and degrees of governance exist and as a result, scholars have moved away from anarchy and toward research that examines how functions of governance are performed and by whom (for an overview see Daase et al., introduction to this volume). These might include quasi-public regulation by private actors,[57] contracts or coordination among legal equals,[58] Great Power leadership or dominion,[59] pooled sovereignty organizations,[60] transnational class factions,[61] and other legitimated international institutions.[62] While none of these meet a formalist's definition of "government," they provide evidence of disaggregated governance among states and sometimes exercise great influence over the processes of international (and perhaps domestic) life. Harold Koh suggests that we should think of state sovereignty in terms of the functions performed by a sovereign (rather than the centralized bureaucracy that often houses those functions), in which case these diverse institutions of international governance might be said to exercise sovereignty.[63]

If one accepts that "governance without government" exists at the international level,[64] then two possibilities are worth considering as locations for international "government," which might be regulated by the international rule of law: strong states and the UN system. First, the international legal system might be seen as granting the most powerful states a governance role over the community of states, and in this case one can ask whether these agents of governance are subordinate to international law. It is often said that certain states (or the Great Powers as a class) have special responsibilities toward the international system, composed of rights and obligations for the maintenance of international order that do not attach to rank-and-file states. Claims about the importance of Great Power leadership, about hegemonic stability, and about collective security all rest on this premise.[65] In this view, Tamanaha's category of "government limited by law" might be satisfied in the international system by ensuring that the strongest states be bound by international law in their governance of the system. This certainly are in a formal sense, but it is unlikely that the international rule of law can rest on the degree to which the international community or some "leading" states are bound by the law as it is written. On the contrary, it is common to see customary law as changing due to changes in state practice, especially by "leading" states. This is true for both customary law and treaty law and it ensures that the law does not stray too far from the desires of the strongest states. The practice of treating abstentions by permanent members in the Security Council as something other than a veto arose in this way. This has been the consistent practice since the earliest days of the Council and yet it contradicts the plain meaning of the Charter clause that regulates voting in the Council. The first time it was done (in 1946) the irate ambassador from the Soviet Union stormed from the room in protest but its repeated use and its practical advantages quickly extinguished any controversy.[66] Today, it is widely accepted as an informal revision of the Charter, and was affirmed by the ICJ in a 1971 opinion that rejected South Africa's claim that a resolution against it was illegal because three permanent members had abstained when it was passed.[67]

One might alternately identify international "government" with the United Nations or another formal international organization (see contributions by Sending and Witt, this volume). It would then be normal to ask how that body is limited by international law. This may amount to seeing the UN Charter as the constitution of the international system but it need not go that far.[68] The argument is particularly relevant for the UN Security Council with its decisive governing authority over the member states of the UN under the Charter. Its powers include the right to decide when to use force against member states, the right to act on behalf of all states when taking a decision, and the right to decide on its own sphere on competence. Together, these look very much like the Weberian definition of a state: a centralized agent that holds a legal monopoly on the legitimate use of force, and the Security Council may be a kind of world government.[69] Moreover, the Council undoubtedly has the authority to make law that is binding on all states, both in relation to specific threats to international peace and security and more generally in its recent "legislative" mode, insisting on certain policies of all states.[70]

But of course, the Security Council is defined in the Charter as a political rather than a legal organ. Its mandate refers to "threats to international peace and security" rather than violations of international law. Subsequent practice has upheld the view that the Council does not decide legal issues.[71] Council decisions using its powers in Chapter VII are legal demands regarding political policy choices rather than settlements of legal disputes themselves. Even the question of whether the Council itself is required to follow international law is open to debate. It is clear that it must abide by the Charter, but it is arguable whether the Council is superior or subordinate to the rest of international law. The argument for its superiority comes from the fact that the Charter authorizes the Council to impose any solution it desires in response to a threat to international peace and security. It is not limited by international law in doing so. The contrary argument rests on the view that since it is *constituted* by international law through the treaty process it is therefore in no position to act outside it. The *Kadi II* decision of the CJEU asked but did not answer the key question of whether that court could invalidate a duly passed resolution of the Council that conflicts with European law.

It is clear that international organizations are in general bound by international law though with some exceptions whose parameters are debatable: the UN Security Council when acting under Chapter VII of the Charter; the ICJ when deciding a case *ex aequo et bono* under Article 38(2) of the ICJ Statute. But it is equally clear that domestic ideal of a government subordinated under law does not apply unproblematically to the international context since it presumes answers to a host of deep (and perhaps unanswerable) questions about the nature and location of government or governance at the international level.

Rules Applied Consistently across Cases?

The third element commonly cited in the domestic rule of law is that rules should be applied dispassionately and similarly across similar cases. This suggests that the content of the law should be constant, and be applied constantly, regardless of the identity of the actor. As with the other two elements, this idea meets decisive obstacles in the international realm in that international legal obligations are founded on precisely the opposite principle: that the identity of the state is an essential consideration in assessing the international lawfulness of an act.

At one level, the idea of legal equality is central to the self-understanding of international law in that each sovereign state is said to begin as a legal person with equal rights and obligations to all other states. Article 2(1) of the UN Charter codifies this into what amounts to a legal foundation for the interstate system: "The Organization is based on the principle of the sovereign equality of all its Members." In practice, however, this expression of sovereign equality moves the international legal–political system *away from* rather than toward the idea of legal equality as imagined in the domestic rule of law. As authors of their own legal obligations, states are in a different position toward the equal application of the law than are individuals. States' legal rights and obligations cease to be equal as soon as some of them consent to treaties.

Each acquires a distinctive portfolio of obligations, with the effect noted above that the lawfulness of a particular act is therefore variable and depends on which state is doing it. And further, the absence of compulsory jurisdiction means that court decisions must be particularistic rather than general, since states are assumed to *not* be bound by the legal decisions of others. This is explicit in the ICJ Statute, which says

Court decisions "have no binding force except between the parties and in respect of that particular case."[72] Moreover, states have unequal influence on making and remaking international rules, so much so that it is widely accepted that the statements, acts, and interests of some count for more in international legalization, both formally and informally.[73] This is equally true of customary international law as it is of treaties.[74] And while this is sometimes dismissed as merely a deviation from the ideal of equality, it is in fact well integrated into the practices and institutions of legalization and legal interpretation – it has been "normalized" as Simpson and others have shown.[75]

In many areas of international law, there can be no general answer to the legality of an act: from torture to nuclear research to labor standards, to determine what actions are lawful for a state one must first know what rules it has accepted and what reservations or understandings it has imposed on those acceptances. States possess more freedom toward particular rules of international law than is compatible with the rule of law as understood in domestic affairs. They have the legal right to accept or reject rules, and some practical capacity to redefine them. This is particularly striking for strong states, as these are given greater weight in the ongoing interpretation of rules in practice and have greater capacity to write, resist, and enforce rules as they wish.

The international rule of law cannot be deduced from the domestic version, but how then to reconstruct the idea of the rule of law on foundations that make sense in the interstate context? Those same features that differentiate domestic from international show a path to thinking clearly about the international rule of law as a structure of political authority. The particularism of states' specific legal obligations contrasts with the universalism of the rule-of-law ideology. The tension between specific and universalism, contested and accepted, shows a way forward for thinking about the international rule of law. The uncontested universal is the general expectation that states will act in accordance with international law (i.e., the international rule of law); the specific are the particular obligations of individual states. The commitment to the international rule of law creates a political structure in which governments exist. Shirley Scott calls it an ideology.[76]

The International Rule of Law as Political Authority Structure

The use of international law as a legitimating discourse is pervasive in contemporary international politics. This is the constitutional metanorm that makes international diplomacy and politics recognizably contemporary: giving, receiving, and arguing over the legal reasoning that authorizes state acts.[77] States almost without fail provide public explanations for how their behavior is consistent with their legal obligations and they routinely use the charge of "illegality" to delegitimate the acts of others which they oppose. This practice, and the expectation that others will engage in it, provides the structure for world politics. Law is the language that states use to understand and explain their acts, goals, and desires and is both internal and external to state interests.

Taking this approach changes how research is designed on the relations between international law and international politics. It requires abandoning the liberal presumption that the rule of law is a neutral, nonpolitical framework for politics and instead opens up three new lines of inquiry. First, it suggests an explicitly instrumental approach to international law.[78] It is normal for states to construct justificatory arguments for their political positions using the legal resources of the past, adapted to present needs. Legal resources and categories are used to legitimate them by showing them to be lawful. These legal justifications are self-interested and instrumental, but draw on communal resources of international law with its internal logic and particular structure.[79] States are continually engaged in showing that they are complying with their obligations. This is a dialogic process as described by Charles Taylor and shows law to be both constraining and empowering.[80]

Second, it undermines the central role often given to the concept of "compliance" in discussions of international law. The conventional approach to international law operationalizes compliance as "the degree to which state behavior conforms to what an agreement prescribes or proscribes."[81] It is fundamentally positivist, in a social-science sense. When states change their policies to conform to a rule, it is taken as evidence that the rule is having an effect, that the state is a good international citizen, and that the international order is well-functioning. But the political impact of the use of legal justification does not come from the correspondence (or lack thereof) between that justification and an objective measure of compliance; it comes instead from the political process of presenting and contesting the legal justification itself. I take seriously the fact that states routinely construct legal narratives of compliance around their behavior and these are naturally contested by those who oppose that behavior. These narratives are important political contributions[82] – they are productive, and juris-generative, in the process of being fought over.[83] When the core of the rule of law is identified as the use of legal forms in legitimation struggles then the question of whether a state is "complying" with its obligations loses some of its meaning.

Finally, this leads to the inescapable connection between law and power. The ability to provide a legal justification is itself a source of power for states. The inability to do so is disempowering. The utility of legal justification proves its power. This contradicts both the liberal institutionalists, who commonly see legalization as a means to avoid power politics, and the IR realists, who see law's utility in the hands of Great Powers as a reason to pay less attention to legalization. Both have it wrong. The political appeal of "legality" for states is strongly compelling as it gives states the ability to portray their acts as lawful, which brings with it more power. That states value this capacity is evident in the degree to which they strive to justify their acts using the resources of international law, and only by investing in legal justifications can a state get access to their legitimating power.

Conclusion

The domestic rule of law is an invention that is designed to deal with problems arising from the hierarchical arrangement of political power inside a state. The international rule of law addresses a different problem: interdependence among actors and the externalities that arise when jurisdictions are free to make their own decisions. Almost without exception, states invest in explanations that situate their behavior within the law and they promote those aspects of international law that favor their interests. This instrumental use of the law is not a failure of the law, nor is it a problem to be fixed; it is instead the system operating as it was designed. It affirms the concept of the international rule of law: for these justifications to work, there must already exist a widespread belief in the importance of law, compliance, and the rule of law in general. Without a generalized commitment to the rule of law among states, the legitimating function of claims to compliance would not take place.

This image of the international rule of law leads to very different political conclusions regarding the contribution of international law to "global order." It makes it impossible to accept the standard view that international law is a neutral framework for resolving interstate disputes and arranging interstate affairs. It works against the separation of legal from political affairs that is characteristic of the liberal approach to international law and politics. It suggests instead that the effort to structure international politics within a set of rules is a substantive political commitment to the content, not just the form, of those rules, that is: to how it distributes power, resources, opportunity, liability, and more.

References

Alter, Karen. 2013. *The New Terrain of International Law: Courts, Politics, Rights*. Princeton: Princeton University Press.

Ashley, Richard K. 1988. "Untying the Sovereign State: A Double Reading of the Anarchy Problematique." *Millennium* 17(2): 227–262.

Bailey, Sydney D. 1974. "New Light on Abstentions in the UN Security Council." *International Affairs* 50(4): 554–573.

Bingham, Tom. 2010. *The Rule of Law*. London: Penguin.

Bradley, Curtis A. 2007. "Unratified Treaties, Domestic Politics, and the U.S. Constitution." *Harvard International Law Journal* 48: 307–336.

Brooks, Rosa. 2012. "All the Pentagon's Lawyers." *Foreign Policy online* 08/29/12, https://foreignpolicy.com/2012/08/29/all-the-pentagons-lawyers/ [last access 05/12/19].

Brunnée, Jutta, and Stephen J. Toope. 2010. *Legitimacy and Legality in International Law: An Interactional Account*. Cambridge: Cambridge University Press.

Buchanan, Allen. 2007. *Justice, Legitimacy, and Self-Determination: Moral Foundations for International Law*. Oxford: Oxford University Press.

Bull, Hedley. 1977. *The Anarchical Society: A Study in World Order*. Ithaca: Columbia University Press.

Büthe, Tim, and Walter Mattli. 2012. *The New Global Rulers: The Privatization of Regulation in the New Economy*. Princeton: Princeton University Press.

Byers, Michael, and Georg Nolte (eds.). 2003. *United States Hegemony and the Foundations of International Law*. Cambridge: Cambridge University Press.

Cane, Peter. 2002. *Responsibility in Law and Morality*. Oxford: Hart.

Carothers, Tom (ed.). 2006. *Promoting the Rule of Law Abroad: In Search of Knowledge*. New York: Carnegie Endowment for International Peace.

Carr, E. H. 1939. *The Twenty-Years Crisis 1919–1939*. London: Macmillan.

Chesterman, Simon. 2008. "An International Rule of Law?" *American Journal of Comparative Law* 56(2): 331–361.

Chimni, B. S. 2004. "International Institutions Today: An Imperial Global State in the Making." *European Journal of International Law* 15(1): 1–37.

Coulson, David.A. 1986. "How Persistent Must the Persistent Objector Be?" *Washington Law Review* 61: 957–970.

Deitelhoff, Nicole, and Lisbeth Zimmerman. 2020. "Things We Lost in the Fire: How Different Types of Contestation Affect the Robustness of International Norms." *International Studies Review* 22(1): 51–76.

Doyle, Michael W. 2009. "The UN Charter: A Global Constitution?" in Jeffrey L. Dunoff, and Joel P. Trachtman (eds.), *Ruling the World? Constitutionalism, International Law, and Global Governance*. Cambridge: Cambridge University Press, pp. 113–132.

Dumberry, Patrick. 2010. "Incoherent and Ineffective: The Concept of the Persistent Objector Revisisted." *International and Comparative Law Quarterly* 59: 779–802.

Dunoff, Jeffrey L. 2009. "The Politics of International Constitutions: The Curious Case of the World Trade Organization," in Jeffrey L. Dunoff, and Joel P. Trachtman (eds.), *Ruling the World? Constitutionalism, International*

Law, and Global Governance. Cambridge: Cambridge University Press, pp. 178–205.

Dworkin, Ronald. 1986. *Law's Empire*. Cambridge: Belknap Press.

Epstein, Charlotte. 2008. *The Power of Words in International Relations: Birth of an Anti-Whaling Discourse*. Cambridge: MIT Press.

Farrall, Jeremy M. 2007. *United Nations Sanctions and the Rule of Law*. Cambridge: Cambridge University Press.

Foot, Rosemary, S. Neil MacFarlane, and Michael Mastanduno. 2003. *US Hegemony and International Organizations*. Oxford: Oxford University Press.

Forst, Rainer. 2013. *Justification and Critique: Toward a Critical Theory of Politics*. Malden MA: Polity.

Franck, Thomas. 1990. *The Power of Legitimacy among Nations*. Oxford: Oxford University Press.

Fuller, Lon. 1969. *Morality of Law*. New Haven: Yale University Press.

Ginsburg, Tom and Tamir Moustafa (eds.). 2008. *Rule by Law: The Politics of Courts in Authoritarian Regimes*. Cambridge: Cambridge University Press.

Goldsmith, Jack L., and Eric A. Posner. 2006. *The Limits of International Law*. Oxford: Oxford University Press.

Goldstein, Judith, Miles Kahler, Robert O. Keohane, and Anne-Marie Slaughter. 2000. "Introduction: Legalization and World Politics." *International Organization* 54(3): 385–399.

Grenfell, Laura. 2013. *Promoting the Rule of Law in Post-Conflict Societies*. Cambridge: Cambridge University Press.

Hardt, Michael, and Antonio Negri. 2000. *Empire*. Cambridge: Harvard University Press.

Hathaway, Oona. 2007. "Why We Need International Law," *The Nation* 11/01/07, www.thenation.com/article/why-we-need-international-law/ [last access 05/13/19].

Hathaway, Oona A. and Scott J. Shapiro. 2017. *The Internationalists: How a Radical Plan to Outlaw War Remade the World.* New York: Simon & Shuster.

Hayek, Friedrich. 1960. *The Constitution of Liberty*. Abingdon: Routledge.

Hayek, Friedrich A. 1994. *The Road to Serfdom.* Chicago: University of Chicago Press.

Helfer, Lawrence R. 2005. "Exiting Treaties." *Virginia Law Review* 91: 1579–1648.

Higgins, Rosalyn. 1963. *The Development of International Law through the Political Organs of the United Nations*. Oxford: Oxford University Press.

Hurd, Ian. 1997. "Security Council Reform: Informal Membership and Practice," in Bruce Russett, and Ian Hurd (eds.), *The Once and Future Security Council.* New York: St. Martin's Press, pp. 135–152.

Hurd, Ian. 2007. *After Anarchy: Legitimacy and Power in the UN Security Council.* Princeton: Princeton University Press.

Hurd, Ian. 2016. "The Permissive Power of the Ban on War." *European Journal of International Security* 2: 1–18.

Hurd, Ian. 2017. *How to Do Things with International Law*. Princeton: Princeton University Press.

Hurd, Ian. 2020. *International Organizations: Politics, Law, Practice*. 4th ed. Cambridge: Cambridge University Press.

Ikenberry, G. John. 2001. *After Victory: Institutions, Strategic Restraint, and the Rebuilding of Order after Major Wars*. Princeton: Princeton University Press.

Ikenberry, G. John. 2011. *Liberal Leviathan: The Origins, Crisis, and Transformation of the American World Order*. Princeton: Princeton University Press.

Johnson, Paul. 1999. "Laying Down the Law." *The Wall Street Journal* 03/10/99.

Johnstone, Ian. 2008. "The UN Security Council as Legislature," in Bruce Cronin, and Ian Hurd (eds.), *The UN Security Council and the Politics of International Authority*. London: Routledge, pp. 80–104.

Jones, Bruce, Carlos Pascual, and Stephen J. Stedman. 2009. *Power and Responsibility: Building International Order in an Era of Transnational Threats*. Washington DC: Brookings.

Kant, Immanuel. 1983. *Perpetual Peace and Other Essays*. Indianapolis: Hackett.

Koh, Harold H. 1991. "International Public Law Litigation." *Yale Law Journal* 100(8):2347–2402.

Koskenniemi, Martti. 2001. *The Gentle Civilizer of Nations: The Rise and Fall of International Law 1870–1960*. Cambridge: Cambridge University Press.

Koskenniemi, Martti. 2007. "Constitution as Mindset: Reflections on Kantian Themes About International Law and Globalization." *Theoretical Inquiries in Law* 8(1):9–36.

Koskenniemi, Martti. 2009. "The Advantage of Treaties: International Law in the Enlightenment." *The Edinburgh Law Review* 13(1): 27–67.

Kratochwil, Friedrich. 1989. *Rules, Norms, and Decisions: On the Conditions of Legal Reasoning in International Relations and Domestic Affairs*. Cambridge: Cambridge University Press.

Kratochwil, Friedrich. 2014. *The Status of Law in World Society: Meditations on the Role and Rule of Law*. Cambridge: Cambridge University Press.

Krisch, Nico. 2005. "International Law in Times of Hegemony: Unequal Power and the Shaping of the International Legal Order." *European Journal of International Law* 16(3), 369–408.

Lake, David A. 2009. *Hierarchy in International Relations*. Ithaca: Cornell University Press.

Liptak, Adam. 2016. "Donald Trump Could Threaten U.S. Rule of Law, Scholars Say." *New York Times* 06/03/16, www.nytimes.com/2016/06/04/us/politics/donald-trump-constitution-power.html [last access 05/13/19].

McCormick, John P. 2004. "Identifying or Exploiting the Paradoxes of Constitutional Democracy: An Introduction to Carl Schmitt's Legality and Legitimacy," in *Carl Schmitt: Legality and Legitimacy*. Durham: Duke University Press.

Mearsheimer, John J. 1994/95. "The False Promise of International Institutions." *International Security* 19(3): 5–49.

Morgenthau, Hans J. 1967. *Politics among Nations*. New York: Knopf.

Moustafa, Tamir, and Tom Ginsburg. 2008. "Introduction: The Function of Courts in Authoritarian Politics," in Tom Ginsburg, and Tamir Moustafa (eds.), *Rule by Law: The Politics of Courts in Authoritarian Regimes*. Cambridge: Cambridge University Press, pp. 1–22.

Murphy, Colleen. 2005. "Lon Fuller and the Moral Value of the Rule of Law." *Law and Philosophy* 24(3):239–269.

Pauly, Louis, and Edgar Grande. 2005. "Reconstituting Political Authority: Sovereignty, Effectiveness, and Legitimacy in a Transnational Legal Order," in Louis Pauly, and Edgar Grande (eds.), *Complex Sovereignty: Reconstituting Political Authority in the Twenty-First Century*. Toronto: University of Toronto Press, pp. 3–21.

Ratner, Steven R. 2004. "The Security Council and International Law," in David M. Malone (ed.), *The UN Security Council: From the Cold War to the 21st Century*. Boulder: Lynne Rienner, pp. 591–606.

Raz, Joseph. 1977. "The Rule of Law and Its Virtues." *The Law Quarterly Review* 93:195–211.

Reinold, Theresa, and Michael Zürn. 2014. "'Rules about Rules' and the Endogenous Dynamics of International Law." *Global Constitutionalism* 3(2):236–273.

Rosenau, James N., and Ernst-Otto Czempiel (eds.). 1992. *Governance without Government: Order and Change in World Politics*. Cambridge: Cambridge University Press.

Rosenfeld, Michel. 2001. "The Rule of Law and the Legitimacy of Constitutional Democracy." *Southern California Law Review* 74:1307–1351.

Scott, Shirley V. 1994. "International Law as Ideology: Theorizing the Relationship between International Law and International Politics." *European Journal of International Law* 5:313–325.

Secretary-General of the United Nations. 2004. "Report of the Secretary General on 'The Rule of Law and Transitional Justice in Conflict and Post-Conflict Societies.'" S/2004/616.

Shellbourne, Mallory. 2017. "Bharara: Trump Telling DOJ Who to Investigate: 'Terrible' Things for Rule of Law." *The Hill* 11/05/17, https://thehill.com/homenews/sunday-talk-shows/358836-bharara-trump-telling-doj-who-to-investigate-terrible-thing-for [last access 05/13/19].

Simpson, Gerry. 2004. *Great Powers and Outlaw States: Unequal Sovereigns in the International Legal Order*. Cambridge: Cambridge University Press.

Tamanaha, Brian. 2004. *On the Rule of Law: History, Politics, Theory*. Cambridge: Cambridge University Press.

Tamanaha, Brian. 2006. *Law as a Means to an End: The Threat to the Rule of Law*. Cambridge: Cambridge University Press.

Tams, Christian J. 2009. "*Current Developments: Jurisprudence of the International Court of Justice (Case Note: Fisheries Jurisdiction (Spain v Canada) Judgment of 4 December 1998)*," http://papers.ssrn.com/sol3/papers.cfm?abstract_id=1413823 [last access 05/13/19].

Taylor, Charles. 1993. "To Follow a Rule…," in Craig Calhoun, Edward LiPuma, and Moishe Postone (eds.), *Bourdieu: A Critical Reader*. Chicago: University of Chicago Press, 45–61.

Tyler, Tom R. 2006. *Why People Obey the Law*. Princeton: Princeton University Press.

United Nations. 1969. *Vienna Convention on the Law of Treaties*, https://treaties.un.org/doc/Publication/UNTS/Volume%201155/volume-1155-I-18232-English.pdf [last access 05/28/19].

United Nations. 2012. *The Role of the United Nations in International Law*, http://treaties.un.org/doc/source/events/2012/Press_kit/fact_sheet_2_english.pdf [last access 05/13/19]. New York: United Nations.

Veitch, Scott. 2007. *Law and Irresponsibility: On the Legitimation of Human Suffering*. Abingdon: Routledge.
Von Stein, Jana. 2009. "Engines of Compliance," in Jeffrey L. Dunoff, and Joel P. Trachtman (eds.), *Ruling the World? Constitutionalism, International Law, and Global Governance*. Cambridge: Cambridge University Press, pp. 477–501.
Von Stein, Jana. 2017. "Compliance with International Law," *in Oxford Encyclopedia of International Relations*. Oxford: Oxford University Press.
Waltz, Kenneth N. 1979. *Theory of International Politics*. Reading: Addison-Wesley.
Wendt, Alexander E. 1999. *Social Theory of International Politics*. Cambridge: Cambridge University Press.
World Justice Project. 2019. *Research and Data*, www.worldjusticeproject.org/rule-of-law-index [last access 05/28/19].
Wunderlich, Carmen. 2013. "Theoretical Approaches in Norm Dynamics," in Harald Müller, and Carmen Wunderlich (eds.), *Norm Dynamics in Multilateral Arms Control: Interests, Conflicts, and Justice*. Athens: University of Georgia Press, pp. 20–48.

Notes

1 For conversations on these themes and for comments on the manuscript I wish to thank the editors of this volume and its reviewers, as well as Tony Lang, Antje Wiener, Jutta Brunnée, Shirley Scott, Michael Zürn, Rob Howse, Frédéric Mégret, Jennifer Mitzen, Karen Alter, Jens David Ohlin, Sidra Hamidi, Joshua Kleinfeld, and Jan Aart Scholte. This is a revised version of research published in 2015 as "The International rule of law and the domestic analogy" in *Global Constitutionalism* 4(3): 365–395.
2 John H. Jackson in *Restructuring the GATT System* (1990) cited in Dunoff 2009: 185.
3 See for instance Hathaway 2007; Hathaway and Shapiro 2017; von Stein 2017. On liberal order, see Ikenberry 2011. On English School, see Bull 1977. On constructivist rules-based order, see Kratochwil 1989 and 2014. On Marxism, see Chimni 2004.
4 These issues are explored in Hurd 2017.
5 Daase et al., this volume.
6 Daase et al., this volume.
7 For a historical view, see Kant 1983. For a more contemporary perspective, see Bull 1977.
8 Hurd 2017.
9 Scott 1994.
10 Hurd 2016.
11 Brooks 2012; Farrall 2007: 39.
12 In this large literature, see inter alia: Bingham 2010; Ginsburg and Moustafa 2008; Raz 1977; Tamanaha 2004.
13 Tamanaha 2004: chapter 9.
14 Chesterman 2008: 331, 337. Hayek 1960 provides a similar list, with the important addition of a substantive list of rights without which he believes the rule of law cannot exist.
15 Fuller 1969; also Brunnée and Toope 2010 and Murphy 2005.

16 World Justice Project 2019.
17 Raz 1977: 198.
18 Friedrich Hayek, *The Political Ideal of the Rule of Law* (1955) cited in Grenfell 2013: 69.
19 Raz 1977: 198 (emphasis in original).
20 Tamanaha 2004: 114.
21 A.V. Dicey in *An Introduction to the Study of the Law* (1885/1945), cited in Bingham 2010: 4.
22 Alter 2013: 340.
23 Moustafa and Ginsburg 2008.
24 Tamanaha 2004: 126.
25 Raz 1977: 200.
26 Cane 2002; Veitch 2007.
27 Raz 1977: 201.
28 McCormick 2004.
29 See the historical narrative in Bingham 2010.
30 Johnson 1999.
31 See the UN Rule of Law project at www.unrol.org, also Carothers 2006 and Farrall 2007.
32 Tamanaha 2006: 2, chapter 12.
33 For instance, Buchanan 2007. For empirical connections between legitimacy and law, see Dworkin 1986 and Tyler 2006.
34 Liptak 2016; Shellbourne 2017.
35 Lon Fuller cited in Tamanaha 2004: 95.
36 Secretary-General of the United Nations 2004: paragraph 6.
37 Bingham 2010: 9.
38 Raz 1977: 209 (emphasis added); Rosenfeld (2001) observes that the requirements of the rule of law and democracy can conflict.
39 Koskenniemi 2001, 2009.
40 *The Case of the SS. "Lotus" (France* v. *Turkey)*, Judgment of September 7, 1927, PCIJ Series A, No 10, at 18.
41 Reinold and Zürn 2014.
42 Reinold and Zürn 2014: 12.
43 See, for instance, the UN Charter, and United Nations (2012).
44 Goldstein et al. 2000: 385, 387.
45 Franck 1990: 54.
46 Bradley 2007.
47 Helfer 2005.
48 Cited in Hurd 2020.
49 Tams 2009.
50 United Nations 1969.
51 Hurd 2017.
52 Reinold and Zürn 2014: 12.
53 Raz 1977: 203.
54 Hayek 1994.
55 Daase et al., this volume. See also Bull 1977; Waltz 1979; Wendt 1999. The "anarchy problematique" is from Ashley 1988.
56 Kant 1983.
57 Büthe and Mattli 2012.

58 Lake 2009.
59 Simpson 2004.
60 Pauly and Grande 2005.
61 Chimni 2004.
62 For instance, the UN Security Council: Hurd 2007.
63 Koh 1991.
64 The phrase is from Rosenau and Czempiel 1992.
65 The literature on the special role of Great Powers, singly or collectively, in generating international order is large and varied. It includes classical writings on great power politics including Bull 1977; Carr 1939; Morgenthau 1967. It also encompasses significant strands of writing on the needs of US foreign policy such as Ikenberry 2001; Jones et al. 2009. A more critical variant sees it as an aspect of hegemony or empire: Byers and Nolte 2003; Foot et al. 2003; Hardt and Negri 2000; Simpson 2004.
66 Bailey 1974: 554.
67 South Africa's argument does suggest that the consensus is something short of universal, or at least that there remains an opening for the strategic use of their complaint when it serves their interests. On informal Charter amendments, see Hurd 1997.
68 See Doyle 2009.
69 Hurd 2007: chapter 7.
70 The binding quality of Council decisions is established at the intersection of articles 25 and 39 of the Charter. See also Farrall 2007. On the Council's move into something resembling global "legislation" see Johnstone 2008.
71 On the distinction between legal and political matters in the UN, see Higgins 1963 and Ratner 2004.
72 Article 59, Statute of the ICJ.
73 *Inter alia* Krisch 2005: 369.
74 For customary law, state agency is preserved by the persistent objector rule (see Coulson 1986: 957). For a critique of the concept of the persistent objector, see Dumberry 2010: 779.
75 Simpson 2004.
76 Scott 1994: 313.
77 Hurd 2017.
78 I mean "instrumental" here in the sense of being implicated in the agent's interests, in Tamanaha 2004, and not in the sense used by Koskenniemi 2007. Tamanaha warns against instrumentalism, as a nefarious dangerous development, but I suggest it is elemental to the international legal–political system.
79 This makes possible a dynamic interaction between legal resources and state interests, as outlined in Wunderlich 2013.
80 The "sceptics" of international law and institutions generally forget the empowering half of this pair. For instance, Goldsmith and Posner 2006; Mearsheimer 1994/95. Charles Taylor explains dialogic in Taylor 1993.
81 von Stein 2009: 478.
82 For instance Forst 2013.
83 On the productive and law-producing capacity of justifications in world politics, see Epstein 2008. On forms of contestation, see Deitelhoff and Zimmermann 2020.

Part III

Resisting Rule

8 Exploring Relations of Rule and Resistance in Global Politics

Christopher Daase and Nicole Deitelhoff[1]

If rule is theorized at all in International Relations (see Daase et al., this volume), it is mostly conceptualized in terms of obedience and compliance, rather than in terms of resistance or contestation. A legacy of Max Weber, who defined the concept of "rule" first and foremost as *legitimate* rule, that is "authority," this notion has persisted to this day where it prevails in the dominant liberal understanding of rule and international order (see Onuf, this volume). In this chapter, we follow a different path by reconstructing international rule through an analysis of resistance. Conceptualizing rule as "constellations of formally or informally institutionalized sub- and superordination with the aim of affecting the distribution of basic goods and influence and of stabilizing expectations, regardless of whether these constellations are primarily of socio-cultural, economic, or military nature" (Daase et al., this volume), we want to shed light on the relational dimension of rule, by analyzing the dynamic relationship between (forms of) rule and (forms of) resistance at the global level. To this end, we distinguish between two forms of resistance – namely opposition and dissidence – in order to show how resistance and rule implicate and influence each other.

The second part of this chapter begins by discussing our understanding of rule and resistance as part of a reciprocal referential context. We argue that resistance is part and parcel of illegitimate *and* legitimate rule and can therefore help to reconstruct manifestations and transformations of global rule. We distinguish between "opposition," as a form of resistance that accepts the existing political order as such and makes use of the established rules of political involvement to express its dissent, and "dissidence," as a form or resistance that rejects the rules of the political order and chooses unconventional forms of organization and articulation to advance a radical critique of rule. We argue that the mechanisms of transition between opposition and dissidence are linked to the transformation of rule, even though the specific cause-and-effect relationships have to be established on a case-by-case basis. After illustrating our conceptualization based on four short case studies in the third part of this chapter, we address open questions in the conclusion and summarize our plea for an understanding of rule that takes its relational dimension seriously to enable us to better theorize and observe the dynamics of rule in international politics.

Conceptualizing Rule and Resistance

As described in the introductory chapter to this volume, we understand rule as asymmetric power relations that are of a certain duration and are reinforced by formal or informal institutions. Hence, rule signifies a constellation of institutionalized sub- and superordination with the aim of affecting the distribution of basic goods and influence, regardless of whether these constellations are primarily of sociocultural, economic, or military nature (Daase et al., this volume). This broad concept helps us avoid normative connotations as far as the legitimacy of rule is concerned. It neither equates rule with "authority" by conceptualizing rule as the voluntary compliance of subjects and subordinates,[2] nor denounces rule as "domination" by emphasizing coercion and suppression by rulers. In fact, these qualifications refer to various conceptions of rule that we can study, focusing on the extent and quality of resistance exercised by subordinates. This conceptualization also allows us to reconstruct rule in terms of resistance, both empirically and theoretically: Empirically, because rule per se is rarely observable in international politics, becoming visible principally if resistance forms that requires countering, and theoretically, because we believe that rule is more precisely conceptualized through the enforcement of power than through voluntary compliance. Rule, then, is no longer that which is more or less voluntarily obeyed but that which is more or less coercively enforced. This implies that rule requires resistance just as resistance requires rule.[3]

Compliance vs. Resistance

The claim that no rule exists without resistance is controversial, however, and there is continuing interest in identifying rule as voluntary compliance.[4] Hannah Arendt once chose to explain the submission of men and women in totalitarian systems as voluntary obedience and deference.[5] However, focusing on compliance tends to lose sight of resistant practices, as anti-colonial resistance did in Arendt's book on violence[6] or the resistance of Jewish prisoners in concentration camps in her book on Eichmann.[7] Only if rule is seen as necessarily implicating resistance, do such practices become visible and dissent and objection apparent. Undoubtedly, the more totalitarian rule becomes, the more the spaces for resistance shrink. Conversely, the more legitimate a constellation of super- and subordination becomes, the less such spaces are needed. Both of these extreme cases make it rather difficult to identify resistance empirically. And yet, to claim that rule may exist without resistance does not make much sense sociologically. For if that order and obedience coincide, the basic relationship that constitutes rule as a form of sociation (*Vergesellschaftung*) disappears.[8] Totalitarian rule and freedom from rule (*Herrschaftsfreiheit*) would be indistinguishable.

The conceptualization of rule through resistance allows us to grasp the problem of freedom from rule – as a situation in which resistance is no longer necessary – and that of totalitarianism – as a situation, in which resistance is no longer possible – more precisely. Rule is totalitarian if the possibility of resistance is almost completely destroyed. But only *almost* completely, since even if compliance is coerced through the most brutal means and even where domination is exercised through extermination, forms of resistance have existed, which have kept the idea of an alternative political order alive.[9] Only if this idea disappears and all hopes are shattered, could we speak of a completely totalitarian system, but for logical reasons not of totalitarian rule. Similarly, legitimate rule might be a situation in which there is no need for resistance, since almost all men and women in almost all situations believe in the rightfulness and justice of the conditions. That said, there may still be people who feel the need to voice dissent or exercise resistance even if they do not have a good reason to do so, and they need to have the right and the possibility to exercise that resistance. If the right to and possibility of resistance, along with the need to resist, completely disappear, rule too disappears, even legitimate rule.[10]

Rule does not always arise with a claim to legitimacy that justifies its coercive character. Rule can also fail to generate legitimacy. Ultimately, the different claims to legitimacy (and their acceptance) only determine the character of rule (referred to as conceptions in the introduction to this volume), not its existence. Although we consider rule to be a structural phenomenon, our focus nevertheless remains on the actors. They occupy different positions within a constellation of institutionalized super- and subordination, which open up certain possibilities for action and exclude others.[11] The constellation can be uniformly hierarchical, with a clearly recognizable center to which everything is subordinated, one example being the nation-state. But it can just as well rest on a set of institutionalized relations of super- and subordination without a single recognizable center to arbitrate collisions between these relations. Therefore, rule can also be ordered in a "heterarchical" way[12] as a juxtaposition and superimposition of vertically and horizontally structured partial orders.[13]

Constellations of institutionalized super- and subordination can also vary with regard to the form of power they embody. Some are based on formal legal regulation (see chapters by Alter and Hurd, this volume), others rather on discursive or performative power (see Sending 2017; Sending, this volume), on structural power in the classical sense (that is, as the power to set the agenda), or on an unequal distribution of resources (see also Morse and Alter, this volume);[14] but, of course, they can also turn out to involve or produce coercive power strengthened by physical force.[15] Similar to a claim to legitimacy, these different forms of power only represent different manifestations of the exercise of rule, but they do not really help in distinguishing rule from non-rule.

However, the more rule occurs outside the context of formal legal control and the less it relies on or produces direct coercion, the harder it becomes to grasp it empirically. This is particularly problematic at the global level, where it is difficult to identify a uniform system of super- and subordination, but instead there is a myriad of varying constellations of overlapping and competing forms of super- and subordination. Such heterarchical orders of rule can rarely be analyzed as manifestly coercive arrangements (such as, e.g., in the case of colonial power) or asymmetrical institutions (such as in the case of unequal treaties). Instead, they need to be identified in discourse, in the presence and absence of bodies of rules, and in the analysis of possibilities of and limits to action (see also Lake, this volume, drawing on ecology theory).[16] This is why they can best be described on the basis of resistance. The study of resistance makes asymmetrical power relations visible and unveils the mechanisms of generating obedience. Rule, as institutionalized power, does have a tendency to marginalize resistance, whether by generating legitimacy and voluntary compliance or through coercion and oppression, but resistance remains a necessary component of rule, whether the latter is exercised subtly or with brute force.

While a focus on resistance can help to identify structures of rule in the context of international institutions that often go unnoticed with more conventional approaches, it is not able to determine the legitimacy or illegitimacy of such structures by itself.[17] Right-wing dissidents criticizing the international financial order might portray transnational banks as an expression of a global Jewish conspiracy. Such protest highlights structures of rule situated in transnational banks, especially the international regulation of these banks, but the kind of power behind it is misinterpreted. Thus, while our approach follows the logic of a sociology of critique that starts from the subjects of rule, we do not overestimate the cognitive capacities of these subjects but trace their resistance and contrast it with an analysis of the respective institutional structures.

Opposition and Dissidence as Forms of Resistance

Drawing on the discussion above, rule always entails resistance because it ultimately rests on coercion. Nevertheless, the quality and extent of resistance that rule gives rise to can vary. It can be limited to individual decisions (or nondecisions) of specific regulatory bodies or *policies*; it can focus on decision-making structures and institutions (*politics*); or it can reject the political order in its entirety, that is, the fundamental norms and principles, rules, and institutions of that order (*polity*).

Furthermore, resistance can also employ different means: It can draw on the applicable rules of the game of political participation accepted in a given political order, or, it can reject these rules and resort to means that lie outside the realm of accepted engagement. We refer to the former form of resistance as opposition and to the latter as dissidence. Think, for example, of signature campaigns by Greenpeace, on the one hand, and arson attacks by the Earth Liberation Front, on the other, as different forms of articulating resistance to the logging of old-growth forests.[18] Common to both forms is that they formulate – albeit in varying degrees – political alternatives to the ruling order, but they differ quite fundamentally over whether they accept that order and the applicable rules of the game of political participation and comply with them (opposition) or whether they reject or deliberately violate these rules (dissidence). Of course, opposition and dissidence are ideal types, and especially in the context of group phenomena, we would not expect to find them in pure form, but rather to observe approximations of one of the two types.

In addition, we would also expect transitions between these forms. The development of the student protest into an urban guerilla movement and then into the terrorist attacks of the Red Army Faction in Germany would be an extreme example of such a transition from opposition to dissidence. Conversely, the evolution of the IRA into Sinn Féin in Northern Ireland might be an example of a transition from dissidence into opposition. Some would also argue that Greenpeace has taken this path, becoming increasingly more mainstream in its environmental protection activities. What then does this tell us about the nature of rule?

Drawing on empirical research on democracy in the tradition of Robert Dahl, we come to the conclusion that the nature and extent of resistance within a political order is an expression of its level of democracy. For Dahl, the right to engage in opposition represents a key step in the (historical) democratization of Western societies (in addition to the right to representation and the right to vote).[19] The more structures of rule provided their members with spaces to articulate dissent and resistance, the stronger the principle of political equality became in the respective systems.[20] At the same time – and this is the central observation for our purpose – this involved the moderation of dissent. In other words, the greater the opportunities to participate in the system of rule and the more space accorded to resistance, the more the resistance lost its radical dissident character (in Dahl's words "system opposition" or "revolutionary opposition") and turned into opposition that seeks to exercise influence from within the applicable rules of the game.[21] A key factor in explaining the transition from dissidence to opposition is the character of the structure of rule and the changes it undergoes.

However, this process can go in both directions. It can also lead from opposition to dissidence, which becomes likely when the spaces for articulating resistance and for political participation begin to shrink. Dahl was not as concerned with autocratic systems as we are today. He was more concerned with the structural changes in the modes of governance of modern nation-states that emerged after the end of World War II. He feared that classical political arenas would be circumvented and the spaces of resistance in political decision-making would shrink, thus rendering political participation ineffective.[22] The more policy-making withdraws from political institutions, such as parliament, and migrates into informal or international bodies, such as policy networks or negotiation systems, the less opportunity there is for dissent to gain a hearing. According to Dahl, this would result in an alienation of the citizens from their system,[23] which renders a radicalization of resistance more likely.[24] Similarly, research on radicalization in social movements has demonstrated that the likelihood of radicalization increases, the more repression a movement meets with and the more it is ignored.[25]

Turning to our focus, the relational dimension of rule, we would assume that the nature of resistance is impacted by the nature of rule. Hence, we would assume that the more radical the resistance (dissidence), the more closed the ruling order, achieved either by narrowing down opportunities for political participation or by avoiding political debate (circumventing arenas of political debate). While we cannot test this assumption in any meaningful way in this chapter, we will demonstrate its usefulness for a study of international rule, applying it to four short case studies of typical expressions of resistance and the changes they have undergone in international politics. A note of caution is in order, however, because we do not expect to observe a clear-cut causal relationship between rule and resistance. Rule and resistance are interdependent, but the way in which they impact each other might vary greatly: Neither do we know for certain what is cause and what is effect in this relationship, nor do we know what kind of context conditions apply to a particular relationship in a given context. Identifying the factors that drive the dynamics of rule and resistance would be the main task for a research program that places the problem of rule at the center of an analysis of global politics.

Illustrative Case Studies

If rule and resistance are impacting each other, as we have tried to demonstrate in the previous section, it should also be possible to draw conclusions from the analysis of resistance regarding the nature of rule and its transformations. To illustrate this, we draw on four case studies of resistance toward international institutions. Our cases refer to (the change in) the Indian government's resistance toward the nuclear non-proliferation regime, the radicalization of resistance by African states vis-à-vis the International Criminal Court (ICC), the ebbs and flows in the resistance of the alterglobalization movement against global economic institutions, and the increasing resistance of states toward the international whaling regime. Taken together, our cases cover a broad range of policy issues, from nuclear arms control to environmental protection, free trade, and human rights protection. They include both non-state and state opponents and range from very narrow to very broad objectives of resistance. However, all four cases display a clear dynamic of radicalizing resistance that we can trace back to the evolution of constellations of rule, embodied in the institutions and institutional fields they address. Our first two cases highlight radicalization in reaction to a closing off of rule vis-à-vis opposition. The increasing radicalization of the resistance of the Indian government to the Treaty on the Non-Proliferation of Nuclear Weapons (NPT) to the point of dissidence, which culminated in the open testing of its own nuclear weapons, corresponds to significant change in the NPT regime that drastically reduced the space for legitimate opposition. Similarly, the radicalization of state resistance toward the international whaling regime in the 1990s and 2000s relates to an institutional dynamic in which a group of states used established procedures to reduce the space for opposition. The situation is less clear in the two remaining cases. In the case of non-state resistance, radicalization within the anti-globalization movement directed at the global economic institutions can be observed, although the institutions under attack began to open up to criticism.[26] Hence, radicalization followed an extension of opportunities for political participation. In a similar vein, the radicalization of resistance, on the part of several African countries and the African Union (AU), in particular, toward the ICC seems to have occurred despite an institutional context with broad and equal opportunities for participation. However, we will show that radicalization in these two cases also corresponded to a shrinking of space for participation. Neither the opening up of the world economic institutions nor the extensive rights to participate in the ICC constituted effective rights to participation. When this became apparent to the opponents, radicalization set in.

Nuclear Dissidence and the System of Rule of Nonproliferation

The nuclear nonproliferation regime has been described as a normative order based on a strong norm of prohibition in the form of the "nuclear taboo."[27] So far, the taboo has been interpreted as relating to the *use* of nuclear weapons, but it also refers to the possession of nuclear weapons, which, according to the NPT, is permitted only to those states that initiated a nuclear explosion before January 1, 1967. For all other states, possession of nuclear weapons is strictly prohibited. To the extent that this prohibition extends beyond the members of the NPT, we can speak of a taboo also with regard to the possession of nuclear weapons.[28] India's breaking of this taboo through its nuclear testing in 1998 and its development of nuclear weapons has been interpreted as an expression of the pursuit of power by an emergent regional hegemon or as an effect of a regional arms race on the Indian subcontinent. But if Indian foreign and security policy is seen in relation to the taboo of possession and as a shift from nuclear opposition to nuclear dissidence, it becomes clear that the nuclear order had become an increasingly rigid system of rule, leaving ever-diminishing space for justified dissent.

The indefinite extension of the NPT in 1995 was a crucial moment for India's change in policy and decision to test nuclear weapons. India had been a proponent of nuclear disarmament since its independence[29] but at the same time kept the option of acquiring its own nuclear arsenal open.[30] Thus, although Jawaharlal Nehru advocated the development of a military nuclear infrastructure, he spoke out against building nuclear weapons. In 1967, India voted against the NPT and, to this day, has remained one of its most vehement critics on account of the treaty's "discriminatory" character. In 1974, after the third Indo-Pakistani War and in the wake of the arrival of the Seventh U.S. Fleet, which Henry Kissinger sent into the Bay of Bengal to intimidate India, India decided to conduct its first nuclear test, which it described as a "peaceful nuclear explosion." Despite this move, India avoided testing nuclear weapons over the next 24 years and pursued a policy of nuclear opposition, calling for full nuclear disarmament. It was only in 1998, shortly after the indefinite extension of the NPT and under the government of the nationalist Bharatiya Janata Party (BJP), that India decided to conduct open nuclear weapons tests, thus opting for nuclear dissidence.

It cannot be claimed that the indefinite extension of the NPT was the direct cause of India's nuclear weapons tests, no more than the Indian nuclear bomb is the cause of the crisis of the nonproliferation regime. But it is evident that the two events are in a reciprocal relation of rule and resistance and that the international nuclear order was destabilized when the nuclear weapon states tried to entrench their nuclear rule indefinitely. To understand the causal mechanism behind the delegitimation of the original regime, it is important to understand the nuclear taboo not only as a prohibition norm[31] but as a social hierarchy.[32] Sociologically speaking, taboos serve to stabilize asymmetric structures of rule through the "direct harnessing of religion to extra-religious purposes."[33] In this sense, the nuclear taboo has not only prohibited the use of nuclear weapons but also established an unequal social order based on the distinctions between conventional and nuclear weapons, between military and political use, and between the legitimate and illegitimate possession of those weapons. The foundation of this system of rule is the shared conviction that nuclear weapons are singular insofar as they confer not only material but also, as it were, spiritual power. It is this power that has made the nuclear weapon states into something akin to the charismatic "priests" of the global nuclear order, whose task is to uphold the central classifications of the taboo.

In 1995, this order crumbled when, by extending the treaty indefinitely, the nuclear weapon states tried to transform the inherently transitory charismatic order into a legal order that promised to be more durable. Max Weber describes the legalization of charisma as "routinization" by which power and status owing to extraordinary events or abilities are turned "into a permanent possession of everyday life."[34] This is what the nuclear weapon states did. They turned their charismatic rule into legal rule. But instead of stabilizing the nuclear order, they destabilized it by undermining the legitimacy of the nuclear taboo.

The date of January 1, 1967, as an abstract criterion of the legitimate possession of nuclear weapons, was only a weak obfuscation of an inherently arbitrary classification that favored the states already possessing nuclear weapons.[35] But from the beginning of the NPT negotiations, the willingness of the non-nuclear weapon states to accept this classification and to recognize the nuclear charisma of the nuclear weapon states was subject to a reservation enshrined in Article VI of the NPT, namely the *bona fide* intention on the part of the nuclear weapon states to take effective measures to achieve complete nuclear disarmament. The establishment of regular review conferences – a novelty in diplomacy – served to maintain the balance between respect and rejection of nuclear rule: respect for the legitimate order of inequality and rejection of the illegitimate claim for domination of the nuclear haves over the nuclear have-nots.[36] Only because the non-nuclear weapon states periodically had the opportunity to extend the NPT for a further five-year period or to withdraw their consent could they consider the inequality of the treaty not to be pure domination but instead a temporary requirement for a stable nuclear order. It was precisely the conditionality and the provisional nature of the regime that guaranteed its legitimacy and fragile stability.

This changed with the indefinite extension of the NPT. Although the extension was welcomed in principle, the contradiction in the global nuclear order was exacerbated and the erosion of the regime accelerated. The "great bargain" that non-nuclear weapon states refrain from acquiring and possessing nuclear weapons as long as the nuclear weapon states engage in nuclear disarmament had lost its logical link. From 1995 on, the rule of the nuclear weapon states rested on a statutory system, which transformed the nondiscriminatory taboo into a discriminatory legal norm. Contradictions in charismatic leadership remain latent as long as the duration of the claim to rule is indeterminate and the social order it creates is regarded as temporary. But contradictions become manifest if charismatic leadership is turned into legal rule, which is designed to be permanent and whose institutions claim indefinite validity. This is the reason why the classification into nuclear weapon states and non-nuclear weapon states was acceptable during the Cold War but could not serve as the basis of legal rule in a multipolar world.

The first round of nuclear dissidence was dominated by states such as India, Pakistan, Libya, Iran, and North Korea, which for various reasons challenged nuclear rule by producing or attempting to produce nuclear weapons themselves. A different kind of resistance to the nuclear order emerged after the NPT Review Conference in 2010, a resistance that initially articulated itself as opposition but has increasingly presented itself as a dissident movement by offering a counter-norm of nuclear abolition.[37] In 2017, 122 nations voted for a Treaty on the Prohibition of Nuclear Weapons calling for their total elimination. Both, the nuclear dissidence of unofficial nuclear weapon states like India and the nuclear opposition of states promoting nuclear prohibition is not only a sign of global "impatience"[38] but a sign of growing resistance to nuclear rule.

The Turn to Dissidence in the International Whaling Commission

Whaling may not be the first thing that comes to mind in a discussion about international resistance, yet the moratorium on commercial whaling, as agreed upon by the International Whaling Commission (IWC), has attracted resistance from the very beginning. This resistance increasingly turned into dissidence once it became obvious that what was initially thought of as a temporary ban (technically not even a ban but a reduction of catch quotas to zero) was to be transformed into a permanent prohibition norm by its proponents.[39]

In 1946, the International Convention for the Regulation of Whaling (ICRW) was adopted. It was designed to collect data on whale stocks to secure their conservation in the future and to help the whaling industry develop a proper basis. To do so, states created the IWC to coordinate and commission the collection of data and to agree on adequate catch quotas for the specific whale populations. Because the commission was deeply influenced by the whaling industry, whale stocks nevertheless soon became exhausted.[40]

Faced with an impassioned dynamic environmental movement that began to emerge in the 1960s and 1970s, the IWC increasingly came under pressure to do something about commercial whaling. The movement aimed at a complete ban on all whaling activities. It was particularly successful in the USA, which changed its position on whaling and became an outspoken opponent. In the years that followed, many former whaling states joined the US and became opponents of whaling as well. In 1982, the IWC agreed on a moratorium on commercial whaling. This shift in the IWC's position was also the result of a number of non-whaling states entering the commission and changing the power relations between whaling states and their opponents.[41]

The moratorium came into force in 1986. It prohibits commercial whaling (by reducing catch quotas to zero) but allows whaling for scientific reasons and aboriginal subsistence whaling. The moratorium was supposed to stay in place until more reliable data was available on the restoration of whale stocks so that new catch quotas could be agreed upon.[42] Since then, however, the anti-whaling states have prevented all attempts to lift the ban, also utilizing an institutional feature of the IWC. To change the IWC schedule responsible for setting catch quotas, a three-quarters supermajority of all member states is required. Since anti-whaling states were at least a blocking minority, they could hijack the IWC, preventing even so much as a debate on the moratorium. Thus, what was meant to be a temporary ban to allow whale populations to recover in fact became a permanent prohibition norm.[43]

From the beginning, several states (including Japan, Norway, Iceland, and the Soviet Union) were opposed to the moratorium, lodging their objections with the IWC, while only one state, Canada, withdrew from the commission and the convention altogether. Nevertheless, also as a result of increasing pressure from the US government, most whaling states had ceased their whaling programs by the end of the 1980s.[44]

While discourses within the IWC on the precise meaning of scientific whaling and aboriginal subsistence whaling continued throughout this time, things changed dramatically once it became clear that what was introduced as a temporary ban in the 1980s was now being pursued as a permanent prohibition. Throughout the 1990s, pro-whaling states called for a new assessment of the ban, arguing that whale stocks should have recovered to varying degrees. However, the anti-whaling states prevented that any agreement could be reached on that.[45] As a consequence, states such as Norway or Iceland, while being in opposition to the ban all along began to turn into dissidents, rejecting the ban in its entirety and resuming whaling.[46] Norway resumed commercial whaling in 1993, Iceland officially resumed scientific whaling in 2002 and commercial whaling in 2006. Japan started scientific whaling in 1987, right after the whaling moratorium came into force, through programs in the Antarctic (JARPA I and II, closed in 2014) and the North Pacific (JARPN I and II, commenced in 1994). Russia, Greenland, St. Vincent and the Grenadines, and the USA have taken up aboriginal whaling. Additionally, resistance to the whaling ban has become increasingly connected to anti-colonialism as it is portrayed as fighting for a right to sustainable use of natural resources and against a "Western" environmental movement making dietary decisions for the rest of the world.[47] This shift is a result of whaling states trying to shift majorities by convincing states of the Global South to join the IWC.

Thus, resistance has increasingly shifted from opposition to dissidence against the institutional rules that have changed the international whaling regime. What began as a temporary ban on commercial whaling was hijacked by anti-whaling states to make it a permanent prohibition of commercial whaling. Making use of the awkward decision-making procedures of the IWC, these states denied the opponents of the ban any chance of even putting the matter on the agenda, thus reducing the space for opposition dramatically. As a consequence, the acceptance of the whaling moratorium plummeted (see also Deitelhoff and Zimmermann 2020: 70).

Dissidence of the Alterglobalization Movement vis-a-vis Global Economic Institutions

The protests of the alterglobalization movement emerged in the 1990s, peaking in the mid-2000s. These protests have become synonymous with resistance to international institutions and their simmering legitimacy crisis. The movement criticizes the hegemony of neoliberal capitalism and the lack of democratic legitimacy of international economic institutions and declares: "Another world is possible."[48] As "resistance"[49] or "globalization from below,"[50] it is sometimes celebrated in post-structuralist and post-Marxist theories as the first genuinely counter-hegemonic movement, if not a "postmodern prince,"[51] with the potential to break up the global neoliberal ruling structures.[52]

Although heterogeneous as regards the goals, strategies, and ideologies of the organizations it brings together,[53] the movement has captured enormous public attention. Its frequent protests have been described as a wave of politicization that places international institutions under pressure to justify their increasingly invasive encroachments on the lives of individual citizens and their lack of democratic legitimacy.[54]

This persistent criticism has not left the global economic institutions unmoved. In search of ways and strategies to restore their legitimacy in the eyes of the public,[55] the institutions reformed their policy guidelines. In addition, they began a gradual opening up of their institutions by establishing dialogue forums for the activists. However, these forums have met with a mixed reception at best. Although non-governmental organizations, in particular, accepted the invitations, a majority of the opponents – chiefly activist groups – rejected it and intensified their resistance. As they saw it, the forums were a thinly disguised attempt to divide the movement and silence its critics.[56] Although the global economic institutions, in particular the World Bank and World Trade Organization, seemed to create more space for political participation, no moderation of the resistance could be observed (or if it was, it was only sporadic). On the contrary, in fact, if anything, it was radicalization that was seen. At first glance, this development speaks against the assumption that restricted spaces for resistance lead to a radicalization of international resistance as well. However, a closer look at the dialogue forums shows that they did not really represent any kind of expansion of the scope for political participation.

The forums were extremely narrowly defined across the board, as O'Brien et al. show in a systematic study of the interaction between transnational social movements and global economic institutions.[57] This already began with the fact that the institutions were very selective in the invitations they issued to the forums, addressing them primarily to their moderate critics, while more radical voices were often not admitted in the first place.[58] Conversely, when access was open, the forums themselves were correspondingly restricted in their mandate. Activists were permitted to ask questions, for example, but only on predefined topics and under narrow time constraints that largely precluded discussion.

O'Brien et al. even conjecture that the global economic institutions deliberately used these forums to split and diffuse the growing resistance and to guarantee the smooth operation of the institutions.[59] In this respect, dialogue forums were more of an attempt to restore the consensus on the rationality of the institutions and were not conceived as an opening up to the critics.

In short, the forums did not permit equal access to or opportunities to exercise influence over decision-making. Instead they restricted the political alternatives to predetermined criteria that corresponded to the rationality of the institution and systematically excluded more radical voices.[60] In particular, even if they had had a chance to participate at the start, the majority of the activist groups within the alterglobalization movement ultimately turned their back on the forums.[61] They regard the global economic institutions across the board as so entangled in a hegemonic discourse of neoliberal ideology that any interaction could only lead to co-optation or, even worse, to a reinforcement of this discourse.[62] Thus these activist groups express a form of dissidence. Because of their intransigence, these groupings were increasingly described as apolitical. Their stress on street protest, civil disobedience, and carnivalesque forms of protest was branded as irrational, given that they had the opportunity to participate in "normal" politics.[63] An increase in repressive measures can also be observed in dealings with the groups within the movement. These include the by now almost military security cordons around the buildings in which major summits are held, heightened police repression of such direct action at transnational summits, and the relocation of summits to regions with comparatively weak human rights protection regimes. In sum, the opening up to political participation as promoted by global economic institutions in response to growing opposition to their policies was often more of a tactic to avoid political debate and an empty promise of participation that frustrated critics.[64]

Dissidence in the International Criminal Court

Our last case concerns the rising resistance to the ICC seen on the African continent, which is often described as either a result of the unjustified focus of the court's investigations on the African continent or as an acknowledgment by African governments that they had no control over the court. While both lines of argument certainly feed into the pattern of resistance to the court, a perspective on rule highlights that radicalization was equally fueled by superficial opportunities for participation that were perceived as a betrayal (see Deitelhoff 2020).

The ICC is usually heralded as a major normative innovation in the international system. For the first time, a permanent court had been established, mandated to prosecute individuals for core crimes under international law, including war crimes, genocide, crimes against humanity, and more recently even the crime of aggression.[65] Nevertheless, the court has attracted substantial resistance in the last decade, specifically from the AU and several African countries.[66]

Resistance on the African continent already emerged in the context of the court's early investigations in Uganda and the Democratic Republic of Congo. However, this resistance was rather modest, questioning the prosecutor's specific activities but not the court as such. This changed dramatically in the aftermath of the court's investigation following the arrest warrant for Omar Al-Bashir, then President of the Sudan. Unlike its earlier cases on the African continent, the investigation of the situation in Darfur was based on a referral to the court by the UN Security Council in 2005, that is, without the consent of the Sudanese government (UNSC Resolution 1593/2005). Once the ICC prosecutor had issued a warrant for the arrest of Omar Al-Bashir in 2009, the AU and several African states strongly criticized the court (and the UNSC) for risking potential peace negotiations in the region. Consequently, the AU filed a petition to the UN Security Council asking it to use its powers to block the court's investigation in Sudan (based on Art. 16 of the Rome statute). The UNSC decided not to discuss the petition but only "took note" of it. Outraged at this, the AU issued the so-called Sirte Declaration in response, asking AU member states not to cooperate with the ICC in the matter of the arrest warrant for Sudan's president Omar al-Bashir.[67]

Resistance was further fueled in the wake of the ICC investigation regarding post-election violence in Kenya in 2007/2008. The Kenya case was based on the *proprio motu* powers of the ICC prosecutor who has the right to initiate an investigation as long as the alleged crimes have been committed on the territory of a state party, such as Kenya. However, with arrest warrants issued for the then deputy prime minister Jomo Kenyatta, resistance to the court once again intensified, beginning to portray the court as a postcolonial instrument of power by the West. The court was framed as an anti-African court, not guided by legal principles but solely by the West's will to dominate[68]: "The ICC, despite being called International Criminal Court, is in fact an International Caucasian Court for the persecution and humiliation of people of color, especially Africans."[69]

Recently, several African states even initiated their withdrawal from the statute, including South Africa, the Gambia, and Burundi. While only Burundi effectively withdrew from the court in the end, there has been a clear line of radicalization of resistance from opposition to dissidence vis-à-vis the court on the African continent over the last decade. In the meantime, the AU has decided to establish an African Court of Justice and Human Rights to sideline the ICC.[70]

This radicalization of resistance to the point of dissidence seems puzzling given that the court has a number of provisions guaranteeing broad and equal participation for states. First of all, state parties can make use of the Assembly of State Parties to make their voices heard regarding the proceedings of the court and indeed the African group is the largest regional group in the Assembly. Beyond that, states can also call upon the UN Security Council to prevent an intervention by the court. The UNSC has the power to ask the court to halt an investigation for a period of 12 months (with scope for extension) by a majority vote.

In fact, the AU and several African member states made use of these opportunities but nevertheless radicalized their stance toward the court to the point of dissidence. This shift toward dissidence can be explained by a closer look at the opportunities for opposition in the ICC context. When it comes to the initial resistance, the topics at stake were issues of complementarity and a claim to prioritize peace over justice. Arguments were largely based on the statute and generally focused on resolving equivocal interpretations within the statute's provisions. This shifted following the arrest warrant for Omar al-Bashir and more specifically in response to the UNSC inaction regarding the request of the AU (and several others thereafter) to block ICC prosecutions in Darfur.[71]

While, up to this point, resistance was still concerned with changing procedures within the court, it then became an attack aimed at the heart of the court, encouraging noncompliance with the court's provisions, questioning its rationale, and, finally, threatening with a mass withdrawal of African countries from the court.[72] The inaction of the UNSC regarding the AU request for deferral created a clear sense of betrayal in many African states. Although they constituted the largest regional group in the court and had been instrumental in bringing the court to life in the first place (out of 121 state parties, 34 are African), their requests were simply ignored. The UNSC had not even officially discussed the matter but had simply "taken note" of the request of the AU, making clear how important it considered the AU and its member states to be.

In sum, African states increasingly perceived the opportunities for participation as superficial if not outright mockery. For these African states, the court was no longer about justice but was in fact a veiled instrument to prolong the colonial rule of major Western states. This perception is hard to uphold if one takes into account that the ICC in fact came about against the widespread opposition of major Western powers, foremost the United States but also, for a long time, France and the UK.[73] It is more an indication of the difficulties of institutions in a political system imbued with formal and informal structures of rule such as is prevalent in the UN Security Council.

Conclusion

Although the cases presented address different issues and involve state and non-state opponents, they demonstrate the utility of a relational understanding of rule that focuses on the link between rule and resistance. In all cases, tracing practices of resistance allows us to identify structures of rule that are often overlooked by traditional approaches. They help us reveal constellations of super- and subordination, even in institutional fields, such as the IWC, that are seemingly based on voluntary commitments. Because classical IR approaches perceive institutions as powerless – they see them as organizations controlled by states or as horizontal cooperative structures to which actors voluntarily submit based on a clearly discernible calculus of utility or normative conviction – these approaches overlook the asymmetrical power relations that become entrenched in international institutions. Focusing on international rule from a relational perspective brings these asymmetries to the fore.

However, focusing on resistance and the changes it undergoes is not sufficient to determine the kind of relationship that exists between resistance and rule in a given context. While it has been shown that both the shrinking of spaces of resistance and the bypassing of those spaces also lead to a radicalization of resistance, the mechanisms that cause or prevent such radicalization are still unclear. Do both types of limitation have similar effects on radicalization, in terms of both their strength and consequences? And how do opponents perceive an opening up of spaces? When do they accept an offer? Is this related to previous beliefs or experiences? In all four cases, we were able to observe forms of opposition and dissidence simultaneously. This illustrates that the political exercise of rule is determined not only by "objective" characteristics of the rulers, but also by subjective assessments of the ruled. How the latter come about is key to understanding the choice between opposition and dissidence, and thus the diversity of domination and resistance.

That said, our cases also point to promising insights that could be used to further develop the research agenda on international rule. In particular, they highlight that resistance is not only a product of rule but that it can also shape constellations of rule. Both in the case of the nuclear nonproliferation system and the global economic order, a strengthening and radicalization of resistance can be observed where rule is manifest, formal, and visible. This is especially apparent in the case of nonproliferation. It was only when the nuclear-armed states tried to convert their informal, charismatic rule into formal, legal rule that opposition became radicalized, because it was only at this point that the inequalities became obvious, on the one hand, and were made permanent through codification, on the other. But parallels can also be drawn for the global economic institutions and resistance to them. Even though this was initially a matter of diffuse protest, resistance became radicalized and focused as soon as institutions for participation were made available, hence, again, when rule assumed a visible form. This resembles the pattern of resistance in the ICC case where dissidence only emerged when the UN Security Council openly disregarded the objection from African states, signaling its disregard for their concerns. Finally, this dynamic can also be detected in the whaling regime. Resistance began to radicalize to the point of dissidence once the anti-whaling states made known their attempt to transform the temporary ban on commercial whaling into a permanent prohibition. Thus, in all our cases, the radicalization of resistance to the point of dissidence corresponds to a closing of opportunities for participation.

These observations imply that the expression of resistance depends on identifiable structures of rule, which places certain limits on our proposal to analyze rule via resistance. Moreover, it also suggests that resistance often forces rule to formalize in order to generate legitimacy and appease that resistance but also to counter it. Our cases show that the formalization of rule is often already a response to resistance, an attempt to legitimize a claim to rule. This dynamic also has a basis in Weber's sociology of rule, which observes a general trend of formalization in modern systems of rule toward more rational-legal bureaucratic forms of rule in order to more effectively stabilize rule as such.

By conceptualizing international relations as a sphere of relations of rule, the various manifestations of conflicts of rule and legitimacy over institutionalized relations of super- and subordination take center stage in international relations. Focusing on the dynamic relationship between rule and resistance proves fruitful for the study of international politics: It allows us to identify relations of rule that have previously been hidden from our analysis, and it offers a promising departure point for exploring the drivers and contexts of rule dynamics beyond the state.

References

Ackerman, Gary A. 2003. "Beyond Arson? A Threat Assessment of the Earth Liberation Front." *Terrorism and Political Violence* 15(4): 143–170.

Andretta, Massimiliano, Donatella della Porta, Lorenzo Mosca, and Herbert Reiter. 2006. *Globalization from Below: Transnational Activists and Protest Networks*. Minneapolis: University of Minnesota Press.

Arendt, Hannah. 1970. *On Violence*. San Diego, CA/New York: Harcourt Brace.

Arendt, Hannah. 1977. *Eichmann in Jerusalem: A Report on the Banality of Evil*. Harmondsworth: Penguin Books.

Arendt, Hannah. 1986 [1951]. *Elemente und Ursprünge totaler Herrschaft*. München: Piper.

Armstrong, David, Theo Farrell, and Bice Maiguashca (eds.). 2003. *Governance and Resistance in World Politics*. Cambridge: Cambridge University Press.

AU. 2009. *Decision on the Meeting of African State Parties to the Rome Statue of the International Criminal Court (ICC)*, https://reliefweb.int/report/sudan/decision-meeting-african-state-parties-rome-statue-international-criminal-court-icc-doc [last access 05/28/19].

Ayres, Jeffrey M. 2003. "Global Governance and Civil Society Collective Action: The Challenge of Complex Transnationalism." *International Journal of Political Economy* 33(4): 84–100.

Badescu, Christina G., and Thomas G. Weiss. 2010. "Misrepresenting R2P and Advancing Norms: An Alternative Spiral?" *International Studies Perspectives* 11(4): 354–374.

Bailey, Jennifer L. 2008. "Arrested Development: The Fight to End Commercial Whaling as a Case of Failed Norm Change." *European Journal of International Relations* 14(2): 289–318.

Bailey, Jennifer L. 2009. "Norway, the United States, and Commercial Whaling: Political Culture and Social Movement Framing." *The Journal of Environment & Development* 18(1): 79–102.

Barnett, Michael, and Raymond Duvall. 2005. "Power in International Politics." *International Organization* 59(1): 39–75.

Bleiker, Roland. 2005. "Seattle and the Struggle for a Global Democratic Ethos," in Eschle, Catherine, and Bice Maiguashca (eds.), *Critical Theories, International Relations and "Anti-Globalisation Movement."* Abingdon: Routledge, pp. 195–212.

Brands, Hal. 2007. "Non-proliferation and the Dynamic of the Middle Cold War: The Superpowers, the MLF, and the NPT." *Cold War History* 7(3): 389–423.

Buckel, Sonja, and Andreas Fischer-Lescano. 2007. "Hegemonie im globalen Recht – Zur Aktualität der Gramscianischen Rechtstheorie," in Buckel, Sonja, and Andreas Fischer-Lescano (eds.), *Hegemonie gepanzert mit Zwang. Baden-Baden: Nomos*, pp. 84–105.

Caygill, Howard. 2013. *On Resistance: A Philosophy of Defiance*. London: Bloomsbury Publishing.

Chacko, Priya, and Alexander E Davis. 2018. "Resignifying 'Responsibility': India, Exceptionalism and Nuclear Non-proliferation." *Asian Journal of Political Science* 26 (3): 352–370.

Clark, John D., and Nuno S. Themudo. 2006. "Linking the Web and the Street: Internet-Based 'Dotcauses' and the 'Anti-globalization' movement." *World Development* 34(1): 50–74.

Crossley, Nick. 2002. "Global Anti-corporate Struggle: A Preliminary Analysis." *British Journal of Sociology* 53(4): 667–691.

Daase, Christopher. 2003. "Der Anfang vom Ende des nuklearen Tabus. Zur Legitimitätskrise der Weltnuklearordnung" *Zeitschrift für Internationale Beziehungen* 10(1): 7–41.

Daase, Christopher, and Nicole Deitelhoff. 2019. "Opposition and Dissidence: Two Modes of Resistance against International Rule." *Journal of International Political Theory* 15(1): 11–30.

Dahl, Robert A. 1965. "Reflections on Opposition in Western Democracies." *Government and Opposition* 1(1): 7–24.

Dahl, Robert A. (ed.). 1966. *Political Oppositions in Western Democracies.* New Haven: Yale University Press.

Deitelhoff, Nicole. 2006. *Überzeugung in der Politik: Grundzüge einer Diskurstheorie Internationalen Regierens*, Frankfurt am Main: Suhrkamp.

Deitelhoff, Nicole. 2009. "The Discursive Process of Legalization: Charting Islands of Persuasion in the ICC Case." *International Organization* 63(1): 33–65.

Deitelhoff, Nicole. 2020. "What's in a Name? Contestation and Backlash against International Norms and Institutions." *British Journal of Politics and International Relations* 22 (4): 715–727.

Deitelhoff, Nicole, Felix Anderl, and Regina Hack. 2019. "Divide and Rule: The Politics of Self-Legitimation in the WTO," in Felix Anderl, Christopher Daase, Nicole Deitelhoff, Jannik Pfister, Victor Kempf, and Philip Wallmeier (eds.), *The Transnationalization of Rule and Resistance: Contestation, Escalation, Exit.* Lanham: Rowman and Littlefield.

Deitelhoff, Nicole, and Lisbeth Zimmermann. 2020. "Things We Lost in the Fire. How Different Types of Contestation Affect the Validity of Norms." *International Studies Review* 22(1): 51–76.

Della Porta, Donatella. 1995. *Social Movements, Political Violence, and the State: A Comparative Analysis of Italy and Germany.* Cambridge: Cambridge University Press.

Donnelly, Jack. 2009. "Rethinking Political Structures: From 'Ordering Principles' to 'Vertical Differentiation' – and Beyond." *International Theory* 1(1): 49–86.

Douglas, Mary. 1966. *Purity and Danger: An Analysis of the Concepts of Pollution and Taboo.* New York: Praeger.

Du Plessis, M. 2010. "The International Criminal Court That Africa Wants." ISS Monograph 172. Pretoria: Institute for Security Studies.

Egeland, Kjolv. 2017. The Road to Prohibition: Nuclear Hierarchy and Disarmament, 1968–2017. DPhil Dissertation, Oxford University.

Falk, Richard. 2000. "Resisting 'Globalization-from-Above' through Globalization-from-Below," in Barry K. Gills (ed.), *Globalization and the Politics of Resistance.* Basingstoke: Palgrave Macmillan, pp. 46–56.

Gibson, John. 2008. "The Myth of the Multitude: The Endogenous Demise of Alter-Globalist Politics." *Global Society* 22(2): 253–275.

Gill, Stephen. 2000. "Toward a Postmodern Prince? The Battle of Seattle as a Moment in the New Politics of Globalisation." *Millennium* 29(1): 131–140.

Gill, Stephen. 2003. *Power and Resistance in the New World Order*. Basingstoke: Palgrave Macmillan.

Guzzini, Stefano. 2005. "The Concept of Power. A Constructivist Analysis." *Millennium* 33(3): 495–521.

Hardt, Michael, and Antonio Negri. 2000: *Empire*. Cambridge: Harvard University Press.

Hay, Colin. 2007. *Why We Hate Politics*. Cambridge: Polity Press.

Hedlund, Gunnar, and Dag Rolander. 1990. "Actions in Heterarchies: New Approaches to Manage the MNC," in Christopher Bartlett, Yves Doz, and Gunnar Hedlund (eds.), *Managing the Global Firm*, London: Routledge, pp. 15–46.

Helms, Ludger. 2004. "Five Ways of Institutionalizing Political Opposition: Lessons from the Advanced Democracies." *Government and Opposition* 39(1): 22–54.

Hirschman, Albert O. 1970. *Exit, Voice, and Loyalty: Responses to Decline in Firms, Organizations, and States*. Cambridge: Harvard University Press.

Higgott, Richard. 2000. "Contested Globalization: The Changing Context and Normative Challenges." *Review of International Studies* 26: 131–153.

Hooghe, Liesbet, and Gary Marks. 2015. "Delegation and Pooling in International Organizations," *Review of International Organizations* 10(3): 305–328.

Hoover, Dean, and David Kovalewski. 1992. "Dynamic Models of Dissent and Repression." *Journal of Conflict Resolution* 36(1): 150–182.

Hurd, Ian. 2007. *After Anarchy. Legitimacy and Power in the United Nations Security Council*. Princeton: Princeton University Press.

Hurd, Ian. 2012. "Almost Saving Whales: The Ambiguity of Success at the International Whaling Commission." *Ethics & International Affairs* 26(1): 103–112.

Jain, Jagdish P. (ed.). 1974. *India and Disarmament: Nehru Era*, Vol. I. New Dehli: Radiant Publisher.

Jalloh, Charles C. 2017. "The African Union, the Security Council, and the International Criminal Court," in Charles C. Jalloh, and Ilias Bantekas (eds.), *The International Criminal Court and Africa*. Oxford: Oxford University Press, pp. 181–213.

Juris, Jeffrey S. 2005. "Violence Performed and Imagined: Militant Action, the Black Bloc and the Mass Media in Genoa." *Critique of Anthropology* 25(4): 413–432.

Kalland, Arne. 2009. *Unveiling the Whale: Discourses on Whales and Whaling*. New York: Berghahn Books.

Kapur, Ashok. 1978. "The Canada-India Nuclear Negotiations: Some Hypotheses and Lessons." *The World Today* 34(8): 311–320.

Kelley, Judith. 2007. "Who Keeps International Commitments and Why? The International Criminal Court and Bilateral Nonsurrender Agreements." *American Political Science Review* 101(3): 573–589.

Kirchheimer, Otto. 1957. "The Waning of Political Opposition in Parliamentary Regimes." *Social Research* 25: 381–414.

Lake, David. 2009. *Hierarchy in International Relations*. Ithaca: Cornell University Press.

Langbein, Hermann. 1986. "Dem brutalsten Terror zum Trotz. Widerstand in den nationalsozialistischen Konzentrationslagern 1939–1945," in Bundeszentrale für politische Bildung (ed.), *Widerstand und Exil 1933–1945*, Bonn: Bundeszentrale für Politische Bildung, pp. 159–168.

Sarah, Lieberman, Gray Tim, A. J. R. Groom. 2011. "Moratoria in International Politics: A Comparative Analysis of the Moratoria on Genetically Modified Products and Commercial Whaling." *The British Journal of Politics & International Relations* 14(4): 518–533.

Lukes, Steven. 1974. *Power: A Radical View*. London: Macmillan.

Meyer, Paul, and Tom Sauer. 2018. "The Nuclear Ban Treaty: A Sign of Global Impatience." *Survival*, 60(2): 61–72.

Mills, Kurt, and Allan Bloomfield. 2017. "African Resistance to the International Criminal Court: Halting the Advance of the Anti-impunity Norm." *Review of International Studies* 44(1): 101–127.

Nagtzaam, Gary. 2017. *From Environmental Action to Ecoterrorism?* Cheltenham: Edward Elgar.

O'Brien, Robert, Amme M. Goetz, Jan A. Scxholte, and Marc Williams. 2000. *Contesting Global Governance. Multilateral Economic Institutions and Social Movements*. Cambridge: Cambridge University Press.

Offe, Claus, and Ulrich K. Preuss. 2006. "The Problem of Legitimacy in the European Polity: Is Democratization the Answer?" *Conweb Papers* 6: 1–37.

O'Grady, Siobhán. 2016. "Gambia: The ICC Should Be Called the International Caucasian Court: Gambia Is the Latest Country to Leave the ICC." *Foreign Policy* 10/26/16, https://foreignpolicy.com/2016/10/26/gambia-the-icc-should-be-called-the-international-caucasian-court/ [last access 05/28/19].

Onuf, Nicholas, and Frank F. Klink. 1989. "Anarchy, Authority, Rule." *International Studies Quarterly* 33(2):149–173.

Ottaway, Marina. 2001. "Corporatism Goes Global: International Organizations, Nongovernmental Organization Networks, and Transnational Business." *Global Governance* 7: 265–292.

Paul, T. V. 2009. *The Tradition of Non-Use of Nuclear Weapons*. Stanford: Stanford University Press.

Sakaguchi, Isao. 2013. "The Roles of Activist NGOs in the Development and Transformation of IWC Regime: The Interaction of Norms and Power." *Journal of Environmental Studies and Sciences* 3(2), 194–208.

Schabas, William A. 2017. *An Introduction to the International Criminal Court*. 5th ed. Cambridge: Cambridge University Press, pp. 61–65.

Simmel, Georg. 1983 [1908]. *Soziologie: Untersuchungen über die Formen der Vergesellschaftung*. Berlin: Duncker & Humblot.

Ssenyonjo, Manisuli. 2017. "State Withdrawals of the Rome Statue of the International Criminal Court," in Charles C. Jalloh, and Ilias Bantekas I (eds.), *The International Criminal Court and Africa*. Oxford: Oxford University Press, pp. 214–246.

Tallberg, Jonas, Thomas Sommerer, Theresa Squatrito, and Christer Jönsson. 2013. *The Opening up of International Organizations: Transnational Access in Global Governance*. Cambridge: Cambridge University Press.

Tannenwald, Nina. 2007. *The Nuclear Taboo. The United States and the Non-Use of Nuclear Weapons Since 1945*. Cambridge: Cambridge University Press.
Weber, Max. 1978. *Economy and Society: An Outline of Interpretive Sociology*. Berkeley: University of California Press.
Wiener, Antje. 2014. *A Theory of Contestation*. Berlin: Springer.
Worth, Owen, and Karen Buckley. 2009. "The World Social Forum: Postmodern Prince or Court Jester?" *Third World Quarterly* 30(4): 649–661.
Zürn, Michael. 2012. "Autorität und Legitimität in der postnationalen Konstellation," in Anna Geis, Anna, Frank Nullmeier, Christopher Daase (eds.), *Der Aufstieg der Legitimitätspolitik*. Baden-Baden: Nomos, pp. 41–62.
Zürn, Michael. 2015. "Jenseits der Anarchie: Autorität und Herrschaft in der Global Governance." *Politische Vierteljahresschrift* 56(2): 319–333.
Zürn, Michael, Martin Binder, and Matthias Ecker-Ehrhardt. 2012. "International Authority and Its Politicization." *International Theory* 4(1): 69–106.

Notes

1 This chapter profited enormously from discussions at two workshops in Frankfurt as well as the helpful comments of the anonymous reviewers. Parts of this text are borrowed from an earlier article, see Daase and Deitelhoff 2019.
2 Hooghe and Marks 2015; Hurd 2007; Lake 2009; Zürn 2012.
3 Caygill 2013: 137ff.
4 See Zürn 2015.
5 Arendt [1951] 1986: 609ff.
6 Arendt 1970.
7 Arendt 1977.
8 Simmel [1908] 1983: 101ff.
9 Langbein 1986.
10 We concede that it will be difficult then to analyze what Steven Lukes (1974) has called the third face of power, that is, if power is used to covertly manipulate others to do something they might not actually want to do by changing what they want. Analytical access to this dimension, however, can only be gained through the concept of "false consciousness," something that is difficult to apply empirically.
11 Buckel and Fischer-Lescano 2007: 90.
12 Hedlund and Rolander 1990.
13 Donnelly 2009: 63.
14 See Onuf and Klink 1989.
15 On the polymorphic character of power, see Barnett and Duvall 2005: 40 and Guzzini 2005.
16 For similar observations on heteronomy, see Onuf and Klinke 1989.
17 In a similar vein, norm research in International Relations and International Law has recently turned toward criticism of international norms (framed, in this strand of research, as "contestation" based on the argument that it is conflict around the legitimacy and application of norms that makes normative commitments visible in the first place (see Badescu and Weiss 2010; Deitelhoff and Zimmermann 2020; Wiener 2014), Wiener 2014.

18 Ackerman 2003; Nagtzaam 2017.
19 Dahl 1966: xi.
20 See also Hirschman 1970.
21 See Dahl 1965.
22 See also Kirchheimer 1957.
23 Dahl 1965.
24 Helms 2004: 38; see also Hay 2007; Offe and Preuss 2006: 9–11.
25 della Porta 1995: 190–195; Hoover and Kowalewski 1992: 173; Juris 2005.
26 Deitelhoff et al. 2019; Tallberg et al. 2013.
27 Paul 2009; Tannenwald 2007.
28 Daase 2003.
29 See Jain 1974.
30 See Kapur 1978.
31 See Tannenwald 2007.
32 Chacko and Davis 2018; Daase 2003.
33 Weber 1978: 433; for a similar account, see Douglas 1966.
34 Weber 1978: 1121.
35 The NPT defines the term "nuclear-weapon state" in Article 9, paragraph 3. According to this definition, a "nuclear-weapon state" is "for the purposes of this Treaty" "one which has manufactured or exploded a nuclear weapon or other nuclear explosive device prior to 1 January, 1967." The countries meant were, of course, the United States, the Soviet Union, Great Britain, France, and China.
36 Brands 2007.
37 Egeland 2017.
38 Meyer and Sauer 2018.
39 See also Hurd 2012 and Lieberman et al. 2011: 519.
40 Bailey 2008: 295.
41 Sakaguchi 2013: 119.
42 As Zimmermann (Deitelhoff and Zimmermann 2020) highlights, the commercial whaling ban was actually executed as a procedural move by declaring to reduce all catch quotas to zero for five years to give whale populations a chance to recover.
43 Deitelhoff and Zimmermann 2020.
44 Sakaguchi 2013.
45 Tallberg et al. 2013: 225.
46 See Kalland 2009, also Bailey 2009; for a detailed analysis of contestation of the ban see Deitelhoff and Zimmermann 2020.
47 Deitelhoff and Zimmermann 2020.
48 Andretta et al. 2006.
49 Armstrong et al. 2003.
50 Falk 2000.
51 Gill 2000.
52 Gill 2003; Hardt and Negri 2000.
53 Clark and Themudo 2006; Crossley 2002; Gibson 2008.
54 Zürn et al. 2012.
55 O'Brien et al. 2000.
56 Ayres 2003: 91; Worth and Buckley 2009: 652.

57 O'Brien et al. 2000: 206.
58 See also Higgott 2000: 143.
59 O'Brien et al. 2000: 208f, 222.
60 See, in general, Ottaway 2001.
61 Worth and Buckley 2009: 652.
62 Andretta et al. 2006.
63 See Bleiker 2005; Juris 2005.
64 Still, the strategy paid off. Since the late 2000s, the protests have significantly declined and many activists have gone on to work for change from within their national systems.
65 Schabas 2017: 61–65.
66 At an early stage already, the court faced resistance from the United States, which had in fact tried to prevent it from being set up in the first place (Deitelhoff 2006, 2009). With the court in force and operational in 2002, the United States threatened to pull out their troops from all UN peacekeeping operations unless these troops were granted immunity from prosecution by the court. In a further step, the Bush administration threatened to withhold military aid and other forms of assistance to other states if these did not agree to sign agreements with the US on the new status of forces in which the states would grant each others' troops immunity from the court on their respective territory (Kelley 2007). At the height of US resistance, the United States Congress even sponsored a bill allowing the US government to initiate a military intervention in the Netherlands if the ICC were to indict and arrest a US American servicemember (American Servicemembers Protection Act, ASPA). Contestation of the court by the US has slowly petered out over the last decade. Nevertheless, the US is not even close to submitting to the statute.
67 AU 2009; Jalloh 2017: 204–206.
68 Du Plessis 2010; Jalloh 2017: 188.
69 Quote from the Gambian Information minister in 2006, cited in O'Grady (2016).
70 This court would not be able to prosecute sitting heads of states (see also Ssenyonjo 2017: 241–243).
71 See also Mills and Bloomfield 2017: 109.
72 Mills and Bloomfield 2017: 114–116.
73 For details, see Deitelhoff 2009.

9 The Contested Authority and Legitimacy of International Law

The State Strikes Back

Karen J. Alter[1]

International law (IL) is an essential feature of international rule. Rule is defined by the book's editors as "constellations of formally or informally institutionalized sub- and superordination with the aim of affecting the distribution of basic goods and influence and of stabilizing expectations, regardless of whether these constellations are primarily of sociocultural, economic or military nature" (Daase et al., this volume). IL, initially created by crafting international law through treaties, multilateral actions, and international institutional decisions, is how states collectively rule the international system. Debates about the content, meaning, and application of international law to specific issues and events are a key way that states and other actors adapt, adjust, and contest over the content of international rule as it pertains to political issues of the day. These actions are sociocultural in that they play into legal discourses about proper and legitimate governance, and they are economic and military to the extent that legal interpretations shape, determine, and guide economies and decisions about when and how force is used. State actions that tear at the fabric and place of international law in international politics are how states try to systemically undermine or change rule that is international law, a rule that by all account locks-in and instantiates the dominance of the most powerful states in the international system.[2]

IL rules both by justifying of state consent and by invoking the authority of IL as law. My focus in this chapter is on contestations over international legal authority – the authority granted to international law *as law*. Legal authority is a formal power based in law (a *de jure authority*). Legal authority becomes politically constraining if it can be wielded by actors that hold states accountable to their international legal obligations, at which point the *de jure* becomes a *de facto* international legal authority that allows political and legal actors to influence international politics by authoritatively invoking and naming certain policies or actions as legal or illegal under international law.

International law draws legitimacy and authority from public affirmations of and diffuse support for the rule of law (ROL). Most individuals, businesses, and global governmental and nongovernmental international actors prefer the ROL to the arbitrary or clientelistic exercise of political power, and they associate the ROL with everything state and international actors desire: economic growth, stopping corruption, political stability, building state legitimacy etc.[3] "The rule of law" has for these reasons become a primary legitimator of governments. Since IL draws on its authority as law, the politics through which IL authority is debated, negotiated, and contested are ROL politics. Legal politics are fundamentally different from the politics associated with national political authority (elections, charisma-based politics, etc.) and international politics (power politics, state-to-state diplomacy, reciprocity norms, issue linking etc.). This difference is inherent to and constitutive of the ROL; it is how the ROL achieves its goal of serving as a good governance check on politics.

To agree that IL's authority is associated with ROL politics is to agree that governments see value in being a ROL actor, or at least in being seen as one (see Hurd, this volume). ROL politics, then, revolves around the question of: "what, exactly, does it mean to be a 'rule of law' country/politician/actor?" and "what does respect for the law require?" These questions are answered by legal communities, including by adjudicators who are tasked with ensuring the proper application of law to particular issues, policies, and cases. Because legal communities are the curators and, in some instances, the trustees of the ROL, in consequentially important ways, international legal authority resides in national and transnational legal communities.[4]

The contested authority of international law is a result of two factors that are particular to international ROL politics (as compared to domestic ROL politics). First, the international system is composed of states that have political actors with their own nationally based political and legal authority. This national legal and political authority can become a rival of international legal authority. Second, international law exists in a situation of international regime complexity, a system of international rules that are not hierarchically ordered (on the heterarchy in the international system, see also Daase et al. in the introduction to this volume). The lack of clear agreement about international legal hierarchy allows states to maneuver around the authority of specific international laws by creating or appealing to parallel and at times competing international legal norms.[5] The sovereignty of states and international regime complexity combine so that the larger authority challenge for international law is the irresolvable problem of multiple overlapping legal and political authorities. In other words, within the domestic sphere, there is some agreed-upon means to resolve hierarchy questions, be it elections, the decision of a supreme council, the fiat of a dictator, or supreme court review. At the international level, by contrast, there is no universally accepted means to resolve strongly held hierarchy and interpretive disagreements, and this reality generates the extraordinary contestation discussed in this chapter.

To be clear, this argument is not predicated on an ontological commitment to the notion of an international ROL. The only precondition is a shared belief that the ROL is worth protecting.[6] Moreover, this argument opens the possibility of legal contestation for many reasons. Governments may simply want to escape an inconvenient IL obligation,[7] but national and transnational legal communities of practice may be motivated by constitutional/domestic political concerns, legal substantive, and normative concerns. Because these other concerns are often of primary importance to legal actors, governments must (also) engage legal debates in legal terms. Such engagement involves concessions to principle, which can further entangle governments in ROL politics where the possibility of limitations on their sovereignty always exists.

The first part of this chapter defines a practice-based conception of how international law gains de facto authority, which explains the focus on national and transnational legal communities as the curators of international law's authority. My approach to IL authority rejects the view that legal authority confers, demonstrates, or implies legitimacy. In my view, the question of whether IL is perceived as legitimate (e.g. sociological legitimacy) or deserving of being seen as legitimate (e.g. normative or moral legitimacy) are separate empirical and normative issues that cannot be presumed by conflating authority with legitimacy.[8] This is especially true because like all law, IL is produced through a political process. Political leaders might like everyone to believe that the law they write is inherently legitimate, but there is nothing magical about powerful actors drafting rules that promote their interests or that protect the state-dominated international system that renders these decisions legitimate. The argument of this chapter is that stakeholders are contesting over whether IL authority is legitimate and binding, and this contestation can be democracy enhancing at the same time as it is IL undermining. A further argument is that because IL authority is no longer defined or controlled by states, states are striking back by contesting the legitimacy and authority of IL.

The second part divides ordinary from extraordinary contestation over IL. Ordinary contestation is directly analogous to domestic ROL politics. Ordinary ROL politics takes place within a legal field, when lawyers, stakeholders, judges, and government officials debate and contest over the meaning of international law. Ordinary ROL politics also involves political strategies, including appointment politics and using financial resources to influence legal politics via the shaping legal ideas and via litigation strategies.

Extraordinary contestation over IL authority occurs because powerful domestic or state actors fail to impose their preferred interpretation of IL via ordinary ROL politics, because IL is proving domestically invasive and/or politically constraining, or because a political leader wants to change the international system itself. I discuss three strategies to supplant constraints generated by IL authority: (1) States can seek to replace international law's authority with domestic law's authority; (2) States can pit different international laws against each other by maneuvering within and around international regime complexes. Because these first two strategies do not escape de jure obligations under international law, and thus may not eliminate the costs associated with violating international law, a third strategy (3) involves attacking the legitimacy and authority of international law altogether (or attacking particular international laws).

The last part of this chapter concludes by recapping how each of these forms of contestation has both normatively positive and problematic potentials. If I am right that the value placed in the ROL constrains state actions, and that meanings associated with international law are created, influenced, and sustained by national and transnational legal communities, then IR scholars who hearken back to the political dynamics of state interest and power defined by Machiavelli, Thucydides, Morgenthau, and others import a blind spot; they overlook the importance of ROL politics in international relations today. This claim also means, however, that only where ROL social norms give law authority will the attribute of legality be politically important. Said differently, the permissive condition of people valuing the ROL is what makes international law *as law* a form of authority beyond the nation-state.

As I write, revisionist authoritarian leaders are raising fundamental challenges to the international system created by the West, advocating a return to earlier times. We are thus witnessing an extraordinary effort by a small number of political leaders to change the permissive condition where legality is associated with legitimacy, where legal arbiters get to define legality, and where IL protections afforded to states, self-determination, and fixed borders are the constitutional basis of the international order.

How International Law Gains Legal Authority in Fact and the Resources States and Legal Actors Have to Influence International Law's Content and Authority

Law – both domestic and international – is what communities of practice make of it. Communities of practice are communities of legal experts, people who claim a special expert knowledge about what constitutes (international) law, how (international) law applies, and what (international) legal rules authorize and prohibit. As a formal matter, state actors make the law when they legislate (at the domestic level) and craft treaties or make legally binding decisions and promises (at the international level). As a practical matter, the content of formal law is filled in through its application by those who use the law – lawyers, judges, administrators, private actors, international officials, scholars, and more.

Especially with respect to IL, the important role of communities of practice is widely recognized. Civil law legal systems are predicated on the (increasingly fictional) notion that only formal law is binding, and thus that neither legal precedent nor customary practices are valid sources of law.[9] By contrast, with respect to IL, international and domestic lawyers, national and international judges, and government and international officials have long looked to custom, judicial rulings, and both state and international legal practices to determine what international law requires. For example, the famous United States Supreme Court *Paquete Habana* ruling from 1900 traced the practices of states for hundreds of years to surmise that international law prohibited as prizes of war the seizing of vessels engaged in innocent fishing.[10] The reliance on practice was inscribed into Article 38 of the ICJ's Charter, which lists valid sources of IL: (b) "international custom, as evidence of a general practice accepted as law," (c) "the general principles of law recognized by civilized nations" and (d) "judicial decisions and the teachings of the most highly qualified publicists of the various nations, as subsidiary means" for ascertaining interpretive, customary, and general principle practices that compose IL. More recently, the importance of practices was recognized in international legal efforts to further specify customary international law, where the International Law Commission[11] recognized physical and verbal acts (and non-acts) of states, diplomatic acts and correspondences, resolutions of international organizations, public statements made on behalf of states, official publications, government legal opinions, and more as providing a basis for ascertaining what constitutes customary international law.[12] All of this means that legal practices constitute international law – by design and fact.

For IL, the relevant communities of practice operate simultaneously at the national, international, and transnational levels. At the national level, communities of practice instantiate IL authority by bringing IL into a government's domestic and foreign affairs decision-making;[13] by adjudicating cases that involve international and foreign law; by serving as law professors that write treatises and teach the next generation of lawyers, government officials, and national judges; and by providing expert advice to government agencies, NGOs, businesspeople, and journalists regarding what international law requires at home and abroad.

It matters, however, that the relevant community of practice is also international and transnational. The international and transnational practice of international law includes legal experts who work (for a time) in international institutions, who (often later) staff international consultancies, who provide expert opinions, who negotiate state international legal contracts and transnational business contracts, and who defend states and firms involved in international legal disputes, etc.[14] The international/transnational dimension is important because it undermines a state's ability to impose its preferred international legal interpretation on others. For example, right now, in China and Russia, international legal dogma aligns fairly strongly with a defined set of national interests in ways that affect freedom of thought and freedom of legal practice.[15] This dogma is important for the strategy of substituting domestic for international law (discussed in the section "Contesting the Authority of International Law: Ordinary and Extraordinary Forms"), but Chinese and Russian leaders are unable to impose their dogmatic interpretation of IL to the larger transnational community of IL practice.[16]

How do communities of practice shape IL? If we agree that international law is law, and as such it generates binding legal obligations, reasonable minds will then ask many questions: Is the international law in question valid law (e.g. properly negotiated and ratified)? Is the country bound by the specific international law? Does state policy x fall under a category where state deference is allowed, or where a derogation is permitted? One can also debate what the law means and how conflicts among laws are to be resolved. If international law is seen *as law*, then national and transnational legal communities will collectively debate and determine these legal points.

To be sure, governments are important actors in these international legal politics. Government consent is the origin of IL. Government practices help define customary international law. And governments directly participate in legal debates by raising legal cases and defending the legality of their policy.

Because communities of practice first and foremost shape IL authority, the primary (e.g. most frequent) mode states use to influence IL is communicative action and discursive politics. Communicative action, as discussed in international relations theory, aims to change actor understandings and preferences through the invocation of and debate over validity claims and claims about appropriate action.[17] I will return to this category of contestation when I discuss legitimacy challenges states raise against IL. Discursive legal politics generally operate at a lower level in that participants accept the overall validity claim of IL as law but use rhetorical and legal arguments to influence IL's substantive application for a particular policy areas or state actions.[18] For example, China claims the South China Seas as a territorial piece of China (the so-called 9-dash line). This claim is rejected by most lawyers and leaders outside of China, including an international arbitral panel.[19] China cannot impose on others its views about the legal validity China's oceanic territorial claim or of the legal invalidity of the arbitral ruling that rejected this claim. Instead, Chinese legal advocates are flocking to and engaging in a broad range of international academic, legal, and political forums to argue China's legal position regarding the South China Seas.[20] These legal strategies are supplemented by domestic and international political actions, as I will soon explain.

The relevant point, however, is that governments must operate alongside other states and alongside communities of international legal practice. Moreover, because many legal actors are motivated by de jure conceptions of IL authority, governments may find themselves unable to escape IL's legal authority.

Important consequences follow from my claim that communities of practice are the curators of IL authority. If international law's authority is constituted by practices, it follows that international legal authority is not categorical; an international law can become authoritative to the point that everyone accepts and follows it, but this will not mean that all international law will be equally authoritative. Also, the authority of international law can vary depending on the law in question, and different audiences can respond differently to the very same international law or international legal ruling. In other words, a judge in one country can accept IL authority for one issue area (e.g. trade) and reject international law for another issue area (territorial claims within the sea), while judges in other countries may accept the authority of both ILs. Flagrant rejections of IL authority can undermine political support for IL, but it is not the case that a government or a court's rejection in Country A negates the acceptance in Country B, or that a rejection in one country thereby eliminates IL authority.[21] These qualifiers become relevant when discussing the three strategies used to challenge IL authority.

It is worth underscoring that international rules may or may not be legal rules.[22] Moreover even today, a number of politicians and lawyers dispute the idea that international law is actually law, suggesting that international law is a code of conduct, or a gentlemen's agreement between states, or at most a legal contract with a pay-or-perform logic.[23] These critiques are designed to socially separate the notion that respect for international law is or should be associated with the normative and political value that people ascribe to law and to the ROL. My argument only applies to legal rules, and it only applies to the extent that respect for the ROL is socially valued, which in turn makes the quality of international legality – of actions being congruent with international law – politically valuable.

Meanwhile, while most lawyers will agree that much law is ambiguous and thus subject to divergent interpretation, many will reject my notion that law's authority depends on or is affected by the affirmations of legal communities. For these lawyers, legal obligation exists regardless of whether or not states or certain legal actors recognize this fact. They will also disagree that drawing on national constitutional law can displace IL's authority, since for them an international legal obligation still binds the state, and thus it exists regardless of what national supreme courts say or do. I do not dispute these points; in fact, my argument depends on them. Precisely because transnational and international legal communities involve actors for whom de jure IL generates binding obligations, states may fail to escape IL authority through formal exit or via the contestation strategies discussed in the section "Contesting the Authority of International Law: Ordinary and Extraordinary Forms."

I also want to pause to unpack what is implicit in this argument. Daase, Deitelhoff, and Witt's introduction to this volume deftly explicates scholarly disagreements regarding whether authority implies legitimacy. All involved, they argue, recognize that "authority is intimately tied to legitimacy," yet that not all countries or actors are equally able to reject or contest the legitimacy of international authority claims (see also Zürn, this volume). This chapter sees international authority and IL authority as contested ideas. My claim about IL is that when legal communities of practice embrace the law (e.g. profess and thereby help to instantiate a particular law's authority and its applicability to the situation at hand), and when the "rule of law" is socially valued, these two factors generate IL's de facto authority. Ordinary legal politics accepts the authority and legitimacy of IL, while trying to influence how international legal obligations are understood and how they are applied domestically. The more extraordinary forms of contestation question key aspects of IL's authority claim. This conceptual separation of IL authority and legitimacy will become important when states engage in communicative action to undermine claims about the legitimate authority of IL.

What this discussion and IR theory miss, however, is that states can move outside of law to change the facts on the ground. International law aims to move the needle, to push states in the direction of respecting international law. By changing the facts on the ground, states can pick up and move the location of the needle that legal actors are trying to move. For example, following the old adage that "possession is nine-tenths of the law,"[24] China is converting rocks in the ocean into militarized islands of sovereign control, and Russia is expanding its military hold over parts of Ukraine.[25] The focus on legal politics also deemphasizes how states can claim an existential mandate to supersede and overwhelm what law requires. Changing the facts on the ground and drawing on political authority are readily employed tactics during intense power politics, total-war, and populist revolts where the importance of law gets sidelined more generally. This chapter is mostly focused on ordinary and extraordinary legal politics, but I will return to address this issue of power politics in the chapter's conclusion.

Contesting the Authority of International Law: Ordinary and Extraordinary Forms

This section identifies a number of strategies through which states contest the authority of specific ILs. In ordinary modes of contestation, legal actors work within the law to shift legal understandings or they use power and money to influence the primary interpreters of IL. I then discuss two extraordinary strategies that exploit the Achilles heel of international law, namely the lack of any agreed upon means to resolve questions about hierarchy: seeking to supplant IL authority with domestic legal authority or seeking to supplant inconvenient IL by appealing to a different binding IL. The final extraordinary strategy – challenging the legitimacy of IL – is an avowedly political strategy, and it is only an option because the larger public may or may not accept the legitimacy of legal authority or of the legal actors who act in the name of IL authority.

All of these forms of contestation can be seen as legal means to debate what Lake calls "relational authority," but whereas Lake sees relational authority challenges as an attempt by the ruled to renegotiate the terms of their consent to the power and authority of the hierarchical ruler,[26] the legal debates occur among actors that are – as a formal matter – equals before the law. In this respect, my argument is more similar to Zürn's concept of reflexive authority wherein the terms through which actors agree to defer to law's authority get defined in an interactional and co-constitutive way, and the basis of this authority is epistemic in that it is based on understandings of legal knowledge (see also Zürn, this volume).[27] Although I am more focused on contestation, and I explicitly theorize about legitimacy challenges to law that fulfills the basic criteria of legality, my argument is also similar to the latest formulation of Brunnée and Toope in that I base my arguments in a "practice of legality" that draws on factors that are intrinsic to law.[28]

Ordinary Contestation: In-Field Efforts to Shift Legal Understandings

Pierre Bourdieu developed a theory of professions wherein each profession defined its own norms, values, and modes of appropriate contestation and where actors within the field jockeyed vis-à-vis each other.[29] This mode of analysis has been applied to the study of domestic and international law, and in particular to studies that explain how legal communities shift interpretations of international law over time so as to promote specific political agendas.[30]

I call this ordinary contestation because it is part of practicing law. Lawyers champion their (or their client's) preferred legal arguments; scholars develop elaborate treatises by analyzing case law and advancing normative arguments; judges adjudicate cases pronouncing legal rulings that may then be contested, critiqued, and further developed in subsequent rulings; lawyers and scholars become practitioners who work in governments, at international organizations, as arbiters for hire etc.[31]

Within field legal contestation can also involve more public challenges that attack legality claims that underpin IL authority. Lon Fuller has famously named as essential a set of eight criteria that are generally seen as required for law to be valid. Succinctly summarized:

> Legal norms must be general, prohibiting, requiring, or permitting certain conduct. They must also be promulgated, and therefore accessible to the public, enabling actors to know what the law requires. Law should not be retroactive, but prospective, enabling citizens to take the law into account in their decision making. Actors must also be able to understand what is permitted, prohibited, or required by law – the law must be clear. Law should avoid contradiction, not requiring or permitting and prohibiting at the same time. Law must be realistic and not demand the impossible. Its demands on citizens must remain relatively constant. Finally, there should be congruence between legal norms and the actions of officials operating under the law.[32]

Practitioners and legal advocates can chip away the legal validity of specific international laws by invoking these eight legality criteria to challenge the legality (and thus the legal authority) of specific international legal acts. For example, advocates can argue that the legal rules are fundamentally unclear, that their application is retrospective and thus illegal, that the law contains contradictions, that the expectations of the law are impossible to achieve, and that the general nonenforcement of the law makes its particular enforcement appear arbitrary and capricious, etc. While the target is the validity of a particular IL, these nonetheless are within-field contestations because they are using the criteria of legality and the terminology and tactics of lawyers so as to influence legal understandings. In doing so, these actors reinforce the idea that legally valid laws are to be respected.

Just as reinterpretation can be a powerful mode of institutional change,[33] legal field orchestrated shifts can be very consequential, and they become fodder for legal scholars, historical institutional, and constructivist scholars who study how legal meanings change and are changed. For example, in *The Death of Treaty Supremacy*, David Sloss argues that in-field legal contestation led to a reinterpretation of the United States' Constitution's Supremacy Clause, undermining a historic US commitment to international law. The process took many years of legal argumentation and appointment politics, and it culminated in the *Medillan* v. *Texas* ruling where the United States Supreme Court invalidated a Presidential order designed to comply with an International Court of Justice ruling against the US.[34] Sloss' argument means that even though the US constitution still proclaims that the "constitution, federal laws made pursuant to it, and treaties made under its authority constitute the supreme law of the land,"[35] whether judges or government officials will see duly ratified international treaties as the law of the land in the US, and thus whether IL has de facto authority in the US, is increasingly precarious.

Field base politics can also involve the sorts of strategies that we find in the political realm, namely using appointment politics to influence administrative decision-making and providing financial resources to influence policy debates. For example, in *The Rise of the Conservative Legal Movement: The Battle for Control of the Law,* Stephen Teles describes how wealthy patrons went about building a conservative perspective of the law, and how they then used their financial resources to capture key parts of American legal education and the American judiciary.[36] These investments paid off in redefining key political debates about gun control, health insurance, abortion and religious rights, which have been shaped by and through legal rulings.

Using power, money, appointments etc. to influence the law is all part of the sausage factory of "rule of law" politics, and in this respect, I see domestic and international ROL politics as similar. Yet ROL politics depends on a belief that law and politics are separate domains. Western understandings of the ROL require independent adjudicators to ensure that the two domains are separate, so that the ROL provides a system of checks and balances that ensures that governmental actors are not above the law. This separation is why the Western version of the ROL provides legitimation.[37] The ROL with Chinese characteristics, sometimes called rule by law, subordinates the ROL to the Chinese Communist Party and to Xi Jinping's leadership conducted for the good of the Chinese people. The Chinese version of the ROL relies on the economic performance and the legitimacy of the Communist Party to provide legitimacy for the ROL with Chinese characteristics.[38] The more transparent the political and oligarchic intervention into legal politics, the more public faith in the ROL is likely to erode.

Power attracts politics, which is why international law is increasingly politicized. While power and politics are present in both international and domestic ROL politics, there is an important difference. At the domestic level, should everyday legal politics develop statutory law in undesired ways, politicians can campaign against extant law and eventually use their power as legislators to change the law. This type of political course correction, however, can be more difficult for international law. Meanwhile, because understandings of international law reside in transnational legal communities, a single country may be unable to reinterpret its way out of an international legal obligation. This difference provokes the extraordinary contestation I discuss next.

Extraordinary IL Contestation: Three Ways States Try to Supplant IL Authority

At the domestic level, the executive branch is often advantaged in ROL politics because governments may be able to fairly easily write (and rewrite) the law, change the rules and the composition of the national judiciary, and orchestrate a constitutional amendment to support their political objectives (I will return to this idea in the chapter's conclusion). These same strategies of state control are much harder to deploy at the international level, because consensus rules and global representation goals make it hard to change IL or stack international courts and because legal fields are transnational.[39] This is not to ignore, however, the special powers that states have within international law, where states can sometimes escape IL authority by invoking formal exit rights, by creating exceptions by adding in reservations, by being a "persistent objector," and by shaping customary international law.[40] In what follows, I presume that the unilateral exit option is either undesirable or unavailable.

If the transnational understandings of IL are at odds with the government's strongly held interests, and especially where governments are highly legitimated actors, a legitimation crisis can arise. In such a situation, domestic and external critics are likely to draw on IL to challenge the validity of the state actions that put interest over law. At this point, there are three forms of legitimation politics states can use to justify ignoring an IL obligation: (1) they can seek to supplant IL's authority by drawing on domestic law's authority; (2) they can supplant the authority of the particular IL by drawing on other IL; or (3) they can engage in communicative action that suggests that the IL is itself not worth defending or following. These strategies will not, however, alter the belief of many lawyers that as a formal (e.g. de jure) matter, the state remains obligated to comply with relevant binding IL, and thus these strategies may appease important domestic and foreign audiences, but not necessarily all IL audiences.

Supplanting International Law with Domestic Constitutional Law Should state actors find themselves legally constrained by international law – the state has consented and ratified the international treaty, state-based actors are unable through persuasion, rhetorical, or appointment politics to generate a preferable international legal interpretation, and the international law itself cannot be changed – a possible rule of law respecting legal move involves finding that domestic law prohibits the state from following international law.

This strategy exploits one aspect of IL's hierarchy problem. As a formal matter, states may be bound to follow IL to which they have legally consented. But most international legal conventions do not speak to the legal question of IL's domestic/internal effect. Rather, whether and how IL is domestically binding is usually a question of national law. Of course, ICs have tried to speak to this issue, insisting that international law is supreme to conflicting domestic law. But with the possible exception of *jus cogens,* there is no universally accepted way to adjudicate legal conflict among a set of higher order laws – constitutions, and international laws – that may be supreme within a self-contained legal system. In this respect, IC rulings that claim supremacy of a particular IL may also not be legally dispositive.

Pitting international and constitutional law against each other forces a ROL actor to choose: the national constitution or international law. Usually, this choice is an easy one. Domestic judges are first and foremost bound by the national constitution. This sort of binary – domestic or international – construction is usually intentional, as nearly every direct clash of international and domestic law can be avoided if there is a will to do so.[41] States can also settle disputes outside of court, offering compensation in lieu of compliance. And if all else fails, judges and politicians can pretend that they *are* in fact complying with IL and with the international judicial ruling as they understand it. But if the goal is to escape international legal constraints by erasing the legal obligation, appeals to the supremacy of the national constitution over international law provide a rule-of-law compliant technique of avoidance.

A rather transparent example of this strategy is President Putin's 2015 change of the Russian Constitutional Court's legal statute, authorizing the Court to find the rulings of international human rights bodies "non-executable." This change does not explicitly interfere with the independence and authority of the Constitutional Court, but its objective is apparent to all. Recently, the Russian Constitutional Court has invoked its new powers to render inapplicable adverse European Court of Human Rights rulings concerning the Yukos oil company.[42]

Russia's effort was government-led, and the intentions were clear to all. Returning to the earlier example of how legal understandings regarding the US Constitution's supremacy clause have shifted, Jens Ohlin suggests that more recently "New Realists" provided legal justifications – in scholarly writings and in their positions in the Office of the Legal Counsel – to reject the idea that IL law ought, as a matter of course, be obeyed. Their arguments, he claims, facilitated the executive branch's rejection of international legal obligations, such as the prohibition on torture. The ultimate goal, Ohlin suggests, is to return international legal understandings to a view that only international law that furthers US interests ought to be obeyed.[43]

I do not want to suggest that this strategy of prioritizing the constitution over international law is necessarily illegitimate or that it is necessarily undermining international legal authority. In Brazil and South Africa judges and politicians turned to domestic constitutional provisions to ensure that the WTO's Agreement on Trade-Related Aspects of Intellectual Property Rights did not undermine socioeconomic rights inscribed into national constitutions (and also international law).[44] The contestation reflected the placing of democratic priorities over international law, and it led to a restatement of the WTO agreement to ensure that governments can also protect public health (the so-called Doha Declaration of 2005).[45]

Nor does elevating constitutional law necessarily suppress international law. Elsewhere I discuss how American, German, and Colombian Constitutional courts have applied the supremacy of their respective constitutions to different ends, sometimes aiding in the application of IL and other times undermining its domestic application.[46] My larger point is that this strategy remains an option that advocates can use to entrench international law into domestic law, or to supplant international law by drawing on the rival legal authority of domestic law.

Maneuvering within and around the International Regime Complex A less studied and less documented strategy involves moving around the international regime complex to avoid international law (see also Morse, this volume). This is a similar argument to Nico Krisch's idea of liquid authority[47] and to authority disagreements in polycentric contexts.[48] International regime complexes are "array[s] of elemental institutions with an authority claim for a particular issue area or territory."[49] It is surely true that international regime complexes can generate stable global governance systems wherein conflicts among rules are avoided.[50] Using a regime complex to escape an international legal obligation should only occur when: (1) prevailing IL and international legal understandings cut against a government or firm's preferred scenario; (2) the government is unable to orchestrate a revision of the contested rule or to recast collective understandings of the rule; and (3) the law's practice is proving politically constraining.[51]

The movement to create UNASUR (Union of South American Nations) provides an example of states generating an international regime complex in order to escape constraining regional IL. In Latin America, leftist populist governments were upset by the free-trade orientation of regional integration systems. Venezuelan President Hugo Chavez tried to spearhead a regional revolt, trying to generate Latin American alternatives to the influence of Washington D.C.–based international institutions (in particular the International Monetary Fund, the World Bank, and the Organization of American States).[52] Most of Chavez' grand visions failed to generate rival rules or institutions, but Latin America's leaders did agree in 2004 to unify the Andean and Mercusor regional systems by merging them into UNASUR.[53] Where Chavez largely failed, Ecuador's president Raphael Correa nearly succeeded. Correa became the main driver of UNASUR integration because of his domestic economic troubles. Ecuador's currency is the US dollar. By 2011, Correa faced a dollar crisis due to decreased foreign investment and falling oil prices. Meanwhile, the rising value of the US dollar had rendered regional products less expensive in comparison to very similar locally produced goods. Seeking to stop the outflow of dollars, and the inflow of cheaper foreign goods, Correa adopted a number of policies that targeted his Andean neighbors in direct contradiction of Andean law. Facing numerous legal challenges, Correa's government began to press for implementing legislation to merge the Andean community into a yet-to-be defined UNASUR system.[54] With this new energy, a number of UNASUR initiatives began to take legal shape. Instability within the region then struck. Chavez died and Venezuela's economy and society disintegrated into chaos; Argentina's leftist leader lost power; Brazil's and Peru's presidents were impeached on corruption charges; and term limits ended Correa's rule. The larger point, however, is that a key goal of UNASUR, and a primary motivation for many Leftist leaders, was that through UNASUR leaders could water down of free-trade oriented binding IL commitments.

Creating new or contesting multilateral regimes takes a lot of effort. An easier strategy is to, where possible, repurpose existing understandings of the law. This is the strategy that authoritarian leaders are using to create a less constraining version of international law.[55] China is going so far as to try to recast what the concept of democracy and human rights mean, so that it can claim the legitimacy associated with democracy, human rights, and the ROL.[56]

I do not want to suggest that maneuvering within the international regime complex necessarily undermines the authority of international law. Laurence Helfer documented "regime shifting" where Western states shifted international legal regimes in order to increase international legal obligations to respect protections for intellectual property rights and developing countries regime shifted to claim special protections for indigenous intellectual property.[57] Keohane and Victor note that building international law by creating regime complexes can provide a means to circumvent political opposition and thereby allow like-minded states to proceed where consensus allows.[58] De Burca et al. suggest that building parallel international institutions may also allow for experimentation and increased political input.[59] Auld and Green suggest that legal complexity further empowers international legal actors who become crucial guides to how states can respect a confusing web of international legal rules.[60]

But, this strategy of adding new elemental institutions to a regime complex can also be used to erode the influence and legal authority of existing international regimes. Many worry, for example, that World Trade Organization is being undermined and replaced by the proliferation of preferential trade agreements. Preferential trade agreements have already eroded the most-favored nation promise associated with WTO membership, and some worry that these agreements can come to substitute for the WTO, eliminating the political and legal relevance of WTO legal obligations.[61]

Backlash: Communicative Action Challenges to the Legitimacy and Authority of International Law A final strategy involves a frontal attack on the legitimacy and authority of international law. There is also nothing new about this strategy. International law has long been seen by third-world scholars as a means of lawfare that powerful states and economic actors use to subjugate the developing world.[62] Because of IL's association with imperialism, and the inconsistent way that IL gets invoked and applied, for many actors IL should be resisted.[63] Criticism can come alongside efforts to construct alternatives, so that this third strategy can coexist with the previously discussed strategy. Yet we are also seeing revisionist power plays that try to significantly change the post–World War II international legal and political order.

The legitimacy challenges against the International Criminal Court provide a recent example of weaker powers combining confrontation without tearing the entire extant order down. African critics are not arguing that war crimes do not exist, that the ICC lacks the authority to investigate these crimes, or that war crimes should not be illegal under international law. Indeed, African leaders are pursuing their own institution to address international war crimes, championing an African approach that can better meet the needs of the continent.[64] Meanwhile, African critics focus on the fact that nearly every ICC legal case is targeted against an African Country, suggesting that the ICC is itself an illegitimate institution and that specific indictments and prosecutions are therefore political rather than legal acts.

While the tactic is not new, revisionist powers have been willing to challenge dominant norms and to use force to severe the link between IL, authority, and legitimacy. The most extreme examples include the "Islamic State of Iraq and Syria" (ISIL's) effort to establish a caliphate under Islamic law rule,[65] and Vladimir Putin's use of force to reestablish Russia's "rightful" imperial rule.[66] Both of these efforts can be seen as a retrograde backlash where the goal is to return to a prior international order.[67]

China is also pursuing a more peaceful legal and political revisionism. On the one hand, the Chinese government engages in legal argumentation to support its claim to the South China Seas,[68] but it also is dredging and building compounds in the Spratly and Parcel islands and creating a constant lifeguard presence to bolster its territorial claims, and it is pressuring states to renounce recognition of Taiwan. China has also joined Russia in raising fundamental questions about how international law today currently operates. In 2016, China's government joined with President Putin's government to issue a Joint Declaration on the Promotion of International Law. The declaration includes many pieces, some designed to defend the governments' legal views with respect to important political issues (especially the Crimea and the South China Seas), some designed to reestablish the notion of sovereign immunity, and some designed to counter developments in international humanitarian intervention.[69] The February 2022 Russian-China Joint Statement on International Relations Entering a new Era reiterates ideas about international law as it implicates the two countries' territorial claims, and asserts that there is no single definition of democracy: "A nation can choose [the] forms and methods of implementing democracy that would best suit its particular state … It is only up to the people of the country to decide whether their State is a democratic one."[70]

As with the other forms of contestation, communicative action challenges have both positive and negative potentials. If the contestation enhances IL accountability, then contestation is arguably normatively desirable and perhaps it will serve to enhance the legitimacy of IL. Indeed, elsewhere I argue that from a normative perspective, we should seek and welcome democratic and normative contestation over IL.[71] But this form of contestation can also be used to deflect political responsibility and to justify policies that might be both democratically and normatively illegitimate. For example, Robert Bork famously suggested that neither democratic checks nor international law should get in the way of the higher moral cause of fighting communism by arming foes of Nicaragua's government.[72] I continue this discussion in the next section.

Conclusion: International Rule of Law Politics in a World of Contested Authorities

This chapter, part of a series of recent essays where I consider how the current political crisis facing the international liberal order implicates my earlier research,[73] engages debates that are prevalent in international relations theory, most of which also find analogues in international legal scholarship.

In *The New Terrain of International Law*, I argued that international law draws its legal authority from being law, meaning a set of ratified and binding legal rules that fulfill essential legality criteria that thus has a de jure authority.[74] Because ROL norms have many positive public associations – fairness, predictability, respect for the legal and political rules of the game, and good governance – even authoritarian governments strive to be perceived as ROL actors. Where the ROL genuinely exists, legal communities become the keepers of the keys to legal authority, collectively defining what law means and how law applies to a specific issue or case. In the terms I used, legal communities become compliance partners and compliance supporters who pressure state and sub-state actors to respect international law. Of course, the legal enforcers of IL include more than just legal communities. Foreign donors, investors, consumers, NGOs, and other international actors can be motivated to shun or outcast to show their displeasure with an actor that has behaved "illegally."[75]

Rule of law norms can be eroded. Authoritarian rulers create a charade of the ROL, what scholars have called "rule-by-law." When authoritarian-minded political factions control all branches of government and the national judiciary becomes captured, then political branches can adjust formal laws to serve whatever purpose political leaders choose. Politicians may then wield their control of the law and judiciary to bolster their political power and to punish political opponents. This is what is meant by the term "rule by law," and it is what neo-authoritarian rulers in Venezuela, Poland, Hungary, Turkey, and Russia have been implementing in recent years.[76] Many will see these tactics as both illegal and illegitimate. Yet since authoritarian leaders can claim an electoral mandate and draw on powers that they formally have under the national legal order's constitution, and should charismatic leaders impart their revisionist ideas about law and authority into the popular imaginary, the very meaning of the ROL can be transformed.[77]

This chapter has discussed both legal and political strategies that states can use to escape international legal constraints. Legal strategies included working within the legal field to shift legal understandings, appealing to rival sources of law including domestic constitutions and differing international legal norms. These legal strategies may be mostly a form of politics enacted through the language of law, but they are also legally plausible, and thus legally defensible. The final strategy I discussed – governments directly assaulting the legitimacy of international law – tears at the fabric of international legal authority. This is also an old strategy, which has some moral and political claims to support it. What is different is that this strategy is being newly deployed by powerful states that are upset because the international law has provided a way to challenge their land claims (in Crimea and the South China Seas) and because global economic law is hindering the pursuit of domestically popular policies.

Whether these legal and political strategies undermine the public's perception that international law ought to be obeyed is yet to be seen. The outcome turns on what are two fundamentally empirical questions: (1) will national populations and legal actors abandon their commitment to legality as a requirement for legitimate government action? (2) Will respect for international law become substantively separated from debates about the social good supplied by the ROL? Should either of these developments come to pass, the political power of international law's compliance partners and supporters will be severely diminished.

My argument is focused primarily on empirical developments, but I have not shied away from discussing normative issues as well. Throughout this chapter, and in my scholarship more generally, I have noted how contesting over the legitimacy and binding authority of IL is not necessarily a bad thing. International law by design and intent punishes so as to constrain certain government choices – the choice to kill non-combatants, the choice to enact market protection, the choice to compromise human rights, and the choice to break covenants with foreigners. But the inertia of IL can also trigger legitimacy challenges at the point that international law becomes disconnected from the legitimate needs and desires of countries and peoples. Indeed, in my earlier work, I argued that international court's (and international law's) dependence on compliance constituencies helped to serve the goals of democracy.[78]

The larger point is that where legitimacy challenges voice deeply felt concerns and contribute to needed reforms, then they are a price to be born to ensure that IL remains accountable to a broad range of interests and actors. The greater risk, however, is that the ROL gives way to the rule of dictators. This is the moment we currently face, a moment where democrats and promoters of the ROL are facing off against forces that push toward a post-factual and less free and accountable world.

It is too early to declare a directional trend. The post–World War II era was surely an era of American-led multilateralism, and during this period the salience and value associated with adhering to international law was ascending. The US-led international liberal order might be at an end, but it is too early to say what will happen to the social value that people have associated with democracy and the ROL. What we can say is that some states have been striking back, and increasingly Great Powers are striking back using both ordinary and extraordinary forms of contesting IL authority. And we can say that a fight to defend or destroy the ROL is currently being waged, and that the fate of IL authority is implicated by this fight.

References

Alter, Karen J. 2006. "Delegation to International Courts and the Limits of Recontracting Power," in Darren Hawkins, David A. Lake, Daniel Nielson, and Michael J. Tierney (eds.), *Delegation and Agency in International Organizations*. Cambridge: Cambridge University Press, pp. 312–338.

Alter, Karen J. 2008. "Agent or Trustee: International Courts in Their Political Context." *European Journal of International Relations* 14(1): 33–63.

Alter, Karen J. 2014. *The New Terrain of International Law: Courts, Politics, Rights.* Princeton: Princeton University Press.

Alter, Karen J. 2018a. "Critical Junctures and the Future of International Courts." *iCourts Working Paper Series* 140: 31.

Alter, Karen J. 2018b. "The Future of International Law," in Diana Ayton-Shenker (ed.), *The New Global Agenda.* Lahnham: Rowman & Littlefield, pp. 25–42.

Alter, Karen J. 2018c. "National Perspectives on International Constitutional Review: Diverging Optics," in: Erin Delaney and Rosalind Dixon, *Comparative Judicial Review.* United Kingdom: Edward Elgar Publishing, pp. 244–272.

Alter, Karen J. 2021. "When and How to Legally Challenge Economic Globalization: A Comment on the German Constitutional Court's False Promise." *International Journal of Constitutional Law* 19(1): 269–284.

Alter, Karen J., and Laurence R Helfer. 2017. *Transplanting International Courts: The Law and Politics of the Andean Tribunal of Justice.* Oxford: Oxford University Press.

Alter, Karen J, Helfer, Laurence R. and Mikael Rask Madsen. (eds.) 2018. *International Court Authority.* Oxford: Oxford University Press.

Alter, Karen J., and Ji Li. 2022. "Chinese and Western Perspectives on the Rule of Law and Their International Implications," forthcoming in Ignacio de la Rasilla and Cai Congyan (eds.), *Cambridge Handbook on China and International Law.* Cambridge: Cambridge University Press.

Alter, Karen J., and Kal Raustiala. 2018. "The Rise of International Regime Complexity." *The Annual Review of Law and Social Science* 14: 329–349.

Alter, Karen J., and Michael Zürn. 2020a. "Conceptualizing Backlash Politics: Introduction to a Special Issue on Backlash Politics in Comparison." *British Journal of Politics and International Relations* 22(4): 563–584.

Alter, Karen J., and Michael Zürn. 2020b. "Theorising Backlash Politics: Conclusion to a Special Issue on Backlash Politics in Comparison." *British Journal of Politics and International Relations* 22(4): 739–752.

Anghie, Antony. 2005. *Imperialism, Sovereignty, and the Making of International Law.* Cambridge/New York: Cambridge University Press.

Auld, Graeme, and Jessica F. Green. 2012. "Unbundling the Regime Complex: The Effects of Private Authority." *Osgoode Hall Law School Research Paper Series* 15.

Becker Lorca, Arnulf. 2014. *Mestizo International Law: A Global Intellectual History 1842–1933.* Cambridge: Cambridge University Press.

Benvenisti, Eyal. 2008. "Reclaiming Democracy: The Strategic Uses of Foreign and International Law by National Courts." *American Journal of International Law* 102(2): 241–276.

Benvenisti, Eyal, and Alon Harel. 2017. "Embracing the Tension between National and International Human Rights Law: The Case for Discordant Parity." *International Journal of Constitutional Law* 15(1): 36–59.

Bork, Robert. 1989/90. "The Limits of 'International Law'." *The National Interest* 18: 3–10.

Bourdieu, Pierre. 1987. "Force of Law: Toward a Sociology of the Juridical Field." *Hastings Law Journal* 38(July): 805–853.

Brunnée, Jutta, and Stephen J. Toope. 2011. "Interactional International Law: An Introduction." *International Theory* 3(2): 307–318.

Brunee, Jutta, and Stephen J. Toope. 2017. "Interactional Legal Theory, the International Rule of Law and Global Constitutionalism," in Antony F. Lane and Antje Wieder (eds.), *Handbook on Global Constitutionalism*. Cheltanham: Edward Elgar Publishing, pp. 170–182.

Capps, Patrick, and Henrik Palmer Olsen. 2018. *Legal Authority beyond the State*. Cambridge: Cambridge University Press.

Carothers, Thomas. 1998. "The Rule of Law Revival." *Foreign Affairs* 77(2): 95–106.

Chayes, Abram. 1974. *The Cuban Missile Crisis: International Crises and the Role of Law*. New York: Oxford University Press.

Chimni, Bhupinder, S. 2018. "Customary International Law: A Third World Perspective," *American Journal of International Law* 112(1): 1–46.

Cottier, Thomas, Charlotte Sieber-Gasser, and Gabriela Wermelinger. 2015. "The Dialectical Relationship of Preferential and Multilateral Trade Agreements" in Andreas Dür and Manfred Elsig, *Trade Cooperation: The Purpose, Design and Effects of Preferential Trade Agreement World Trade Forum*. Cambridge: Cambridge University Press, pp. 465–496.

Cottee, Simon. 2017. "What Isis Really Wants" Revisited: Religion Matters in Jihadist Violence, but How? *Studies in Conflict and Terrorism* 40(6): 439–454.

De Búrca, Gráinne, Robert O. Keohane, and Charles Sabel. 2014. "Global Experimentalist Governance." *British Journal of Political Science* 44(3): 477–486.

Delisle, Jacques. 2000. *China's Approach to International Law: A Historical Perspective*. Washington: Cambridge University Press.

Dezalay, Yves, and Bryant G. Garth. 1996. *Dealing in Virtue: International Commercial Arbitration and the Construction of a Transnational Legal Order, Language and Legal Discourse*. Chicago: University of Chicago Press.

Dezalay, Yves, and Bryant G. Garth. 2006. "From the Cold War to Kosovo: The Renewal of the Field of International Human Rights." *Annual Review of Law and Social Science* 2: 231–255.

Dezalay, Yves, and Mikael Rask Madsen. 2012. "The Force of Law and Lawyers: Pierre Bourdieu and the Reflexive Sociology of Law." *Annual Review of Law and Social Science* 8(1): 433–452.

Dodge, William S. 2015. "International Comity in American Law." *Columbia Law Review* 115(8): 2071–2141.

Finnemore, Martha. 1999. "Are Legal Norms Distinct?" *Journal of International Law and Politics* 32: 699–706.

Gehring, Thomas, and Benjamin Faude. 2013. "The Dynamics of Regime Complexes: Microfoundations and Systemic Effects." *Global Governance* 19(1): 119–130.

Ginsburg, Tom. 2020. "Authoritarian International Law?" *American Journal of International Law* 114(2): 221–260.

Ginsburg, Tom, and Tamir Moustafa. 2008. *Rule by Law: The Politics of Courts in Authoritarian Regimes*. Cambridge/New York: Cambridge University Press.

Goldsmith, Jack L., and Eric A. Posner. 2005. *The Limits of International Law*. Oxford/New York: Oxford University Press.

Green, James A. 2016. *The Persistent Objector Rule in International Law.* Oxford: Oxford University Press.

Haggard, Stephan, Andrew Macintyre, and Lydia Tiede. 2008. "The Rule of Law and Economic Development." *Annual Review of Political Science* 11(1): 205–234.

Hakimi, Monica. 2017. "Constructing an International Community." *American Journal of International Law* 111(2): 317–356.

Hathaway, Oona, and Scott J. Shapiro. 2011. "Outcasting: Enforcement in Domestic and International Law." *Yale Law Journal* 121(2): 252–469.

Helfer, Laurence. 2004. "Regime Shifting: The TRIPS Agreement and the New Dynamics of International Intellectual Property Making." *Yale Journal of International Law* 29: 1–81.

Helfer, Laurence. 2005. "Exiting Treaties." *Virginia Law Review* 91: 1579–1648.

Hestermeyer, Holger. 2007. *Human Rights and the WTO: The Case of Patents and Access to Medicines.* Oxford/New York: Oxford University Press.

Hull, Isabel V. 2014. *A Scrap of Paper: Breaking and Making International Law during the Great War.* Ithaca: Cornell University Press.

Ikenberry, G. John. 2001. *After Victory: Institutions, Strategic Restraint, and the Rebuilding of Order after Major Wars.* Princeton: Princeton University Press.

Kalb, Marvin L. 2015. *Imperial Gamble: Putin, Ukraine, and the New Cold War.* Washington, D.C: Brookings Institution Press.

Kelley, Judith. 2007. "Who Keeps International Commitments and Why? The International Criminal Court and Bilateral Nonsurrender Agreements." *American Political Science Review* 101(3): 573–589.

Keohane, Robert O., and David G. Victor. 2011. "The Regime Complex for Climate Change." *Perspectives on Politics* 9(1): 7–23.

Kittrie, Orde F. 2016. *Lawfare: Law as a Weapon of War.* Oxford: Oxford University Press.

Koinova, Maria, Maryam Zarnegar Deloffre, Frank Gadinger, Zeynep Sahin Mencutek, Jan Aart Scholte, and Jens Steffek. 2021. "It's Ordered Chaos: What Really Makes Polycentrism Work." *International Studies Review* 23(4): 1988–2018.

Krisch, Nico. 2017. "Liquid Authority in Global Governance." *International Theory* 9(2): 237–260.

Lake, David A. 2009. *Hierarchy in International Relations.* Ithaca: Cornell University Press.

Madsen, Michael Rask. 2009. "Legal Diplomacy: Law Politics and the Genesis of Postwar European Human Rights," in Stefan-Ludwig Hoffmann (ed.), *Human Rights in the Twentieth Century: A Critical History.* Cambridge: Cambridge University Press, pp. 62–84.

Madsen, Mikael Rask. 2013. "Unpacking Legal Network Power: The Structural Construction of Transnational Legal Expert Networks," in Mark Fenwick, Stephen Van Uytsel, and Stephen Wrbka (eds.), *Networked Governance, Transnational Business and the Law.* Berlin: Springer Verlag, pp. 39–56.

Mälksoo, Lauri. 2015. *Russian Approaches to International Law.* Oxford: Oxford University Press.

Marchuk, Iryna. 2017. "Flexing Its Muscles (Once Again): The Russian Constitutional Court's Defiance of the Authority of the ECtHR in the Yukos

Case." *EJIL: Talk!* 02/13/17, www.ejiltalk.org/flexing-muscles-yet-again-the-russian-constitutional-courts-defiance-of-the-authority-of-the-ecthr-in-the-yukos-case/ [last access 05/12/19].

Merryman, John Henry, and Rogelio Pérez-Perdomo. 2007. *The Civil Law Tradition*. Stanford: Stanford University Press.

Morse, Julia, and Robert Keohane. 2014. "Contested Multilateralism." *The Review of International Organizations* 9(4): 385–412.

Natarajan, Usha, John Reynolds, Amar Bhatia, and Sujith Xavier. 2016. "Introduction: TWAIL – on Praxis and the Intellectual." *Third World Quarterly* 37(11): 1946–1956.

Ohlin, Jens David. 2015. *The Assault on International Law*. Oxford: Oxford University Press.

Ohnesorge, John K. M. 2007. "The Rule of Law." *Annual Review of Law and Social Science* (3): 99–114.

Peters, Anne. 2017. "The Refinement of International Law: From Fragmentation to Regime Interaction and Politicization." *I•CON* 15(3): 671–704.

Posner, Eric, and Alan Sykes. 2011. "Efficient Breach of International Law: Optimal Remedies, 'Legalized Noncompliance,' and Related Issues." *Michigan Law Review* 110: 243–294.

Pratt, Tyler. 2018. "Deference and Hierarchy in International Regime Complexes." *International Organization* 72(3): 561–590.

Reus-Smit, Christian. 2011. "Obligation through Practice." *International Theory* 3(2): 339–347.

Risse, Thomas. 2000. "'Lets Argue': Communicative Action in World Politics." *International Organization* 34(1): 1–39.

Roberts, Anthea. 2017. *Is International Law International?* New York: Oxford University Press.

Sanahuja, José Antonio. 2012. "Post-Liberal Regionalism in South America: The Case of Unasur." *EUI Working Papers* 2012/05.

Scheppele, Kim Lane. 2018. "Autocratic Legalism." *University of Chicago Law Review* 85(2): 545–583.

Sirleaf, Matiangai. 2017. "The African Justice Cascade and the Malabo Protocol." *International Journal of Transitional Justice* 11(1): 71–91.

Sloss, David. 2016. *The Death of Treaty Supremacy: An Invisible Constitutional Change*. Oxford: Oxford University Press.

Specia, Megan, Takkunen, Mikko 2018. "South China Seas Photos Suggest a Military Building Spree from China." *The New York Times* 02/08/18, www.nytimes.com/2018/02/08/world/asia/south-china-seas-photos.html [last access 05/12/19].

Stone Sweet, Alec, and Thomas Brunell. 2013. "Trustee Courts and the Judicialization of International Regimes: The Politics of Majoritarian Activism in the ECHR, the EU and the WTO." *Journal of Law and Courts* 1(1): 61–88.

Streeck, Wolfgang, and Kathleen Ann Thelen. 2005. *Beyond Continuity: Institutional Change in Advanced Political Economies*. Oxford/New York: Oxford University Press.

Sutherland, Peter, Jagdish Bhagwati, Kwesi Botchwey, Niall Fitzgerald, Koichi Hamada, John H. Jackson, Celso Lafer, and Theirry de Montbrial. 2004. *The Future of the WTO: Addressing Institutional Challenges in the New Millennium*. Lausanne: The World Trade Organization.

Tamanaha, Brian Z. 2004. *On the Rule of Law: History, Politics, Theory.* Cambridge: Cambridge University Press.

Teles, Stephen M. 2009. *The Rise of the Conservative Legal Movement: The Battle for Control of the Law.* Princeton: Princeton University Press.

The Ministry of Foreign Affairs of the Russian Federation. 2016. *The Declaration of the Russian Federation and the People's Republic of China on the Promotion of International Law,* www.mid.ru/en/foreign_policy/position_word_order/-/asset_publisher/6S4RuXfeYlKr/content/id/2331698 [last access 05/28/19].

UN Office of Legal Affairs. 2019. *International Law Commission,* http://legal.un.org/ilc/ [last access 05/12/19].

Venzke, Ingo. 2018. "Semantic Authority, Legal Change and the Dynamics of International Law," in Patrick Capps, and Henrik Palmer Olsen (eds.), *Legal Authority beyond the State.* Cambridge: Cambridge University Press, pp. 102–126.

Winters, Alan I. 2015. "The WTO and Regional Trade Agreements: Is It All Over for Multilateralism?" in Manfred Elsig, Bernard Hoekman, and Joost Pauwelyn (eds.), *Assessing the World Trade Organization: Fit for Purpose.* Cambridge: Cambridge University Press, pp. 344–375.

WTO 2001. *Declaration on the TRIPS Agreement and Public Health,* www.wto.org/english/thewto_e/minist_e/min01_e/mindecl_trips_e.htm, [last access 05/12/19].

Zürn, Michael. 2018. *A Theory of Global Governance.* Oxford: Oxford University Press.

Notes

1 The author acknowledges the helpful feedback of participants in the "Beyond Anarchy: Rule and Authority in the International System" workshop and Benjamin Faude, Yoram Haftel, Jessica Tobin, and two anonymous reviewers.

2 Ikenberry 2001.

3 Carothers 1998; Haggard et al. 2008; Ohnesorge 2007.

4 My trustee argument is similar yet somewhat different to that of Alec Stone Sweet and Thomas Brunell 2013. For more, see Alter 2008, 2014: chapter 2.

5 Legal scholars tend to debate this notion by discussing the fragmented and pluralistic nature of international law. Whereas some legal scholars seek to overcome or resolve fragmentation and pluralism, others accept that no solution to the hierarchy problem will emerge so that international law will remain fragmented and pluralistic. See, for example, Capps and Olsen 2018: Introduction.

6 Christian Reus-Smit 2011 points out that this shared commitment may be historically contingent. It may also be a particularly Western notion.

7 Although as Judith Kelley 2007 demonstrates, governments may also make costly principle decisions based on their respect for the rule of law.

8 Alter et al. 2018: chapter 1.

9 Merryman and Pérez-Perdomo 2007.

10 The Paquete Habana, 175 U.S. 677, 20 S. Ct. 290, 44 L. Ed. 320, 1900 U.S. LEXIS 1714 (U.S. Jan. 8, 1900).

11 The Law Commission is a United Nations Agency with an explicit mandate to "initiate studies and make recommendations for the purpose of … encouraging the progressive development of international law and its codification" (UN Office of Legal Affairs 2019).
12 Chimni 2018: 2–5 (esp. notes 7 and 11).
13 Chayes 1974; Hull 2014.
14 Madsen 2013; Roberts 2017: 110–124.
15 Chinese and Russian leaders are working hard to ensure that legal scholars echo and amplify the government's position regarding international law with Russian and Chinese characteristics. Delisle 2000; Mälksoo 2015.
16 Alter and Li 2022.
17 Risse 2000: 7.
18 I do not mean anything complicated in this reference to discursive politics, and indeed my notion is compatible with Venzke's argument about "semantic authority as an actor's capacity to find recognition for their claims in about international law and to establish reference points for legal discourse that others actors can hardly escape." Venzke goes on to parse these theoretical categories even further, see Venzke 2018: 104.
19 Arbitration between the Republic of the Philippines and the People's Republic of China, PCA Case No. 2013–19, Jurisdiction and Admissibility (Oct. 29, 2015), www.pca-cpa.org [hereinafter Award on Jurisdiction]; *In re* Arbitration Between the Republic of the Philippines and the People's Republic of China, PCA Case No. 2013–19, Award (July 12, 2016), www.pca-cpa.org.
20 Roberts 2017: 240–254.
21 Alter et al. 2018: chapter 1.
22 Finnemore 1999.
23 Goldsmith and Posner 2005; Posner and Sykes 2011.
24 This principle holds because dispossessing a country of land is difficult. Moreover, the common law even recognizes this adage through the principle of adverse possession.
25 Specia and Takkunen 2018.
26 Lake 2009: 28–44.
27 Zürn 2018: chapter 2.
28 Brunee and Toope 2017.
29 Bourdieu 1987; Dezalay and Madsen 2012.
30 Becker Lorca 2014; Dezalay and Garth 1996, 2006; Madsen 2009.
31 Roberts 2017: 23–43.
32 Brunnée and Toope 2011: 310 (citing Murphy 2005: 240–241).
33 See the discussion of gradual institutional change via conversion Streeck and Thelen 2005: 26–29.
34 Sloss 2016.
35 Article 6(2) of the Constitution of the United States (1789).
36 Teles 2009.
37 Tamanaha 2004.
38 This is the so-called Three Supremes doctrine. For a discussion of differences between Chinese and Western understandings and their ROL implications, see Alter and Li 2022.

39 Alter 2006.
40 Exit can sometimes be used to escape IL obligations, but not all IL obligations can be exited, see Helfer 2005. Reservations are formal legal exceptions that states can (when legally permitted) add during international treaty ratification. "Persistent objector" is another international legal notion wherein states that persistently object can escape from what might otherwise be a universal customary international law, see Green 2016.
41 Comity (the notion of mutual respect for the legal decisions of other courts) and coordinationism (finding complementarities) are the standard means judges use to avoid contradictions in legal rulings, see Dodge 2015.
42 Marchuk 2017.
43 Ohlin 2015.
44 Hestermeyer 2007: 1–17.
45 WTO 2001.
46 Alter 2018c.
47 Krisch 2017.
48 Koinova et al. 2021.
49 Alter and Raustiala 2018: 332.
50 Gehring and Faude 2013: 120; Pratt 2018.
51 Morse and Keohane 2014 create the term "contested multilateralism" to capture this scenario, except that for Morse and Keohane the goal of contested multilateralism is not to escape an international legal obligation per se (see also Morse, this volume). I am sticking with the original concept of maneuvering around the regime complex because the fundamental point is that the absence of hierarchy is what makes this strategy a tool that can be used to legitimate ignoring a parallel international legal obligation. For more, see Alter and Raustiala 2018.
52 Chavez tried to create counter-hegemonic Latin American alternatives to the Washington D.C. institutions. His first effort involved created the Bolivarian Alliance for the Peoples of Our America, or ALBA, but few other states joined. Later, in 2006 Chavez switched his economic allegiance from the Andean Community – a regional free-trade oriented trading system that included Venezuela, Colombia, Peru, Bolivia and Ecuador – to Mercosur, a different regional economic trading system that included Argentina, Brazil, Paraguay and Uruguay. At the time, both Brazil and Argentina had leftist political leaders who Chavez hoped to co-opt.
53 Sanahuja 2012.
54 Alter and Helfer 2017: 184–192.
55 Ginsburg 2020 calls this strategy mimic, recast, and repurpose.
56 One sees these goals in the Russia-China Joint statements on international law, discussed later in this chapter.
57 Helfer 2004.
58 Keohane and Victor 2011.
59 De Búrca et al. 2014.
60 Auld and Green 2012.
61 Cottier et al. 2015; Sutherland et al. 2004: chapter 2; Winters 2015.
62 Lawfare involves leveraging law, as an alternative to military force, to coerce others, see Kittrie 2016.

63 See the manifesto for "Third World Approaches to International Law" (TWAIL), Natarajan et al. 2016. A concrete example of this perspective is that for many years, international law applied only to "civilized nations." For uncivilized nations, pretty much every form of subjugation, violence, and entrapment was permissible, Anghie 2005: chapter 2; Becker Lorca 2014: chapter 5.
64 Sirleaf 2017.
65 Cottee 2017.
66 Kalb 2015.
67 See the discussion of backlash as a retrograde strategy involving extraordinary tactics, see Alter and Zürn 2020a.
68 Roberts 2017: 240–254.
69 See the Ministry of Foreign Affairs of the Russian Federation (2016) for an English version of the Joint Declaration.
70 Joint Statement of the Russian Federation and the People's Republic of China on the International Relations Entering a New Era and the Global Sustainable Development, February 4, 2022, available at www.airuniversity.af.edu/Portals/10/CASI/documents/Translations/2022-02-04%20China%20Russia%20joint%20statement%20International%20Relations%20Entering%20a%20New%20Era.pdf
71 Alter 2021
72 Bork 1989/90.
73 See also Alter 2018a, 2018b.
74 Alter 2014.
75 Hathaway and Shapiro 2011.
76 Ginsburg and Moustafa 2008; Scheppele 2018.
77 Alter and Zürn 2020b.
78 Alter 2014: 344; see also Benvenisti 2008; Benvenisti and Harel 2017; Hakimi 2017; Peters 2017.

10 Rule and Resistance in the Anti-globalization Era

Julia C. Morse[1]

> The divide is no longer between the left and the right but between patriots and globalists.
>
> Marine Le Pen, Leader of France's National Front Party, 5 February 2017

Contemporary globalization processes have empowered non-state actors, providing new opportunities for transnational civil society and multinational companies to influence international outcomes. They have also engendered the growth of regime complexes,[2] as states and non-state actors that are dissatisfied with a multilateral institution's rules bypass unilateralism in favor of alternative multilateral venues. Although this process of "contested multilateralism"[3] has led to the formation of overlapping, nonhierarchical institutions, it has also produced regimes that intrude more into the daily lives of citizens around the globe. Transnational networks may continue to grow, but a subset of citizens are in open revolt. These citizens view international arrangements as intrinsically disconnected from their preferences, preferring closed borders to free movement, and trade barriers over expansion. These are the anti-globalists, and they are ready to dismantle global governance.

Scholars have noted the democratic deficit of multilateral institutions for several decades,[4] but recent political developments have made it harder to ignore. In democracy after democracy, voters have shown support for populist leaders who decry multilateral institutions and advocate for significant retrenchment. In the United States, a nationalist anti-globalist won the presidency after campaigning to abandon trade agreements and allies alike. In Italy, an anti-globalization party comprised half of the governing coalition in 2018. And in Britain – a rare case where voters were given control over their multilateral future – anti-globalist sentiment propelled a victory for Brexit.

A desire to overturn the *status quo* is not a new phenomenon in international politics. Coalitions dissatisfied with multilateral institutions frequently seek change. Such efforts may be internal, or if institutional reform is blocked, they may launch contested multilateral challenges to increase bargaining power or find alternative venues. And at the extreme, states may always exit, although in practice this option is rarely pursued. Anti-globalist leaders are thus the latest manifestation of a longstanding practice: The desire of governments to make the international arena align more closely with domestic political goals.

This chapter considers the implication of anti-globalist resistance for international rule and authority. I highlight three ideal types of rule challenges. First, a leader may attempt to dismantle the *status quo* through unilateral action. This pathway includes both minor rule challenges like US President Trump's antagonism toward international trade and major decisions like Britain's exit from the European Union (EU). Second, a dissatisfied coalition may engage with an institution in an effort to reduce rules or obligations. Anti-migration efforts by the "Visegrad Four" group of the Czech Republic, Poland, Slovakia, and Hungary reflect this approach in the EU. Third, a dissatisfied coalition may engage in contested multilateralism, building new institutions or seeking alternative venues that favor state sovereignty over open borders. This strategy could take the form of what Riggirozzi and Tussie have called "post-hegemonic regionalism,"[5] where states and non-state actors redefine the regional space to reflect domestic changes in interests and ideas, while also offering alternative institutional structures to the *status quo*. In Latin America, left-wing politicians have banded together in an effort to reverse conventional economic policies that favor mobile capital and little regulation. A similar strategy could be deployed by right-wing, anti-globalist parties in Europe, where leaders might opt for smaller institutional groupings among states with similar preferences.

In theory, each strategy could be characterized by minor or major resistance. Unilateral action, institutional engagement, and even contested multilateralism do not always overturn international authority. Rather, mild versions of all three approaches may include what Alter terms "ordinary contestation," where states work within existing laws and debates. What makes *anti-globalist* resistance, however, more notable is that dissatisfied actors are more likely to prioritize "extraordinary contestation," working directly to supplant the authority of international law. Anti-globalists come to power on rhetoric of dismantling the international order; their preferred strategies of resistance are more likely to be what Daase and Deitelhoff term "dissidence": a complete rejection of the rules of order (Daase and Deitelhoff, this volume).

Because anti-globalists are defined by this "dissidence" goal, their choice of strategies has different implications for how we understand the sources of rule and authority in the modern international system.

If international authority has moved beyond state consent and international institutions themselves now constitute a legitimate source of authority in the international system, it will be more difficult for anti-globalist leaders to escape the confines of institutional commitments through unilateral action. Powerful states like the United States and the United Kingdom might be able to disrupt the institutional order, but unilateralism is unlikely to undermine global governance unless such states deploy it repeatedly over a long period of time or unless the strategy diffuses to a larger population of states. Alternatively, if rules derive their authority primarily from power disparities across states, then unilateral challenges by countries like the United States and regional hegemons should alter significantly the institutional network governing state conduct.

Anti-globalist leaders form a distinct set of challengers to the global system because they share a common motivation – the desire to regain national sovereignty and reduce the power of international institutions. Because of this ambition, anti-globalist leaders typically resist the international system through unilateral pronouncements, actions, and exit from institutions. Over the last decade, anti-globalist populists have decried long-established international rules on human rights, led campaigns to exit economic institutions, and removed their countries from major climate agreements. In the EU, transnational anti-globalist coalitions have sought to limit the flow of migrants to their countries and to restrict labor mobility. In Latin America, a left-wing backlash to globalization led to the formation of new regional organizations to strengthen cooperation among like-minded states and exclude the United States from regional affairs.[6]

A flurry of activity, and yet to date, such efforts have yielded relatively few results. In some ways, then, unilateral anti-globalist challenges have paradoxically highlighted the strength of international rules and procedures. Anti-globalist sentiment is widespread, yet institutions have adapted little to this preference structure. International organizations continue to exert significant authority over states, even those dissatisfied with multilateralism. The persistence of the current *status quo* suggests that rule and authority in international politics are not simply endogenous to state preferences and that institutions are likely to be continued sources of rule and authority for years to come, even as preferences change.

While governance structures may hold, however, more informal aspects of cooperation could suffer. Anti-globalist challenges have illustrated the degree to which many areas of cooperation are dependent upon norms never set forth in formal rules. Institutions exert influence over states in many ways beyond formal, legally binding rules.[7] States build informal structures in part because such institutions are more flexible and adaptive, yet these very features make them more susceptible to anti-globalist challenges. If informal institutions and norms shift to accommodate new state preferences, this transformation would suggest that while norms might serve to some degree as a source of authority in global governance, they are powerful only to the extent they reflect "buy-in" from all states. Shifting norms may be the first sign of broader changes to come in the years ahead.

Analyzing an emerging trend like anti-globalism presents unique challenges. We observe the independent and dependent variables at an incipient stage and therefore can only speculate about possible long-term effects. However, delineating strategies and thinking through their likely effects on institutions are nonetheless important tasks. Since 1945, an ever-tightening network of institutions, information, and ideas has bound world populations more closely together. This global governance architecture has brought more than one billion people out of poverty and improved health outcomes and quality of life in most countries.[8] Institutions have also promoted closer economic relationships between countries, raising the costs of conflict and facilitating the peaceful settlement of disputes that might otherwise result in war.[9] Yet despite such benefits, many populations in developed countries feel left behind by the globalization process. These individuals often blame global institutions for domestic disparities and their preferred leaders are ones who seek to disrupt the entire global system. Understanding the likely effects of such challenges allows us to probe underlying assumptions about rule and authority, while also anticipating possible policy challenges in the years to come.

Rule and Authority in the International System

To understand the effects of anti-globalist challenges, we must first consider how rule and authority operate more generally in international politics. In the introduction to this volume, Daase, Deitelhoff, and Witt conceptualize rule as including both formal and informal constellations of sub- and superordination: rules can empower or suppress, serving to redistribute material and immaterial goods and stabilize expectations. Following this framework, international rules have varying degrees of power over states, getting them to do what they otherwise would not.[10] While many IR scholars might tie power to coercive authority, David Lake's concept of relational authority is more helpful for thinking through how resistance, which in this chapter takes the form of anti-globalist challenges to the international order, may generate downstream effects for international rule and authority. In Lake's account, authority is a type of social contract where a governing body provides political order that is valuable enough to the governed to offset the loss of freedom.[11] Once relational authority is established, the governing body and the governed are constantly renegotiating the terms of the agreement, determining what is just or legitimate. When the governed view rules as more legitimate, the rules become more authoritative and are thus more likely to be obeyed.[12]

Based on this conceptualization of international authority, global governance expansion occurs when states and non-state actors work to broaden political order while minimizing the loss of freedom. International rules may deepen, touching on new issue areas or creating unforeseen implementation challenges. In the years following the 9/11 terrorist attacks, for example, states built out a massive counterterrorism regime complex consisting of many multilateral and regional organizations that could provide guidance and technical assistance to states around the world. When global governance expands for this type of functional reason, new institutions do not necessarily portend conflict among governing bodies. Organizations may exhibit "institutional deference,"[13] whereby they accept each other's explicit authority and differentiate labor and expertise, or enlist other organizations in pursuit of shared goals.[14] Regime complexes may provide other cooperative benefits, facilitating flexibility across issues and adaptation over time,[15] or positively restructuring an IO's mandate.[16] When a regime complex is organized around a central institution, it may produce positive governance gains,[17] perhaps by increasing the likelihood that potential problems will be addressed by states.[18]

States may also expand global governance out of a desire to resist or renegotiate the existing regime complex. IOs institutionalize formal and informal mechanisms of power and authority. But while initial institutional design features are likely to reflect a clear contract between the governing body and the governed, IOs often struggle to adapt to changes in the distribution of power and interests over time. Indeed, part of the advantages of international organizations are that they lock-in power arrangements that are difficult to change.[19] As a result, institutions are slow to anticipate and adapt to shifting state preferences. Dissatisfaction increases but may not lead to significant change.

When states are dissatisfied with the institutional *status quo,* they can choose several different strategies to renegotiate the social contract and potentially redistribute authority within a regime. A dissatisfied state can unilaterally challenge a regime through noncompliance or threats of withdrawal. Alternatively, a state or coalition might opt to try to engage with a multilateral institution, seeking to redesign the agenda or rules or block future cooperative efforts. Finally, a dissatisfied coalition might use contested multilateralism, repurposing an existing institution or creating a new institution to challenge the *status quo*. A state or coalition's choice of strategy signals something about the nature of rule and authority in the international system and also has long-term consequences for the authoritativeness of the regime complex.

Unilateral Challenges

States often opt for unilateral strategies to contest multilateral rules. This type of strategy can take many forms, including overt withdrawal or resistance, covert noncompliance, or partial compliance. A key aspect of unilateralism is that a state has almost complete control over the extent of resistance or noncompliance and so can better anticipate the impact of its behavior. Unilateral challenges need not create significant disruptions. A dissatisfied state looking only to forgo its own obligations may calculate that weak implementation or hidden noncompliance is the easiest way to shirk authority without bearing broader cooperative costs. Even when states opt for overt resistance, they may view unilateral challenges as efforts to renegotiate rules rather than as complete rejections of institutional authority.

Hungary's approach to the Syrian refugee crisis demonstrates this type of targeted unilateral resistance. The EU's Charter of Fundamental Rights includes the right to asylum, and European states are legally bound to uphold such principles. In September 2017, the European Court of Justice (ECJ) ruled that European officials are legally allowed to order member state governments to take specific quotas of refugees entering the country.[20] Despite such principles and rules, however, Hungary opted instead to close its borders. It erected a fence along its border with Serbia, and if authorities caught undocumented immigrants, Hungarian officials "escorted" them back.[21] The Hungarian government's actions challenged EU norms and principles in a targeted way, challenging authority without forcing the country to endure the loss of cooperative benefits that would accompany full withdrawal. In the short term, the EU proved willing to bear such costs; EU rules continue to exert authority over Hungary despite conflicting domestic preferences. More recently, however, the ECJ pushed back against Hungary's broader authoritarian turn, ruling that the EU can withhold funding from member states that fail to uphold rule-of-law principles.[22]

While mild unilateral challenges can chip away at an institution's authority, stronger unilateral actions – such as threats of exit or actual withdrawal – cause more immediate disruption. A state may use this approach to enhance its bargaining leverage and to push for institutional reform.[23] In some cases, credible exit threats are sufficient to force legal and procedural change. Separatist movements in Quebec, Scotland, and Catalonia, for example, have used such threats as effective bargaining tactics to enhance their own autonomy. The UK's Brexit referendum had similar origins: British Prime Minister David Cameron proposed the vote as a political tactic to increase his party's domestic support and also strengthen negotiating power with the EU.[24] As a bargaining tactic, however, exit threats are somewhat risky: if withdrawal occurs, a state relinquishes any control over the regime. For this reason, full withdrawal is likely to be a policy of last resort.

While unilateral exit clearly challenges global governance authority, its long-term effects are likely to vary across contexts. The United States' withdrawal from the Kyoto Protocol severely weakened the regime, whereas the Paris Agreement persevered even absent the United States. Policymakers have warned for years that North Korea's withdrawal from the Nuclear Non-Proliferation Treaty (NPT) and subsequent missile tests could lead to the collapse of the NPT,[25] and yet, nearly 15 years later, the regime still stands. In some cases, a single state's withdrawal could even paradoxically strengthen an IO if other countries are dissuaded from leaving. The prolonged and messy negotiations over Brexit, for example, sent a clear signal to other countries about the costs of EU extraction and may have made the prospect less appealing for both politicians and the publics in other member states.

Unilateral withdrawal may temporarily weaken a regime; however, its long-term effects on institutional authority are likely to depend in part on the prominence of the exiting country. A central actor exiting an institution will redistribute power across the remaining members. IOs operate based on two sets of principles – sovereign equality and unequal distribution of privileges[26] – and this coincidence means the exit of a powerful country will fundamentally shift how an institution operates, regardless of its official decision-making procedures. Such disruptions renegotiate relational authority and may even create openings for others to challenge the regime. In contrast, if a state is weak or peripheral, exit may have little impact.

The rationale for exit is also likely to moderate its impact on institutional authority. If a state is isolated and continually violating a regime's rules prior to exit, such as the North Korea NPT example, exit may have few effects on the regime. Similarly, when a country exits for domestic political reasons, the remaining member states are unlikely to view the action as an indictment on the institution. Venezuela's recent decision to withdraw from the Organization of American States (OAS), for example, is unlikely to have a significant impact on how other member states view the OAS, since Venezuela decided to withdraw to avoid public condemnation from OAS foreign ministers about the Venezuelan government's handling of ongoing violent protests. However, when an exiting country challenges something fundamental about an institution – such as its rules or decision-making procedures – this action can create broader challenges to regime legitimacy. States adhere to rules in part because they perceive them to be legitimate,[27] and a regime's authority is directly connected to such perceptions.[28] If exit prompts other states to perceive a regime as illegitimate, they may seek alternative venues or outsource governance to transnational organizations, as Lake describes in this volume.

The varied effects of unilateral withdrawal on institutional authority can be seen by comparing several different cases of US "soft" exit. The United States has, on multiple occasions, participated in negotiations over a treaty but failed to ratify the final outcome for domestic political reasons. Such was the case with the UN Convention on the Law of the Sea (UNCLOS) and the Rome Statute for the International Criminal Court (ICC). In both cases, however, the United States took subsequent steps to support the agreements, abiding by UNCLOS norms in practice and supporting the Security Council's referral of the Libya situation to the ICC. This approach is, in some respects, the converse of what Alter describes in this volume: rather than a state supplanting international law with domestic law or pitting international regimes against each other, the US has prioritized standard international law without actually subjecting itself to jurisdiction. As a result, the effect of these soft exits on institutional authority has been relatively limited. On the other hand, US exit from climate agreements has had more varied impacts. The United States' withdrawal from the Kyoto Protocol was based on what many observers considered to be a significant flaw in the agreement: the fact that China did not agree to any emissions reductions. Perhaps as a result, US action permanently damaged the regime. The United States' exit from the Paris Agreement, however, was more neutral: While it undoubtedly damaged the agreement's effectiveness, the regime's normative legitimacy remained unchallenged. The regime was further buttressed with the US reentry in 2021.

Institutional Engagement

A dissatisfied state or coalition might also engage directly with an international institution in order to challenge rules and authority. States frequently work to reshape rules, agenda, or decision-making procedures to more accurately reflect their preferences. As Mahoney and Thelen point out, this effort may be gradual, focused more on implementing existing rules in a new way than on forcing through drastically new standards.[29] Some scholars have argued that states engage with the World Trade Organization's (WTO) dispute settlement body in this way, using cases and legal briefs to establish precedent and shape future trade rules in line with their interests.[30] This strategy is predicated on a long time horizon: While incremental institutional change may gradually alter the nature of relational authority between an institution and its members, it is poorly equipped to respond to significant dissatisfaction in the short term.

To date, few anti-globalist leaders or coalitions have been successful in creating significant institutional change through incrementalism. Such efforts inevitably run into roadblocks set up by the other states that prefer to retain the institutional *status quo*. Italy's former Prime Minister Giuseppe Conte, for example, won the 2018 election on an anti-EU platform that opposed austerity and immigration. But while Prime Minister Conte pushed back against the EU's call for spending cuts and taxes, Germany's Prime Minister Angela Merkel publicly rejected his proposal, pointing out that all EU member states are required to follow the same rules.[31] Even with far-right parties gaining a significant foothold in the European Parliament, such actors have struggled to shape policy outcomes in a significant way.[32] Incremental attempts to adjust rules are unlikely to create significant institutional change unless the perpetrators are powerful countries that can build a strong coalition and know how to wield institutional procedures to their advantage.

Dissatisfied states may also work to block or stonewall institutional activities. If, as Lake suggests, relational authority rests on providing political order that is valuable enough to the governed to offset the loss of freedom, institutional obstruction may be a powerful way of undermining such benefits. States may subject themselves to voluntary subordination because they perceive limits on information and rationality;[33] however, if an IO ceases to function as intended, authority is often undermined. Obstruction can occur through formal mechanisms, such as voting or vetoes, or through informal pathways like agenda setting or bureaucratic oversight.

Obstruction is particularly detrimental when a dissatisfied actor or coalition is powerful. In such circumstances, a state may exercise informal influence over high-stakes issues,[34] or potentially forestall cooperation entirely. During treaty negotiations, a coalition might adopt an untenable position and prevent parties from reaching any type of agreement, as has been the case with the persistently stalled Doha negotiations on trade. In the case of established institutions, dissatisfied actors may simply curtail an institution's agenda or continually introduce resolutions that run against the founding principles. Such efforts can damage the social contract between the governing body and the governed by undermining or narrowing an institution's value, such that even cooperative states are less willing to rely on the institution as a source of authority. When this type of functional damage occurs, the existence of a regime complex may actually help mitigate obstruction, as other institutions can compensate for agenda gaps or losses in legitimacy.

Russian and Chinese engagement with the UN Security Council over the last two decades illustrates this type of obstruction strategy. Although the UN Charter gives the Security Council "primary responsibility for the maintenance of international peace and security," the Council has struggled to respond to many international crises since the late 1990s. In 1999, the United States and United Kingdom were unable to secure UN Security Council authorization for military action in Kosovo, despite unanimity that Yugoslavia was committing massive human rights violations, because Russia and China threatened to veto any authorizing resolution.[35] As a result, Western states used the North Atlantic Treaty Organization (NATO) to authorize military action, challenging the UN Security Council's supremacy. Ironically, the ultimate impact of this case of institutional obstruction was not only to undermine the Security Council's authority as a maintainer of peace and security but also to elevate NATO as a potential alternative source of authority for peace and security. Russia adopted a similar obstructionist approach to the conflict in Syria, preventing the Security Council from passing any meaningful resolution to address the violence and humanitarian catastrophe in the region.

Contested Multilateralism

The third possible strategy is for a dissatisfied coalition to challenge global governance directly through contested multilateralism. Contested multilateralism "occurs when states and/or non-state actors either shift their focus from one existing institution to another or create an alternative multilateral institution to compete with existing ones."[36] Similar to unilateral exit and institutional engagement, contested multilateralism originates with resistance to established international rules or procedures. Unlike engagement, however, the dissatisfied coalition is unable to address the source of dissatisfaction through purely internal means. Institutions may be unable to adapt to changing preferences due to horizontal decision structures or divergent state preferences.[37] The underlying source of dissatisfaction may also be impossible to address within a specific institutional space. Recent work on defensive or post-hegemonic regionalism in Latin American, for example, argues that a core reason for Latin American regional construction is to exclude the United States and Canada from membership.[38] If a coalition's challenge is political or normative in nature, rather than based on specific policy outcomes, institutional adaptation may not be able to achieve the intended objective. In such cases, contested multilateralism offers a viable alternative strategy for shaping global governance.

Morse and Keohane identify two types of contested multilateral challenges.[39] The first is regime shifting, a concept developed by Lawrence Helfer,[40] which occurs when a coalition uses an alternative institution to formulate rules or practices that conflict with the original institution's rules or reduce its authority. The effort by developing countries and European states to increase the UN General Assembly's role in counterterrorism policy and, concomitantly, to deemphasize the UN Security Council's approach provides one such example. In the mid-2000s, developing countries began to advocate for expanding the scope of counterterrorism to include the conditions that give rise to terrorism – a shift that would have redistributed the costs of cooperation toward developed states. At the same time, European countries began to push for more overt references to human rights.[41] The efforts of this unusual coalition eventually led the UN General Assembly to adopt the Global Counter-Terrorism Strategy in 2006, which broadened the scope of counterterrorism to encompass both human rights concerns and conditions conductive to terrorism – two norms underemphasized by the Security Council at that time.

Morse and Keohane also describe a second type of contested multilateralism called competitive regime creation. This strategy occurs when a coalition creates a new, competitor institution that more closely aligns with its interests; as a result, the new institution's rules or procedures conflict with the original institution's rules or reduce its authority. For example, China's drive to create a new forum for development lending, the Asian Infrastructure Investment Bank (AIIB), was tied in large part to years of dissatisfaction with the World Bank. According to Kreuder-Sonnen and Zangl, China and other rising powers were reportedly dissatisfied with the Bank's constraints on infrastructure lending and its institutional accountability mechanisms.[42] Other scholars have suggested the World Bank's unwillingness to increase China's vote share to reflect its increased economic power may have also created dissatisfaction.[43] Regardless of reason, after years of pushing for change in the World Bank, China went outside the institution in 2015 to create the new AIIB, where it holds the only veto over allocation decisions.

US opposition to the AIIB highlights how contested multilateral challenges may be perceived as redistributing global governance authority. The United States publicly opposed the bank's creation, reportedly because the US government worried that the AIIB would fragment global economic standards by forgoing the World Bank's environmental protections, governance standards, and anticorruption measures.[44] From the US perspective, the World Bank's authority was based on providing states funding with key conditions attached to the loans. If the AIIB were to provide loans without those conditions, the World Bank's social contract between the governing body and the governed could be called into question.

Notably, the AIIB example also suggests that competitive regime creation does not always undermine international authority in the long run. As Sending describes in this volume, authority evolves as actors participate in the process of making political rule. Institutions with significant overlapping memberships may promote similar norms and values, particularly if the competitor institution includes countries that were satisfied with the status quo. In the case of the AIIB, China encouraged a broad coalition of countries to join the institution as founding members. Despite US lobbying, many European countries and US allies joined negotiations early on and helped share the new institution's rules and norms. As a result, the AIIB has largely embraced most of the World Bank standards and is cooperating with the Bank on several projects. Overlapping membership may thus mitigate the disruptive effect of contested multilateral challenges on regime authority.

Latin America has experienced an alternative model of competitive regime creation that may be more viable for anti-globalist coalitions. Beginning in the early 2000s, a wave of elections brought a set of radical, left-wing leaders to power in Latin America. These governments explicitly rejected the neoliberal market ideology that was previously the basis of economic integration in the region. As the United States attempted to negotiate a Free Trade Area of the Americas (FTAA), Venezuela led an alternative initiative to create the Bolivarian Alliance for the Peoples of Our America (ALBA). ALBA positioned itself in direct opposition to the ideology of economic integration; indeed, it touted its success in derailing the now-abandoned FTAA and in bringing the state "back in" as an economic actor in order to restrict market forces.[45] ALBA created its own Peoples' Trade Agreement (ALBA-TCP) focused on aligning trade with poverty reduction and cultural identity preservation. Although ALBA started out with only two members, today ALBA-TCP has grown to include nine states. Notably, its membership intentionally excludes Canada and the United States as part of a counter-hegemonic effort to reject North American leadership in the region.[46] A similar, albeit more moderate, effort to build regional integration without US influence also occurred in 2008 with the establishment of the Union of South American Nations (UNASUR). UNASUR includes countries with more diverse preferences vis-à-vis the United States but has served as a venue for conflict resolution between member states while also bolstering Brazil's image as a regional power.[47]

The creation of ALBA and UNASUR in Latin America illustrates a potential model for anti-globalist contested multilateralism while also highlighting the constraints of such an approach. New left leaders in Latin America banded together to form ALBA and UNASUR, and in the process, they successfully derailed a proposed free trade agreement. However, the effects of ALBA and UNASUR on already existing institutions like the OAS remain less clear. Riggirozi argues that UNASUR's role in resolving territorial disputes affects the authority of existing US-led institutions like the OAS[48]; however, other scholars see the new institutions as "hollow institutional shells void of substantive multilateralism, and to which leaders are reluctant to delegate real authority."[49] While the new institutions may have weakened the authority of the OAS, the OAS continues to be the central institution in the region.

Anti-Globalist Contestation

Given these three strategies, how should we expect anti-globalist leaders to engage with the international system and challenge global governance? To answer this question, it is helpful to consider first the specific nature of anti-globalist resistance to the international system. Anti-globalist policy positions often align; many leaders are opposed to free trade and financial integration and support tighter borders and less immigration. The philosophy of nationalism that underlies these preferences, however, is perhaps more important than the actual policy proposals themselves. Anti-globalists share one key defining core belief: A government should reduce the authority of international rules over its citizens. Economic anti-globalists might target trade rules, while environmental anti-globalists might seek to challenge emission commitments. But regardless of issue area, the end objective is the same: These governments want to reconceptualize the social contract. Historian Jeremy Adelman has cautioned that this trend is not the end of integration but rather a move toward the bilateral and imperialist model of global order that dominated so much of history.[50] In this world, the reassertion of national sovereignty is an end in itself.

The anti-globalist distrust of international organizations and their rules often correlates with a deep sense of nativism. Anti-globalist leaders and the citizens who support them typically employ a narrow definition of the homeland and its rightful population. Citizens that are not part of the dominant ethnic majority are deemed illegitimate political actors. In Hungary, Prime Minister Viktor Orban vowed to use his third term to defend the country's "Hungarian culture and Christian culture" against migrants and refugees.[51] Polling data following the Brexit vote in the United Kingdom suggests "leave" voters were more likely to be "ethnic" voters focused on a language and heritage-based version of English identity.[52] In a similar way, anti-globalist leaders object to international organizations that provide foreign populations authority over a country's domestic rules. In his statement to the United Nations, US President Trump argued that "the nation-state remains the best vehicle for elevating the human condition."[53] Marine Le Pen, speaking of the rise of anti-globalist leaders, stated "we will give back to nations reasoned protectionism, economic and cultural patriotism."[54]

Rising anti-globalist sentiment suggests that while global governance has expanded significantly over the seventy years, underlying norms may have failed to keep pace with such expansion. Institutional authority and legitimacy are based in part on performance.[55] Widespread resistance to rule then suggests an underlying problem – the political order provided by international rules is no longer valuable enough to certain communities to offset the loss of autonomy. This perception may or may not be connected to reality. Due to the nature of international cooperation, costs are apparent while the benefits are diffuse, which makes it more difficult for individuals to recognize their gains. Regardless of the underlying truth, however, a segment of the global population clearly believes that their countries are worse off under globalization. This subpopulation is likely to channel such discontent toward global governance institutions, which have promoted and intensified the economic, informational, and technological processes that leave many individuals feeling disconnected and left behind.

With their streamlined preferences, anti-globalist leaders provide a unique opportunity to understand the nature of international rule today. While dissatisfied states have historically sought to shift and transform international rules, current anti-globalists seek to undermine or dismantle the system. These challenges test the limits of international obligations, serving as a type of stress test for international organizations. Understanding the conditions under which rules will persist in the face of such challenges will shed significant light on the underlying strength of global governance.

Anti-Globalist Unilateralism

Anti-globalist resistance could readily take the form of unilateral noncompliance or exit. Unilateralism is the lowest cost and fastest way for a country to challenge an institution's governing authority. In principle, withdrawing from an institution is a direct path to authority reclamation, allowing the governed country to eliminate its international obligations. In practice, however, leaders often want to retain some of the cooperative benefits of the institution, which makes exit much more complicated to negotiate. Supporters of Brexit – the most striking example of anti-globalist contestation to-date – encountered such a problem. They wanted to close borders and limit immigration, while also maintaining close economic ties to Europe. These conflicting goals proved difficult to achieve in practice, and five years after the vote, new border and immigration arrangements continue to disrupt trade and labor supply.[56]

Britain's struggles highlight key downsides of unilateral challenges. In almost all cases, anti-globalist leaders will want to retain at least some benefits of international agreements after exit. Institutions thus have additional negotiating leverage compared to the withdrawing state. Furthermore, while an anti-globalist leader may personally view an institution as illegitimate, he may also recognize that global governance structures have broader legitimacy, both within domestic populations and across international borders. Scholarship on compliance has pointed out that domestic actors may respond to government noncompliance by appealing to international agreements,[57] while transnational civil society may also use international norms to criticize states that fail to meet such standards.[58] Such arguments suggest that anti-globalist leaders have incentives to avoid unilateral challenges to authority, particularly in issue areas where global governance is highly institutionalized.

Unilateral exit may also be a costly strategy because it requires states to relinquish control over institutional outcomes. Unilateral exit will rarely dismantle institutional structures – instead, institutions will continue to exist and exercise authority, but without the input of anti-globalist countries. The United States' decision to withdraw from the Trans-Pacific Partnership did not dismantle the agreement; instead, the remaining countries pushed forward with the Comprehensive and Progressive Trans-Pacific Partnership, which was signed in March 2018.[59] The potential costs of absence can be quite high. Institutional rules may deviate further from state preferences, and while former members may no longer be subject to the rules themselves, the institution may still shape broader norms or conduct across states. Finally, and perhaps most significantly, unilateral exit enables rival states to use institutions to further their own agenda. The Soviet Union's boycott of the Security Council did little damage to the Council's legitimacy, but it did allow the United States to put forward a resolution authorizing military action in the Korean peninsula.

Coordinated multilateral exit may be a more appealing alternative to unilateral exit as it avoids some of the downsides of unilateral action. An anti-globalist coalition could decide to exit an organization together as part of an effort to bring back more domestic control while also minimizing political costs. Yet even when leaders are ideologically aligned, they may still struggle to carry out such plans. In January 2017, for example, the African Union (AU) approved a nonbinding resolution calling for AU member states to investigate the idea of collective withdrawal from the ICC. While many AU countries were dissatisfied with the ICC due to a perceived anti-African bias, several AU members vocally opposed the resolution and it ultimately accomplished very little.[60] Indeed, of the three AU members that had signaled their intention to leave the ICC,[61] only one (Burundi) ultimately withdrew from the Court.

Anti-Globalist Institutional Engagement

Faced with such constraints, anti-globalist leaders and coalitions might instead opt for the other two types of challenges – institutional engagement and contested multilateralism. Institutional engagement could take one of two forms. Leaders might work to obstruct institutions in a way that prevents them from making new rules or furthering cooperative gains. US-Soviet disagreements during the Cold War, for example, blocked the UN Security Council from responding to many international crises. Anti-globalist leadership in a powerful country could produce a similar outcome if the government has a controlling vote share in an international body or if institutional procedures are based on consensus. A coalition of weaker countries might also be able to block specific multilateral policy outcomes, such as when a small group of Caribbean islands blocked a 2017 OAS resolution to condemn Venezuela's President for his repressive actions.[62]

An alternative engagement strategy could be to push for institutional adaptation. In some ways, direct institutional engagement may be the best option for anti-globalists because they have an opportunity to renegotiate and reduce institutional authority. For powerful countries in particular, such a strategy may be even more beneficial than unilateralism – whereas unilateral withdrawal might collapse an institution, institutional engagement and renegotiation provides an opportunity to transform rules in a nationalist way. But such efforts will also encounter roadblocks from other states that may be unwilling to engage in piecemeal cooperation. During Brexit negotiations, for example, UK Prime Minister Theresa May proposed a "three-basket approach" wherein Britain would stick to EU rules in some areas, diverge moderately in others, and opt for distinctly different solutions in the rest, but EU officials strongly rejected such selective access to the common market.[63]

Anti-globalist institutional engagement might also target norms rather than formal rules or policies. This strategy could be particularly effective at undermining multilateral authority because it highlights the degree to which global governance operates based on informal understandings and procedures. Perhaps the best example of anti-globalist norm contestation is US President Trump's approach to the G-7 and the WTO. Over the last forty years, informal groupings of countries (known as the G-7/G-8, and in recent years, the G-20) have become an increasingly important feature of informal governance.[64] Since the first meeting in 1975, these summits have always resulted in some type of final statement or recap, which lays out a shared geopolitical vision and policy agenda. Yet in 2018, US President Trump refused to sign the final G-7 Communique, breaking an unofficial norm and reducing the authoritativeness of the final statement. Trump also challenged multilateral norms in the area of trade, invoking the WTO's national security exception to justify tariffs. Although the provision is technically part of the WTO rules, states rarely invoke the provision. Instead, avoiding abuse has depended on restraint by WTO members.[65] The US violation of the non-use norm may encourage other states to violate in a similar fashion. Such challenges to international norms illustrate both the degree to which norms are a source of authority in the international system and also the fragility of norm-related governance.

Anti-Globalist Contested Multilateralism

If all other strategies fail, anti-globalist leaders may opt for contested multilateralism to challenge global governance. In some ways, the idea of anti-globalist-led contested multilateralism seems paradoxical – why would coalitions that prefer to dismantle international order seek to do so through international institutions? And yet, there are some incentives for leaders to engage with the international system in this way. From a domestic standpoint, most anti-globalist movements are pluralities within their countries, which means they are likely to encounter strong domestic resistance if they seek to challenge international rules unilaterally. If, instead, anti-globalist leaders opt to form international anti-globalist coalitions, they create new allies for their policies. Perhaps more importantly, an anti-globalist effort to create or repurpose an international institution is likely to have broader legitimacy among pro-globalist domestic populations, potentially expanding a leader's base of support.

Anti-globalist contested multilateralism could take several forms. Anti-globalist leaders might be inclined to join an alternative multilateral venue that espouses weaker rules or obligations, in order to reduce the authority of a *status quo* institution. European states, for example, might challenge the supremacy of the EU by joining the Eurasian Economic Union – a strategy that would allow anti-globalists to forum shop between the two organizations, while also undermining the EU's centrality in Europe. A dissatisfied coalition might also try to repurpose an alternative institution to pursue an anti-globalist agenda. This latter approach, however, is likely to be constrained by issue area. If a large enough coalition of states opposed the cooperative *status quo* in climate change, it might be possible to find an alternative institution with fewer rules and requirements. In issue areas like trade or immigration, however, anti-globalist coalitions will find few alternative institutions that can be easily co-opted.

Anti-globalist contested multilateralism could also take the form of competitive regime creation. If anti-globalist sentiment increases and such leaders gain control of more countries, governments may find it easier to form coalitions and build new institutions. Anti-globalist coalitions might seek to build issue-specific institutional partnerships on issues like migration or certain types of trade. Alternatively, they might build more fluid, overarching institutions designed to normatively contest international rules as Latin American states have done with ALBA. Given the broader distrust of delegated authority, however, anti-globalist countries will have incentives to opt for informal institutions that allow direct more control and facilitate less transparency.

Long-Term Effects of Anti-Globalist Challenges

Regardless of strategy, anti-globalist dissatisfaction with international institutions is likely to transform the global system. The overarching consequences, however, will depend on the leaders' choice of strategy. A small set of anti-globalist leaders opting for unilateral resistance may gradually decrease institutional authority, but so far, international institutions seem poised to withstand such challenges, even from powerful countries. Similarly, while obstructionist action may stall institutions and prevent countries from making any future progress, this strategy is unlikely to undermine the overarching authority of a regime in an irreparable manner. The UN Security Council, after all, was weakened by great power conflict for nearly four decades, yet states continued to participate throughout this period.

Multilateral engagement, on the other hand, could lead to a complete renegotiation of rules and a weakening of institutional authority. If anti-globalist leaders assemble a coalition that is large enough to push through significant changes to institutional rules, such action could drastically reshape the relationship between an institution and the governed states. An EU controlled by anti-globalist parties, for example, would probably find itself with a restricted mandate and less power in the global arena. Similarly, if anti-globalist leaders follow the Trump administration's approach to WTO dispute settlement, the global trade regime will weaken significantly.

Equally troublesome is the idea that anti-globalists might actually create their own multilateral institutions to try to disrupt global norms. Such an institution might be similar to the once-proposed "Alliance of Democracies,"[66] but instead of being bound by political system, countries would unite around normative dissatisfaction with the global order. In the counterterrorism regime complex, the Shanghai Cooperation Organization (SCO) has played such a role, adopting a set of counterterrorism rules in 2004 that directly conflict with UN human rights standards. The SCO rules espouse a very expansive definition of terrorism, equating terrorist acts with the co-equal "evils" of separatism and extremism, and obligating states to extradite and deny asylum to individuals suspected of such activities.[67] If anti-globalists were to create a similar institution, challenging global norms on issues like refugees or trade, such action could have long-term consequences; not only would it challenge the normative legitimacy of existing institutions, it would also politicize global governance in a way that has, so far, been rare. Although ideology often shapes the way leaders engage with multilateral institutions, there are few cases where multilateral institutions are directly linked to political ideology. Indeed, one of the hallmarks of global governance is that politicians, regardless of party, continue to participate in the same institutions as their predecessors. The formation of new institutions based on ideology would represent a departure from this norm, creating the possibility that global governance could become a battle ground for domestic politics. While the influx of domestic politics into international institutions might make them less stable, it could also potentially enhance the democratic legitimacy of such institutions.

Conclusion

The surge in anti-globalist sentiment will undoubtedly have long-term repercussions for international institutions. As anti-globalist leaders obtain positions of power, they are likely to seek out strategies to weaken international rules and challenge the international order. Unilateral action is often the most accessible option. By publicly flouting rules or withdrawing from institutions or agreements, anti-globalists can directly appease their supporters and address sources of discontent. Unilateralism, however, has key drawbacks. It requires diminishing or relinquishing control even as other states continue to follow institutional rules. A state may exit an agreement but find that the institution's procedures and norms continue to exert influence over international politics. Opting out reduces formal control but not always informal significance.

Without massive exits, institutions have largely persevered, and this resilience reveals much about rule and authority in international politics today. Institutional rules may start off endogenous to state preferences, but they are slow to adapt to changing sentiment. Even in the EU, where anti-globalist fervor has swept through a number of member states, leaders continue to abide by institutional rules that diverge significantly from popular opinion. States continue to comply generally with international rules, despite this domestic-international disconnect. Global governance has become its own source of authority.

Yet anti-globalist challenges may also portend larger threats to come. Authority depends in part on institutions providing services that are desirable enough to offset the loss of national autonomy. If domestic populations no longer want the policies in question, institutions will eventually face crises of legitimacy. Global governance thus sits at a crossroads. On the one hand, institutional authority is powerful enough to constrain those governments most committed to enhancing national sovereignty. On the other, even as anti-globalist leaders are hindered, the surge in nationalist sentiment suggests the system is failing in key ways.

For strategic anti-globalists, then, the optimal way to undermine cooperation may be to work within the system itself. Institutional rules might be slow to change, but informal norms can shift rapidly, and the long-term consequences of such efforts could shake the very foundations of the post-1945 order. Institutions might continue to govern the conduct of states, but the informal norms that underlie such bodies would be deeply damaged. The end result would be a reduced, fragmented, and potentially illiberal global governance authority. Ultimately, an anti-globalist coalition may upend the *status quo* more readily through active participation than direct confrontation or unilateral exit.

References

ALBA. 2018. *What Is the ALBA?* https://albainfo.org/what-is-the-alba/ (last access July 19, 2022).

Abbott, Kenneth W., and Duncan Snidal. 2000. "Hard and Soft Law in International Governance." *International Organization* 54(3): 421–456.

Abbott, Kenneth W., Philipp Genschel, Duncan Snidal, and Bernhard Zangl (eds.). 2015. *International Organizations as Orchestrators*. New York: Cambridge University Press.

Adelman, Jeremy. 2017. "A More Dangerous Globalism." *The Japan Times: Opinion Section* 03/26/19, www.japantimes.co.jp/opinion/2017/03/26/commentary/world-commentary/a-more-dangerous-globalism/ (last access July 19, 2022).

Alter, Karen, and Sophie Meunier. 2009. "The Politics of International Regime Complexity." *Perspectives on Politics* 7(1): 13–24.

Bach, David, and Abraham L. Newman. 2007. "The European Regulatory State and Global Public Policy: Micro-institutions, Macro-influence." *Journal of European Public Policy* 14(6): 827–846.

Baczynska, Gabriela. 2018. "EU Rejects Three-Pronged British Approach to New Ties after Brexit." *Reuters* 02/22/18, www.reuters.com/article/us-britain-eu-baskets/eu-rejects-three-pronged-british-approach-to-new-ties-after-brexit-idUSKCN1G61VM. (last access July 19, 2022).

Barbero, Michele. 2021. "Europe's Far-Right Seeks to Unite." *Foreign Policy* 4/23/21, https://foreignpolicy.com/2021/04/23/europe-far-right-division-european-parliament-poland-hungary/. (last access July 19, 2022).

Bershidsky, Leonid. 2018. "Hungary Is Winning Its War on Muslim Immigrants." *Bloomberg* 04/13/18, www.bloomberg.com/view/articles/2018-04-13/hungary-is-winning-its-war-on-muslim-immigrants (last access July 19, 2022).

Betts, Alexander. 2013. "Regime Complexity and International Organizations: UNHCR as a Challenged Institution." *Global Governance* 19(1): 69–81.

Bexell, Magdalena, Jonas Tallberg, and Anders Uhlin. 2010. "Democracy in Global Governance: The Promises and Pitfalls of Transnational Actors." *Global Governance* 16(1): 81–101.

Breuilly, John. 2016. "Nationalism and Brexit." *Oxford University Press Blog* 12/18/16, https://blog.oup.com/2016/12/nationalism-brexit-identity-referendum/ (last access July 19, 2022).

Brummer, Chris. 2010. "Why Soft Law Dominates International Finance – and Not Trade." *Journal of International Economic Law* 13(3): 623–643.

Busch, Marc L. 2007. "Overlapping Institutions, Forum Shopping, and Dispute Settlement in International Trade." *International Organization* 61(4): 735–761.

Büthe, Tim and Walter Mattli. 2011. *The New Global Rulers: The Privatization of Regulation in the World Economy*. Princeton: Princeton University Press.

Carrel-Billiard, Francois, and Christine Wing. 2010. *Nuclear Energy, Nonproliferation, and Disarmament: Briefing Notes for the 2010 NPT Review Conference*. New York: International Peace Institute.

Copeland, Dale. 2015. *Economic Interdependence and War*. Princeton: Princeton University Press.

Daalder, Ivo. H. and James Lindsay. 2004. "An Alliance of Democracies." *The Washington Post* 05/23/04.

Dahl, Robert A. 1957. "The Concept of Power." *Behavioral Science* 2(3): 201–215.

Dai, Xinyuan. 2007. *International Institutions and National Policies*. New York: Cambridge University Press.

Davis, Christina L. and Julia C. Morse. 2018. "Protecting Trade by Legalizing Political Disputes: Why Countries Bring Cases to the International Court of Justice." *International Studies Quarterly* 62(4): 709–722.

Einhorn, Robert. 2017. "Non-proliferation Challenges Facing the Trump Administration." Arms Control and Non-proliferation Series 15. Washington, DC: Brookings.

Foot, Rosemary. 2007. "The United Nations, Counter Terrorism and Human Rights: Institutional Adaptation and Embedded Ideas." *Human Rights Quarterly* 29(2): 489–514.

Ganley, Elaine. 2017. "Le Pen's world: French nationalism at heart of her campaign." *AP News* 12/01/17, https://apnews.com/237b06a4076e4f4184d3338f 6f22241f (last access July 19, 2022).

Gutteridge, Nick. 2017. "'This Won't End Well' EU Judges REJECT Eastern European Case against Migrant Quota Scheme." *Sunday Express* 09/06/17, www.express.co.uk/news/politics/850538/Migrant-crisis-ECJ-rejects-Hungary-Slovakia-claim-refugee-quotas (last access July 19, 2022).

Hall, Rodney Bruce, and Thomas J. Biersteker (eds.). 2002. *The Emergence of Private Authority in Global Governance*. New York: Cambridge University Press.

Helfer, Laurence R. 2004. "Regime Shifting: The TRIPs Agreement and New Dynamics of International Intellectual Property Lawmaking." *Yale Journal of International Law* 29(1): 1–83.

Helfer, Laurence R. 2009. "Regime Shifting in the International Intellectual Property System." *Perspectives on Politics* 7(1): 39–44.

HRIC. 2011. "Counter-Terrorism and Human Rights: The Impact of the Shanghai Cooperation Organization." *Human Rights in China Whitepaper*: www.hrichina.org/sites/default/files/publication_pdfs/2011-hric-sco-whitepaper-full.pdf (last access July 19, 2022).

Hurd, Ian. 1999. "Legitimacy and Authority in International Politics." *International Organization* 53(2): 379–408.

Ikenberry, G. John. 2000. *After Victory: Institutions, Strategic Restraint, and the Rebuilding of Order after Major Wars*. Princeton: Princeton University Press.

Kahn, Matthew. 2017. "Pretextual Protectionism? The Perils of Invoking the WTO National Security Exception." *Lawfare* 07/21/17, www.lawfareblog .com/pretextual-protectionism-perils-invoking-wto-national-security-exception (last access July 19, 2022).

Keck, Margaret E. and Kathryn Sikkink. 1998. *Activists Beyond Borders: Advocacy Networks in International Politics*. New York: Cornell University Press.

Keohane, Robert O., and David G. Victor. 2011. "The Regime Complex for Climate Change." *Perspectives on Politics* 9(1): 7–23.

Keohane, Robert O., and Joseph S. Nye Jr. 2000. "Introduction," in Joseph S. Nye, and John D. Donahue (eds.), *Governance in a Globalizing World*. Washington, DC: Brookings Institution Press, pp. 1–44.

Keppler, Elise. 1 February 2017. "AU's 'ICC Withdrawal Strategy' Less than Meets the Eye." *Human Rights Watch,* www.hrw.org/news/2017/02/01/aus-icc-withdrawal-strategy-less-meets-eye (last access June 25, 2022).

Kreuder-Sonnen, Christian, and Bernhard Zangl. 2016. "Varieties of Contested Multilateralism: Positive and Negative Consequences for the Constitutionalization of Multilateral Institutions." *Global Constitutionalism* 5(3): 327–343.

Lake, David A. 2010. "Rightful Rules: Authority, Order, and the Foundations of Global Governance." *International Studies Quarterly* 54(3): 587–613.

Legler, Thomas. 2013. "Post-hegemonic Regionalism and Sovereignty in Latin America: Optimists, Skeptics, and an Emerging Research Agenda." *Contexto Internacional* 35(2): 325–352.

Lesage, Dries, and Thijs van de Graaf. 2013. "Thriving in Complexity? The OECD System's Role in Energy and Taxation." *Global Governance* 19(1): 83–92.

Mahoney, James, and Kathleen Thelen. 2010. "A Theory of Gradual Institutional Change," in James Mahoney, and Kathleen Thelen (eds.), *Explaining Institutional Change: Ambiguity, Agency, and Power.* New York: Cambridge University Press, pp. 1–37.

Mansfield, Edward D., and Jon C. Pevehouse. 2000. "Trade Blocs, Trade Flows, and International Conflict." *International Organizations* 54(4): 775–808.

Mansfield, Edward, and Brian Pollins (eds.). 2003. *Economic Interdependence and International Conflict.* Ann Arbor: University of Michigan Press.

Martill, Benjamin. 2021. "Prisoners of Their Own Device: Brexit as a Failed Negotiating Strategy." *The British Journal of International Relations,* online first, https://doi.org/10.1177%2F13691481211044645.

McBride, James. 2018. "What Is the Trans-Pacific Partnership (TPP)?" *Council on Foreign Relations,* 05/15/18, www.cfr.org/backgrounder/what-trans-pacific-partnership-tpp (last access July 19, 2022).

McLaughlin, Daniel. 2018. "Hungarian NGOs Fear Crackdown as Orban Prepares for New Term." *The Irish Times* 05/07/18, www.irishtimes.com/news/world/europe/hungarian-ngos-fear-crackdown-as-orban-prepares-for-new-term-1.3487116 (last access July 19, 2022).

Moravcsik, Andrew. 2004. "Is There a 'Democratic Deficit' in World Politics? A Framework for Analysis." *Government and Opposition* 39(2): 336–363.

Morse, Julia C., and Robert O. Keohane. 2014. "Contested Multilateralism." *Review of International Organizations* 9(4): 385–412.

Nye Jr., Joseph S. 2001. "Globalization's Democratic Deficit: How to Make International Institutions More Accountable." *Foreign Affairs* 80(4): 2–6.

Orsini, Amandine, Jean-Frédéric Morin, and Oran Young. 2013. "Regime Complexes: A Buzz, a Boom, or a Boost for Global Governance?" *Global Governance* 19: 27–39.

Pelc, Krzysztof J. 2014. "The Politics of Precedent in International Law: A Social Network Application." *American Political Science Review* 108(3): 547–564.

Perlez, Jane. 2015. "China Creates a World Bank of Its Own, and the US Balks." *The New York Times* 12/04/15, www.nytimes.com/2015/12/05/business/international/china-creates-an-asian-bank-as-the-us-stands-aloof.html (last access July 19, 2022).

Pratt, Tyler. 2017. "Angling for Influence." *Working Paper,* https://scholar.princeton.edu/sites/default/files/tylerpratt/files/influence_aug25.pdf (last access May 14, 2019).
Pratt, Tyler. 2018. "Deference and Hierarchy in International Regime Complexes." *International Organization* 72(3): 561–590.
Raustiala, Kal, and David G. Victor. 2004. "The Regime Complex for Plant Genetic Resources." *International Organization* 58(2): 277–309.
Reisen, Helmut. 2015. "Will the AIIB and the NDB Help Reform Multilateral Development Banking?" *Global Policy* 6(3): 297–304.
Riggirozi, Pía. 2012. "Reconstructing Regionalism: What Does Development Have to Do with It?" in Riggirozi, Pía and Tussie, Diana (eds.). *The Rise of Post-Hegemonic Regionalism.* New York: Springer, 17–39.
Riggirozzi, Pia. 2012. "Region, Regionness and Regionalism in Latin America: Towards a New Synthesis." *New Political Economy* 17(4): 421–443.
Riggirozzi, Pia, and Diana Tussie (eds.). 2012. *The Rise of Post-Hegemonic Regionalism: The Case of Latin America.* Dordrecht: Springer.
Russett, Bruce, and John Oneal. 2001. *Triangulating Peace: Democracy, Interdependence, and International Organizations.* New York: Norton.
Sandford, Alasdair. 2022. "Post-Brexit Guide: Where Are We Now – and How Did We Get Here?" *EuroNews* 2/14/2022. www.euronews.com/my-europe/2021/06/23/brexit-draft-deal-first-of-many-hurdles-to-a-smooth-exit (last access February 28, 2022).
Shaffer, Gregory C., and Mark A. Pollack. 2010. "Hard Vs. Soft Law: Alternatives, Complements, and Antagonists in International Governance." *Minnesota Law Review* 94: 706–799.
Simmons, Beth A. 2009. *Mobilizing for Human Rights: International Law in Domestic Politics.* New York: Cambridge University Press.
Ssenyonjo, Manisuli. 2018. "State Withdrawal Notifications from the Rome Statute of the International Criminal Court: South Africa, Burundi, and the Gambia." *Criminal Law Forum* 29: 63–119.
Stevis-Gridneff, Matina, Monika Pronczuk, and Benjamin Novak. 16 Feb 2022. "Top European Court Rules EU Can Freeze Aid to Poland and Hungary." *The New York Times* www.nytimes.com/2022/02/16/world/europe/eu-court-funds-hungary-poland.html (last access January 20, 2023).
Stone, Randall W. 2011. *Controlling Institutions: International Organizations and the Global Economy.* Cambridge: Cambridge University Press.
The White House. 2017. *Remarks by President Trump to the 72nd Session of the United Nations General Assembly,* www.whitehouse.gov/briefings-statements/remarks-president-trump-72nd-session-united-nations-general-assembly/ (last access 05/28/19).
Tussie, Diana. 2016. "Presidential Diplomacy in UNASUR: Coming Together for Crisis Management or Marking Tufts?" in Gordon Mace, Jean-Philippe Therien, Diana Tussie, and Olivier Dabene (eds.), *Summits & Regional Governance: The Americas in Comparative Perspective.* New York: Routledge.
Von Borzyskowski, Inken and Felicity Vabulas. 2022. "When Do Withdrawal Threats Achieve Reform in Intergovernmental Organizations." *Working Paper.*

Weiffen, Brigitte, Leslie Wehner, and Detlef Nolte. 2013. "Overlapping Regional Security Institutions in South America: The Case of OAS and UNASUR." *International Area Studies Review* 16(4): 370–389.

Wheeler, Nicholas J. 2000. "Reflections on the Legality and Legitimacy of NATO's Intervention in Kosovo." *The International Journal of Human Rights* 4(3): 144–163.

Wilkinson, Tracy. 2017. "U.S. Struggles to Unite Countries in Condemning Venezuela." *LA Times* 06/20/17, www.latimes.com/nation/la-fg-trump-latin-america-20170620-story.html (last access July 19, 2022).

Wittner, Lawrence. 2005. "Does the Nuclear Non-Proliferation Treaty Have a Future?", *Nuclear Age Peace Foundation,* www.wagingpeace.org/does-the-nuclear-non-proliferation-treaty-have-a-future/ (last access July 19, 2022).

World Bank Group, and World Trade Organization. 2015. *The Role of Trade in Ending Poverty.* Geneva: World Trade Organization.

Notes

1 I would like to thank Robert Keohane, Tyler Pratt, the editors, and the other contributors to this book for helpful feedback on this chapter.

2 Alter and Meunier 2009; Raustiala and Victor 2004.

3 Morse and Keohane 2014.

4 See, for example, Bexell et al. 2010; Keohane and Nye 2000; Moravcsik 2004; Nye 2001.

5 Riggirozzi and Tussie 2012.

6 Weiffen et al. 2013.

7 For example, see work on "soft law" (Abbott and Snidal 2000; Shaffer and Pollack 2010), regulatory institutions (Bach and Newman 2007; Brummer 2010; Büthe and Mattli 2011; Hall and Biersteker 2002), and informal influence (Stone 2011).

8 World Bank and World Trade Organization 2015.

9 On the link between economic interdependence and conflict, see Copeland 2015; Davis and Morse 2018; Mansfield and Pevehouse 2000; Mansfield and Pollins 2003; Russett and Oneal 2001, among others.

10 This interpretation is in line with the notion of power put forward by Dahl (1957: 202–203), who writes "*A* has power over *B* to the extent that he can get *B* to do something that *B* would otherwise not do."

11 Lake 2010.

12 Hurd 1999.

13 Pratt 2018.

14 Abbott et al. 2015.

15 Keohane and Victor 2011.

16 Betts 2013.

17 Lesage and Van de Graaf 2013.

18 Orsini et al. 2013.

19 Ikenberry 2000.

20 Gutteridge 2017.

21 Bershidsky 2018.

22 Stevis-Gridneff et al. 2022.
23 Von Borzyskowski and Vabulas 2022.
24 Martill 2021.
25 See, for example Carrel-Billiard and Wing 2010; Einhorn 2017; and Wittner 2005 among many others.
26 Onuf, this volume.
27 Hurd 1999.
28 Lake 2010.
29 Mahoney and Thelen 2010.
30 Busch 2007; Pelc 2014.
31 The EU's Stability and Growth Pact requires EU members to have a debt-to-GDP ratio no higher than 60% and a government deficit of no greater than 3% of GDP.
32 Barbero 2021.
33 Zürn, this volume.
34 Stone 2011.
35 Wheeler 2000.
36 Morse and Keohane 2014: 387.
37 Coalitions with outside options may credibly threaten to find alternative institutional arrangements. Even in the face of such threats, however, institutions often fail to adapt as veto players prevent organizational change.
38 Legler 2013.
39 Morse and Keohane 2014.
40 Helfer 2004, 2009.
41 Foot 2007.
42 Kreuder-Sonnen and Zangl 2016.
43 Pratt 2017; Reisen 2015.
44 Perlez 2015.
45 ALBA 2018.
46 Riggirozzi 2012.
47 Tussie 2016.
48 Riggirozi 2012.
49 Legler 2013: 338.
50 Adelman 2017.
51 McLaughlin 2018.
52 Breuilly 2016.
53 The full text of this speech is available at The White House 2017.
54 Ganley 2017.
55 Sending, this volume; Alter, this volume.
56 Sandford 2022.
57 Dai 2007; Simmons 2009.
58 Keck and Sikkink 1998.
59 McBride 2018.
60 Keppler 2017.
61 In 2016, South Africa, Burundi, and the Gambia submitted to the UN Secretary-General written notifications to withdraw from the Rome Statute. For more on the politics surrounding ICC withdrawal in Africa, see Ssenyonjo 2018.

62 Wilkinson 2017.
63 Baczynska 2018.
64 The first G-6 summit was held in 1975 and included France, West Germany, the USA, Japan, the UK, and Italy. In 1976, Canada joined the group; Russia joined in 1998. The G-8 expelled Russia in 2014 in response to the annexation of Crimea. The G-20 includes G-8 countries as well as Argentina, Australia, Brazil, China, India, Indonesia, Korea, Mexico, Saudi Arabia, South Africa, Turkey, and the European Union.
65 Kahn 2017.
66 Daalder and Lindsay 2004.
67 HRIC 2011.

Index

Footnotes are indicated by n. after the page number, and tables are indicated by tab.

www.ingramcontent.com/pod-product-compliance
Ingram Content Group UK Ltd.
Pitfield, Milton Keynes, MK11 3LW, UK
UKHW022012130125
453400UK00021B/300

9 781009 307697